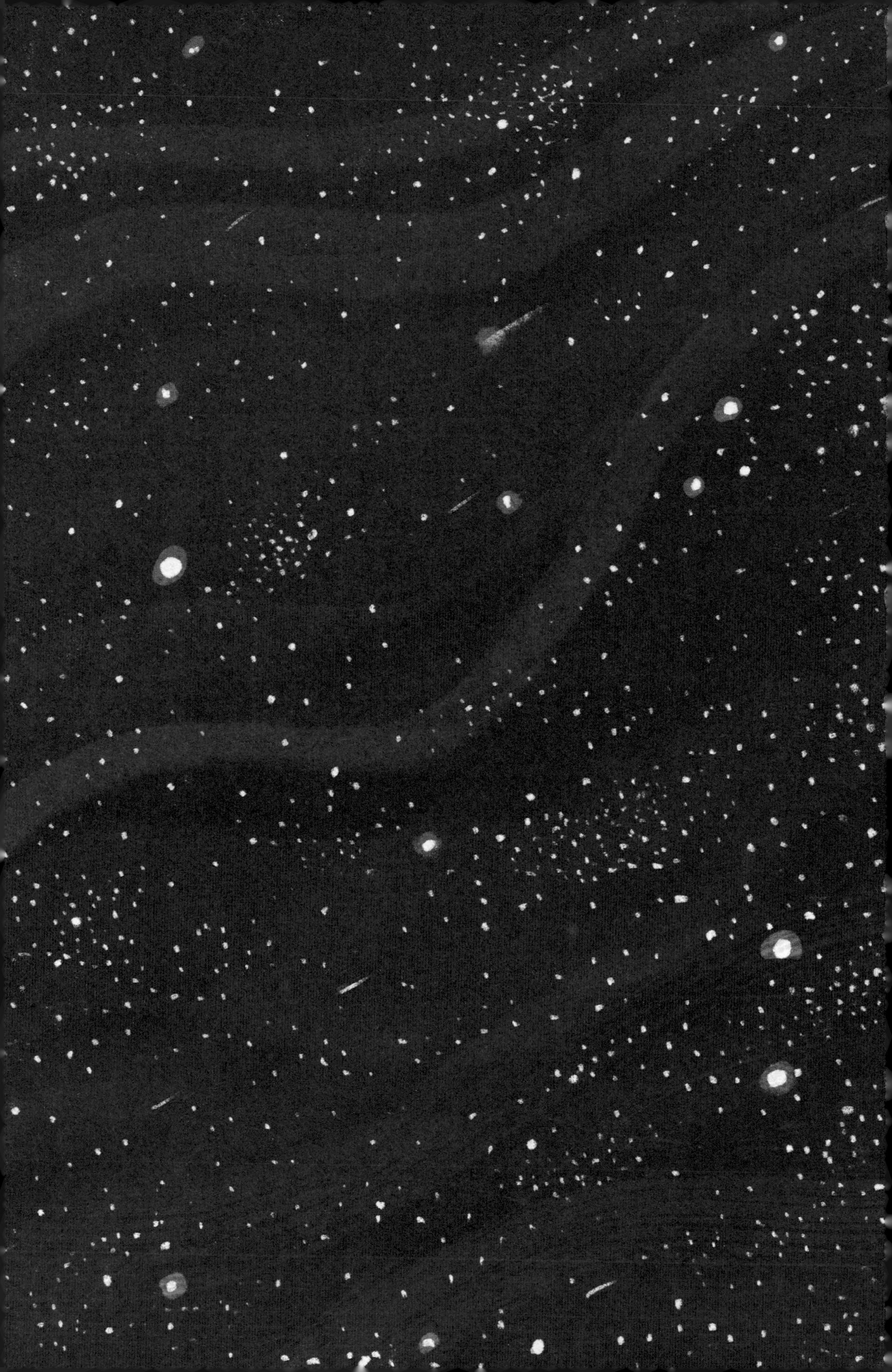

LIGHTS, PLANETS, PEOPLE!

Written by Molly Naylor &
illustrated by Lizzy Stewart

Published by Avery Hill Publishing, 2021

10 9 8 7 6 5 4 3 2 1

First published in the UK in 2021 by Avery Hill Publishing
Unit 8
5 Durham Yard
London
E2 6QF
Printed in Malta

A CIP record for this book is available from the British Library

ISBN: 978-1-910395-61-5

Molly Naylor
www.mollynaylor.com

Lizzy Stewart
www.abouttoday.co.uk

Avery Hill Publishing
www.averyhillpublishing.com

For Karen, who helped make Maggie.

Supported using public funding by

**ARTS COUNCIL
ENGLAND**

LOTTERY FUNDED

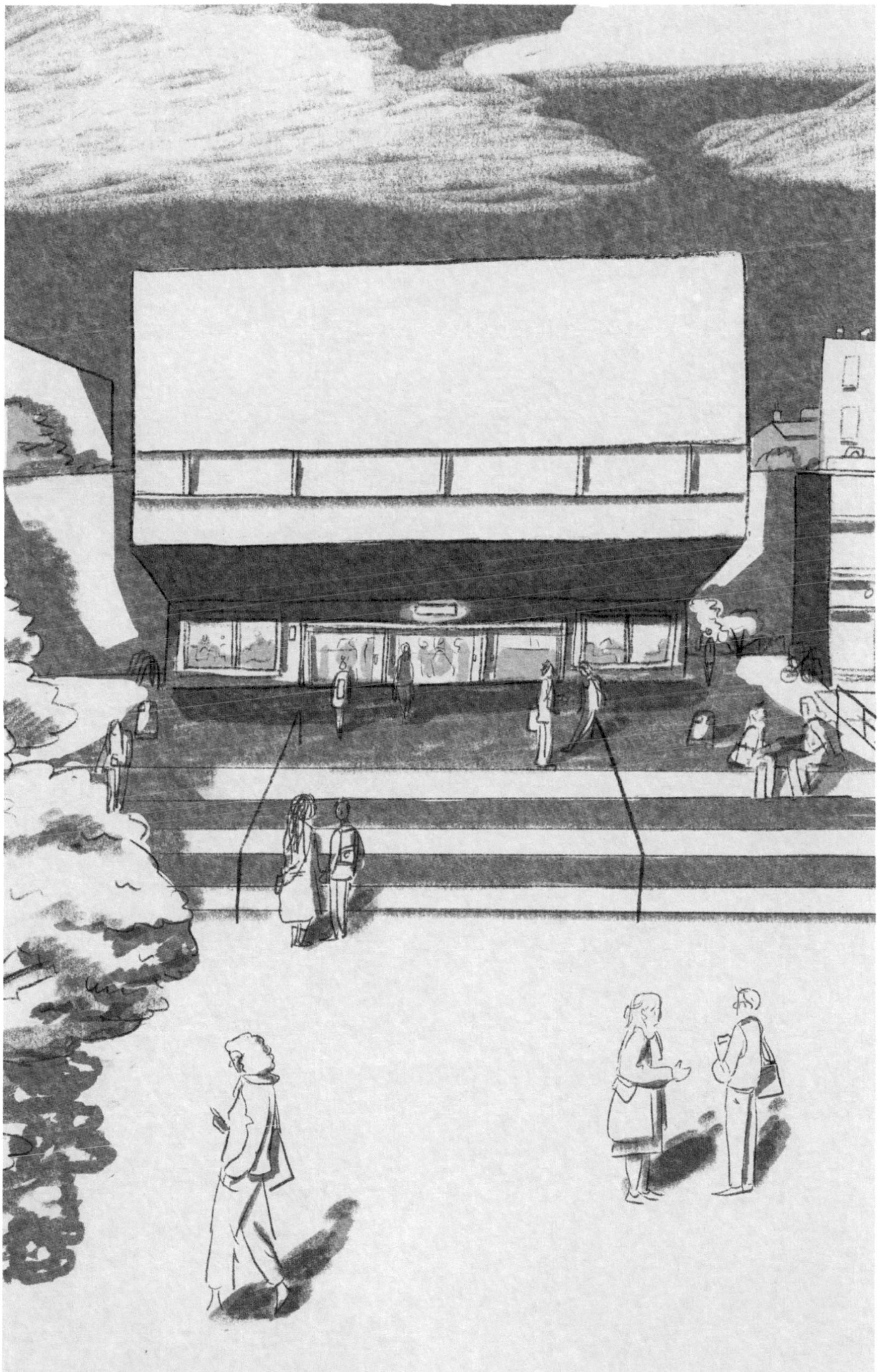

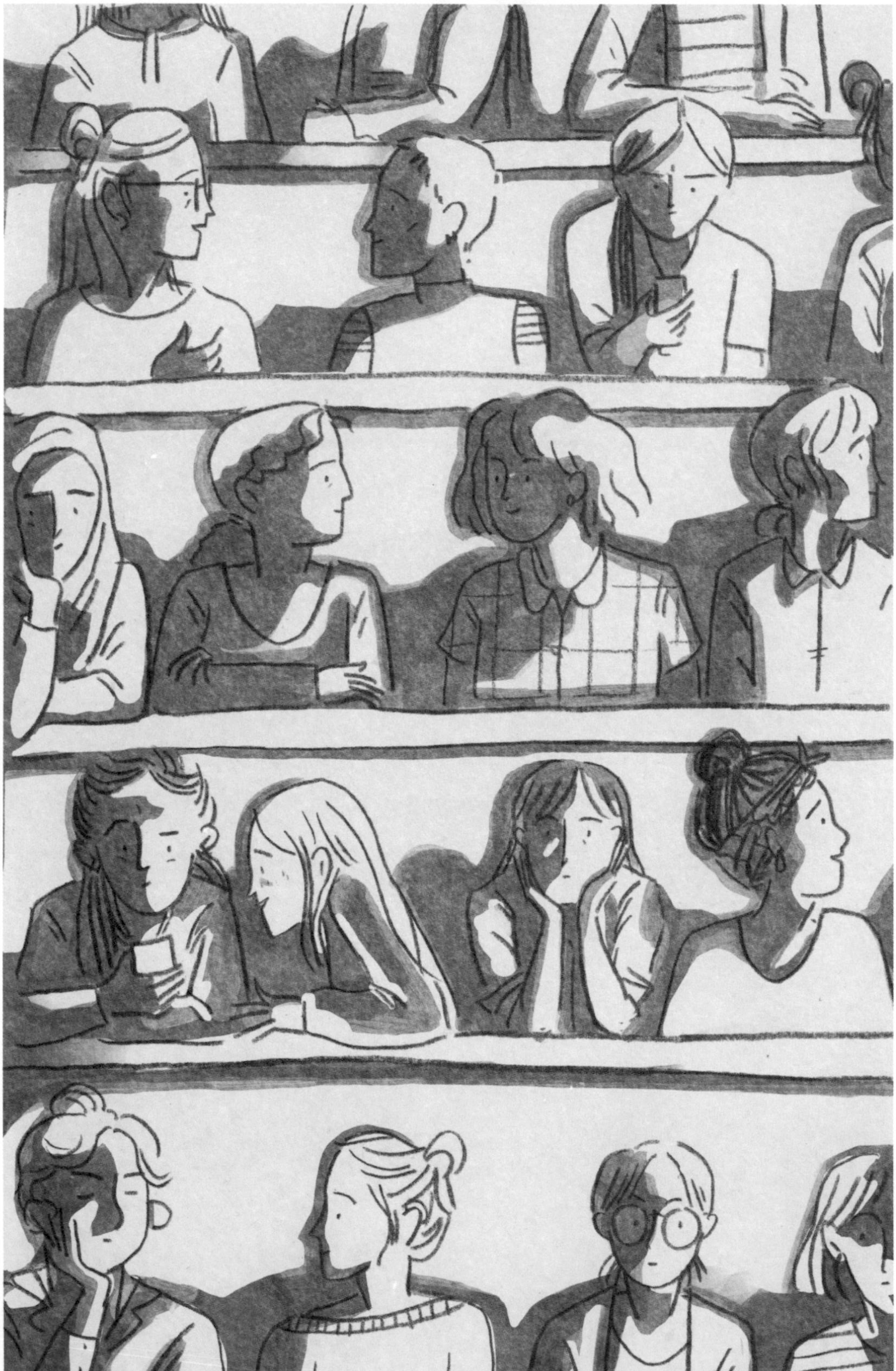

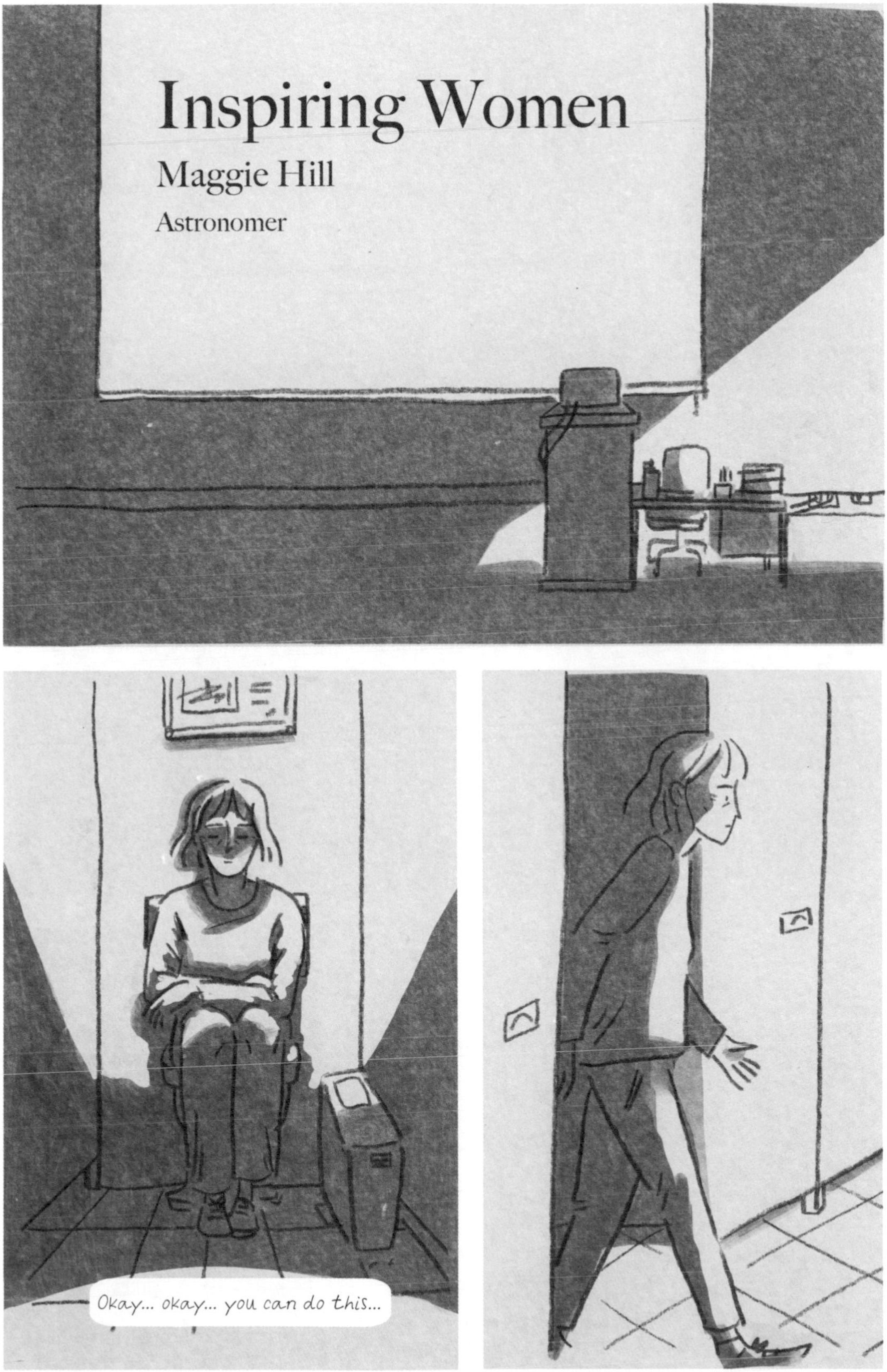
Inspiring Women
Maggie Hill
Astronomer
Okay... okay... you can do this...

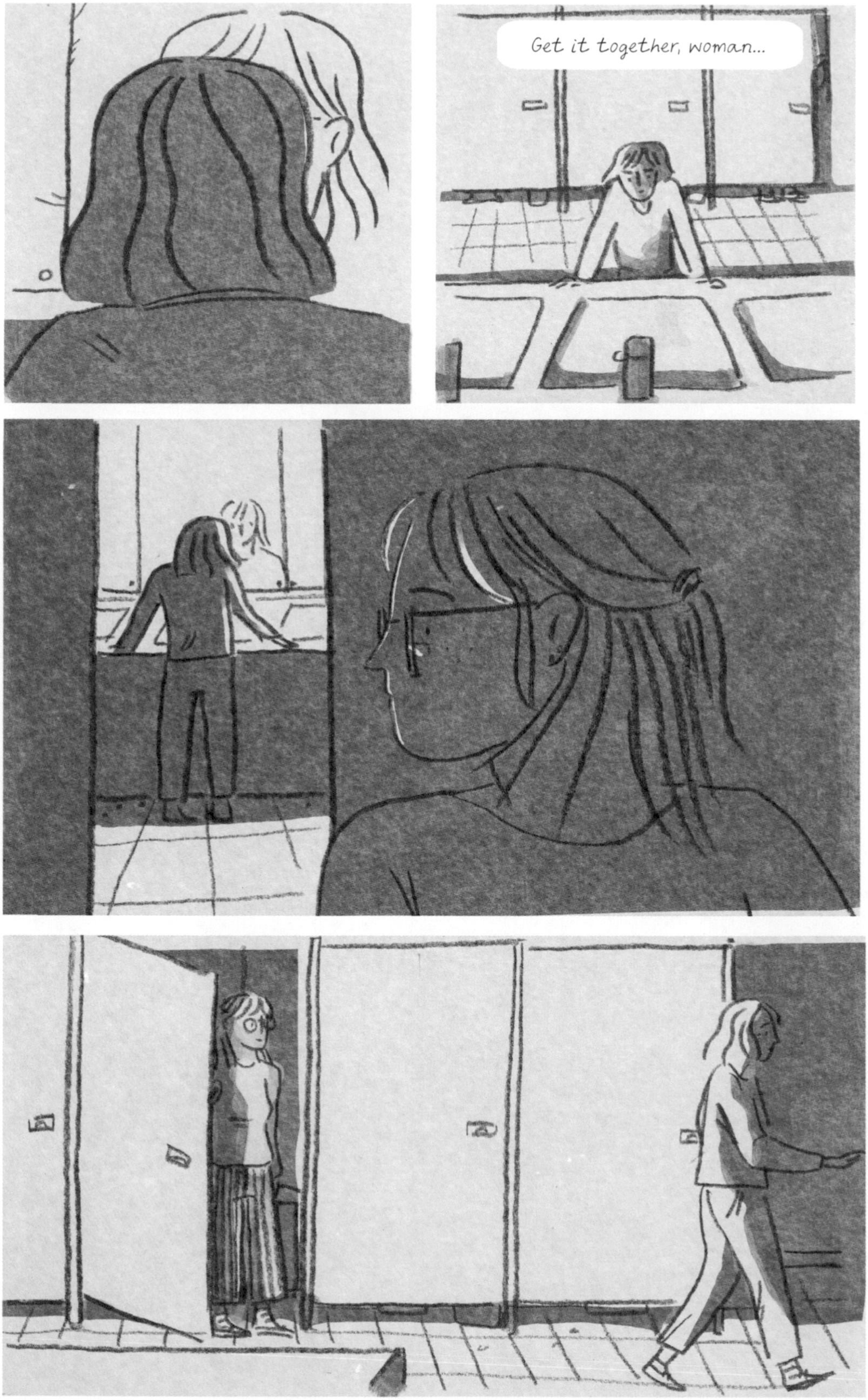
Get it together, woman...

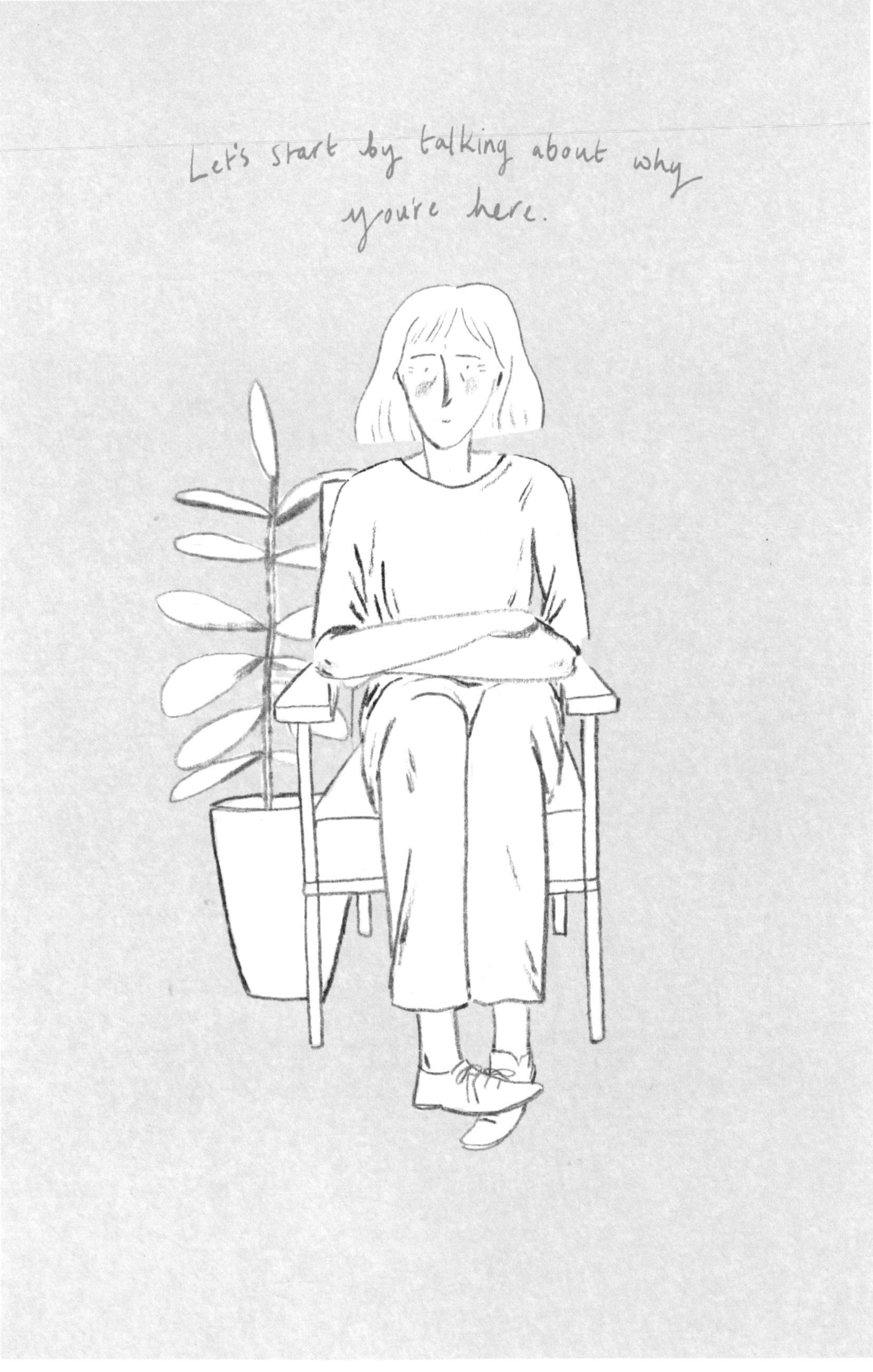
Let's start by talking about why you're here.

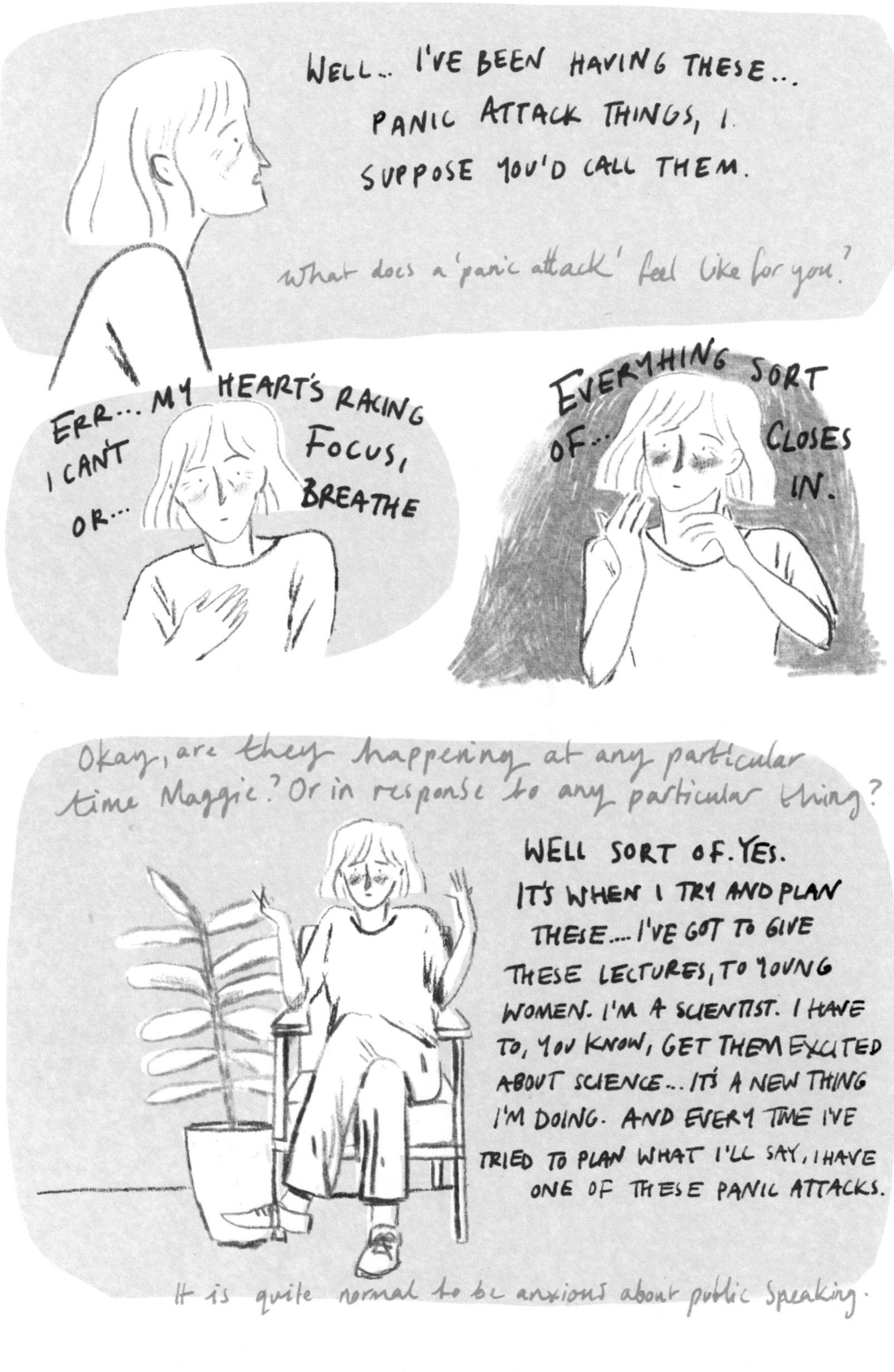
WELL... I'VE BEEN HAVING THESE... PANIC ATTACK THINGS, I SUPPOSE YOU'D CALL THEM.
What does a 'panic attack' feel like for you?
ERR... MY HEART'S RACING
I CAN'T FOCUS,
OR... BREATHE
EVERYTHING SORT OF... CLOSES IN.
Okay, are they happening at any particular time Maggie? Or in response to any particular thing?
WELL SORT OF. YES. IT'S WHEN I TRY AND PLAN THESE.... I'VE GOT TO GIVE THESE LECTURES, TO YOUNG WOMEN. I'M A SCIENTIST. I HAVE TO, YOU KNOW, GET THEM EXCITED ABOUT SCIENCE... IT'S A NEW THING I'M DOING. AND EVERY TIME I'VE TRIED TO PLAN WHAT I'LL SAY, I HAVE ONE OF THESE PANIC ATTACKS.
It is quite normal to be anxious about public speaking.

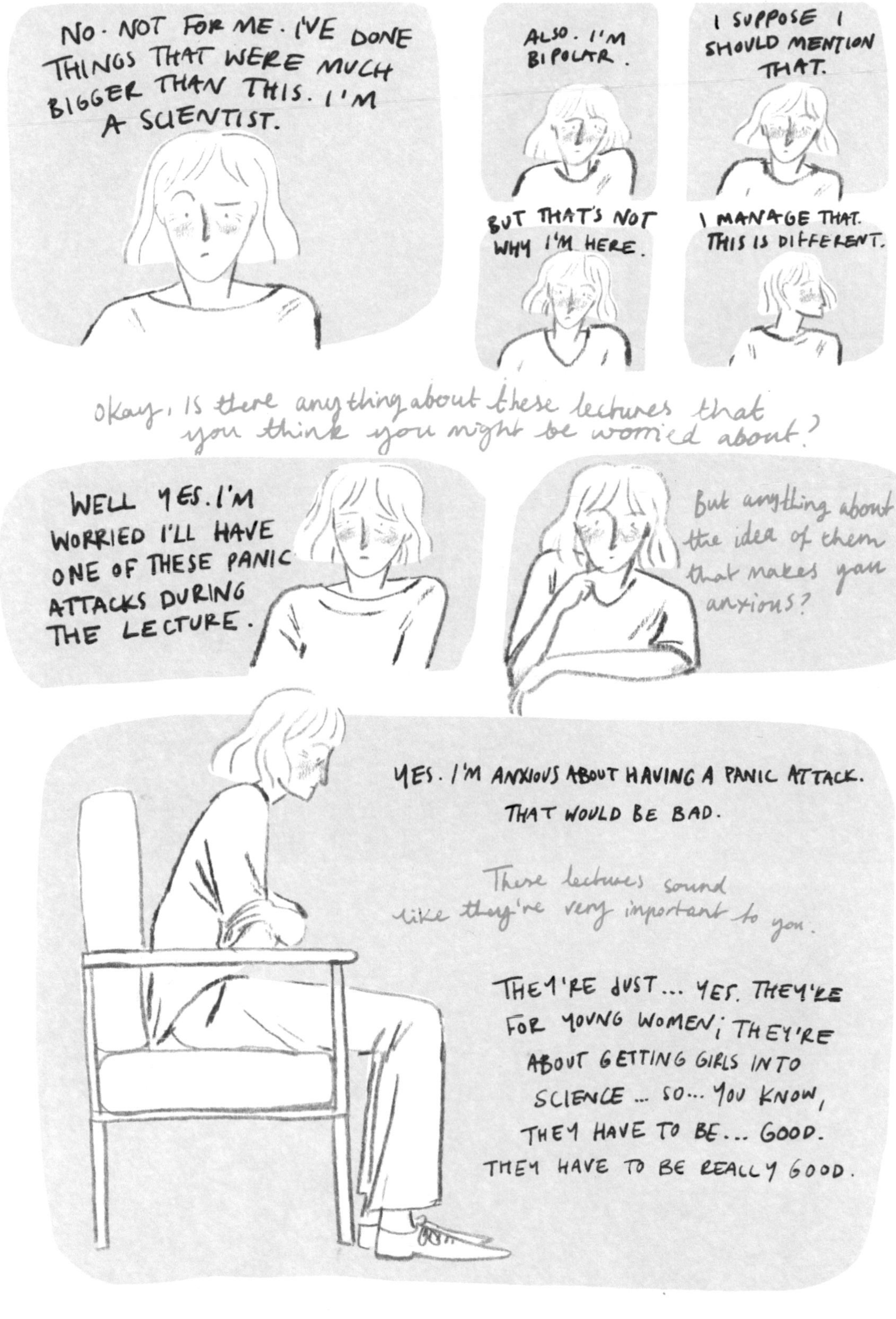

NO. NOT FOR ME. I'VE DONE THINGS THAT WERE MUCH BIGGER THAN THIS. I'M A SCIENTIST.
ALSO. I'M BIPOLAR.
I SUPPOSE I SHOULD MENTION THAT.
BUT THAT'S NOT WHY I'M HERE.
I MANAGE THAT. THIS IS DIFFERENT.
Okay, is there anything about these lectures that you think you might be worried about?
WELL YES. I'M WORRIED I'LL HAVE ONE OF THESE PANIC ATTACKS DURING THE LECTURE.
But anything about the idea of them that makes you anxious?
YES. I'M ANXIOUS ABOUT HAVING A PANIC ATTACK. THAT WOULD BE BAD.
These lectures sound like they're very important to you.
THEY'RE JUST... YES. THEY'RE FOR YOUNG WOMEN; THEY'RE ABOUT GETTING GIRLS INTO SCIENCE... SO... YOU KNOW, THEY HAVE TO BE... GOOD. THEY HAVE TO BE REALLY GOOD.

I'm really sorry about this...

Is there no way of getting someone else to help? I really need the Powerpoint.

We're really pushed. I think we might just have to... go for it if that's okay?

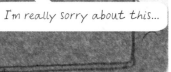

The girls are all waiting, so...

Sorry, is that okay?

I suppose so.

Thank you, sorry again.

Hello everyone. Thanks for coming. This is the first in our series of Inspiring Women talks, and it's my great pleasure to welcome the incredible Maggie Hill.

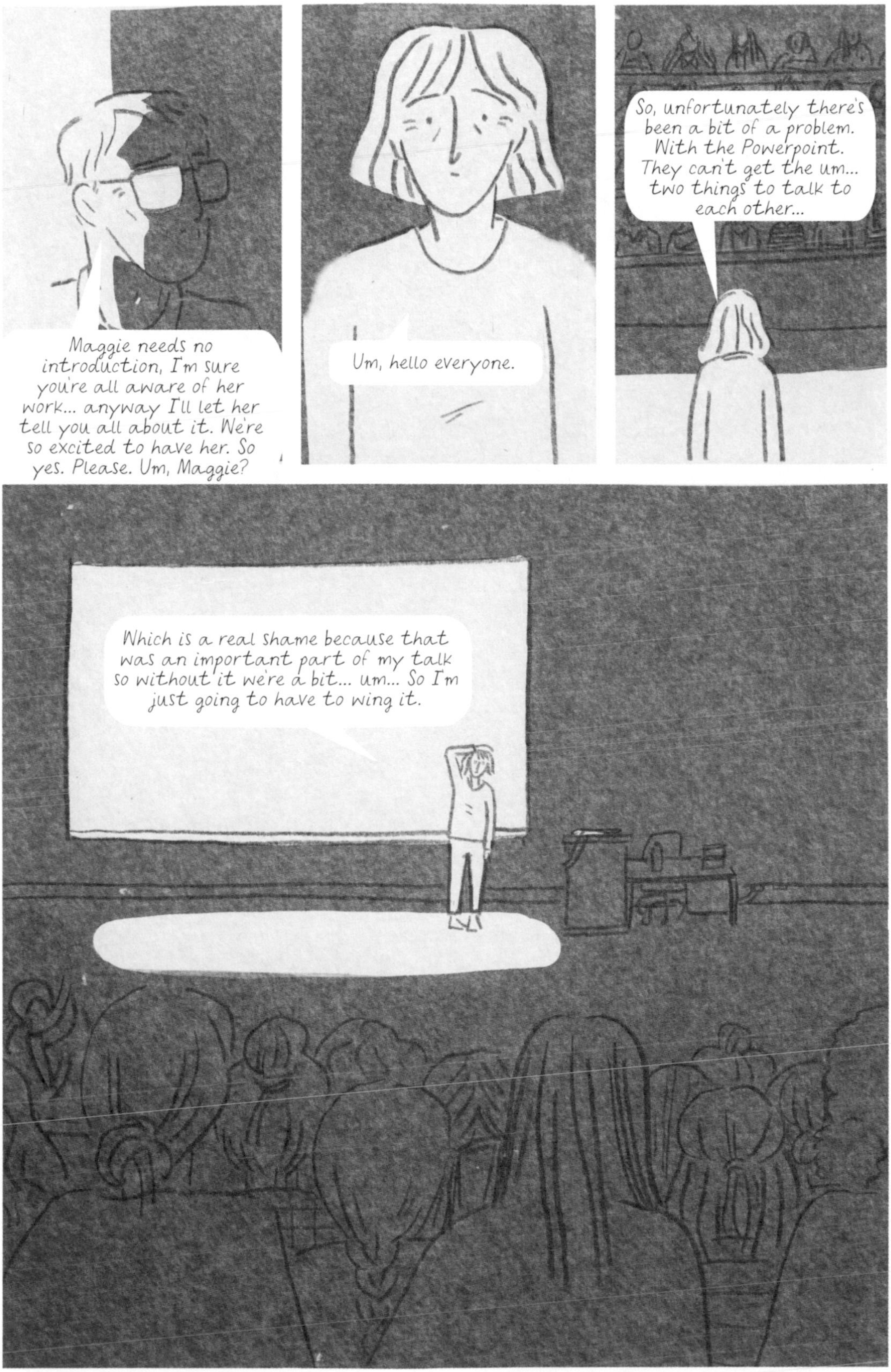
Maggie needs no introduction, I'm sure you're all aware of her work... anyway I'll let her tell you all about it. We're so excited to have her. So yes. Please. Um, Maggie?
Um, hello everyone.
So, unfortunately there's been a bit of a problem. With the Powerpoint. They can't get the um... two things to talk to each other...
Which is a real shame because that was an important part of my talk so without it we're a bit... um... So I'm just going to have to wing it.

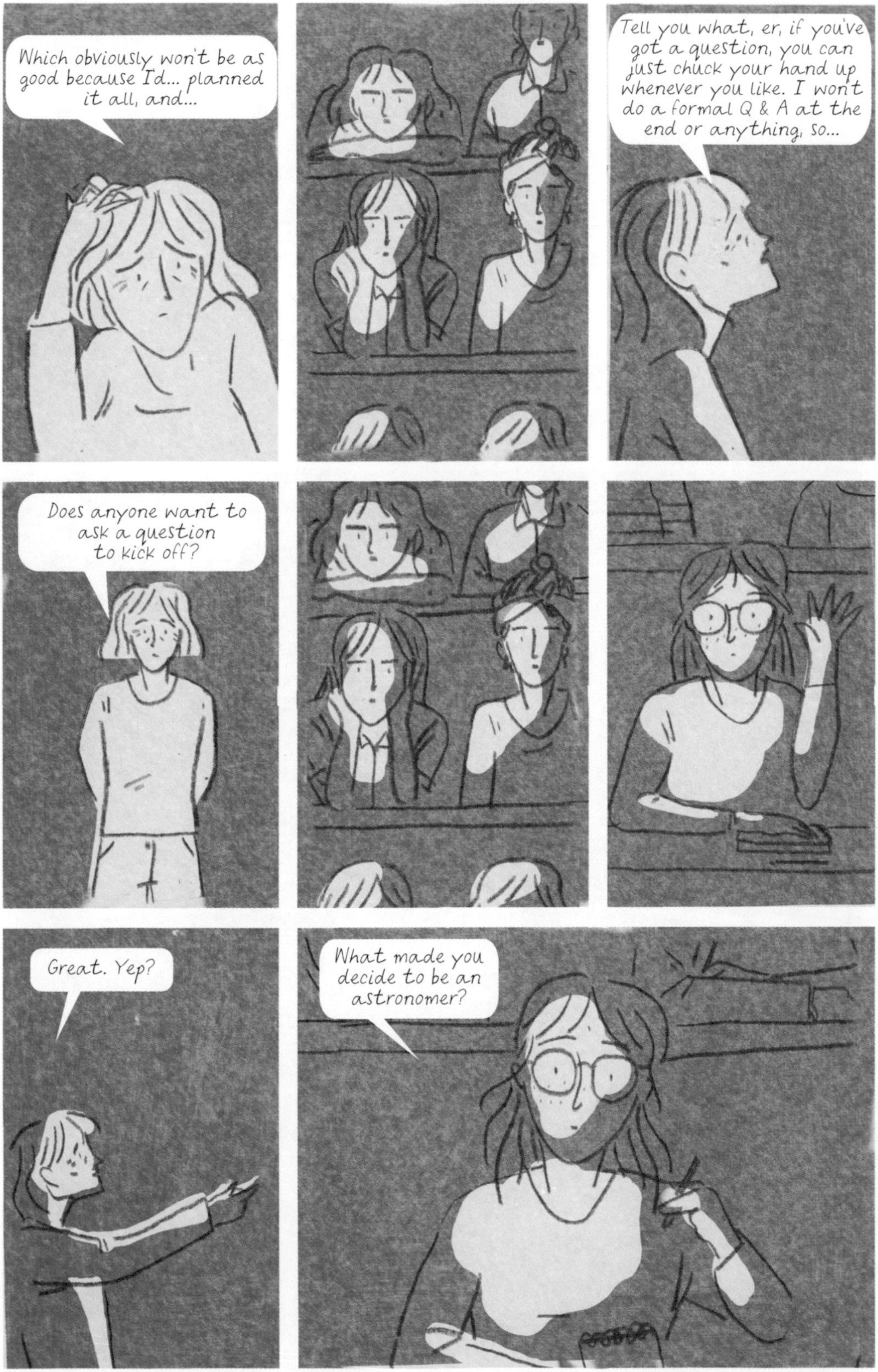

Which obviously won't be as good because I'd... planned it all, and...
Tell you what, er, if you've got a question, you can just chuck your hand up whenever you like. I won't do a formal Q & A at the end or anything, so...
Does anyone want to ask a question to kick off?
Great. Yep?
What made you decide to be an astronomer?

I was ten when I watched the moon-landings. I sat there in my pyjamas, absolutely glued, giddy as you like.

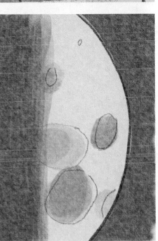

I remember lying in bed that night - my bed was up against the wall - and we had that bobbly Anaglypta wallpaper - I don't know if you know what I mean? And I remember lying there, touching the bobbles, imagining I was touching the surface of the moon. I didn't sleep all night.

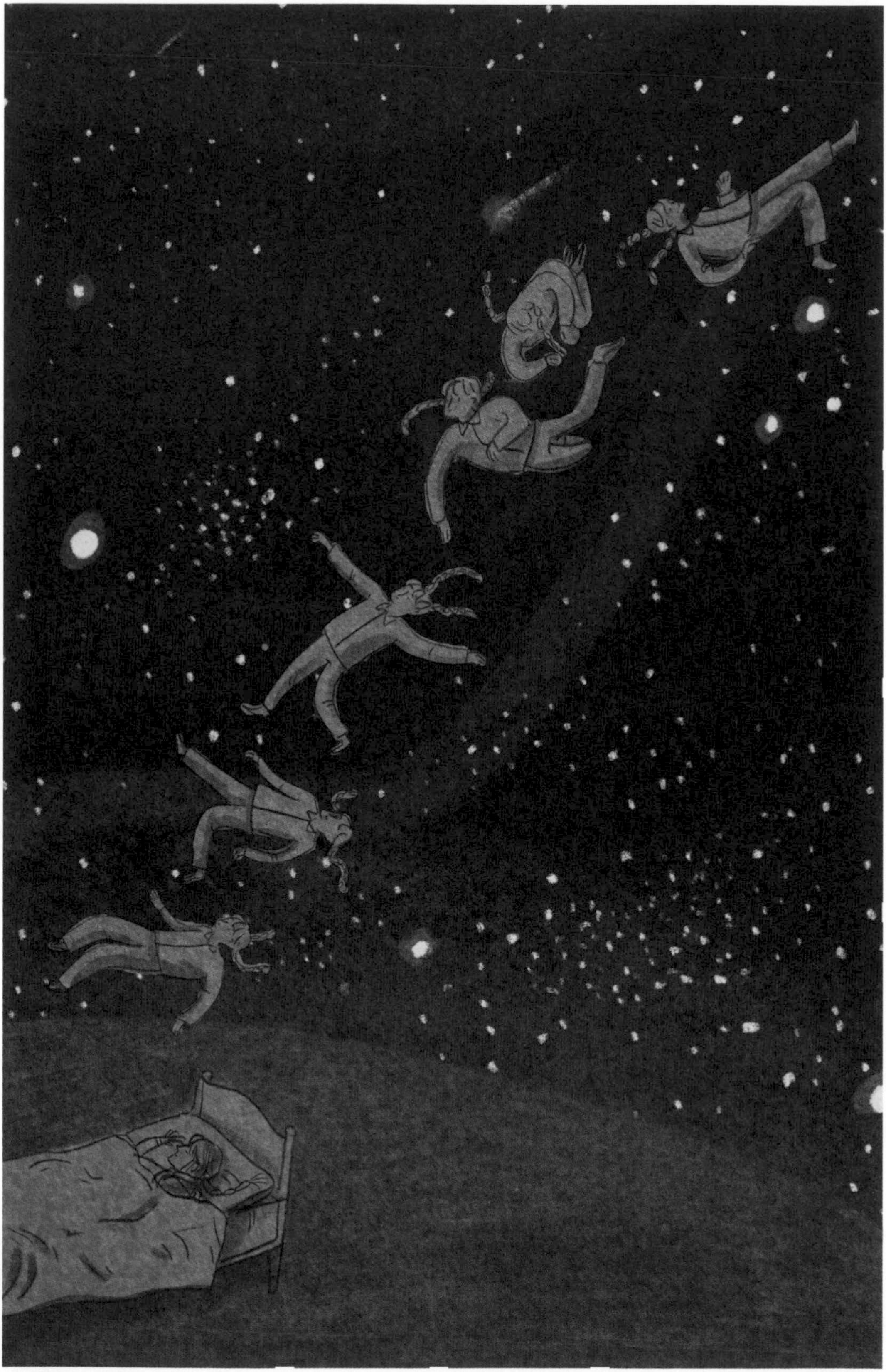

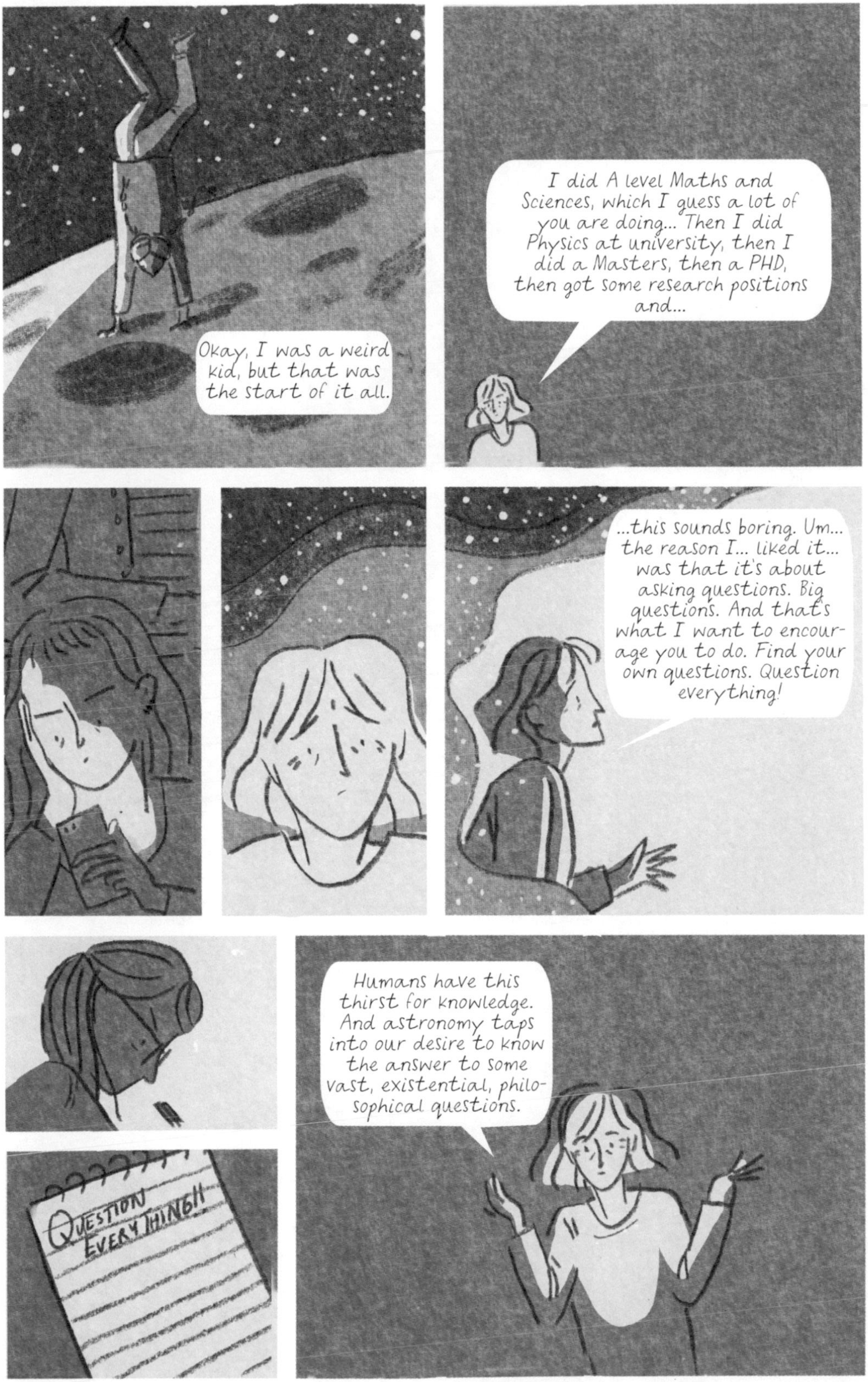
Okay, I was a weird kid, but that was the start of it all.
I did A level Maths and Sciences, which I guess a lot of you are doing... Then I did Physics at university, then I did a Masters, then a PHD, then got some research positions and...
...this sounds boring. Um... the reason I... liked it... was that it's about asking questions. Big questions. And that's what I want to encourage you to do. Find your own questions. Question everything!
QUESTION EVERYTHING!!
Humans have this thirst for knowledge. And astronomy taps into our desire to know the answer to some vast, existential, philosophical questions.

In some ways, sure, it is hard to conceive of sciences more far removed from our lives and our concerns than astronomy and cosmology. Most of the physical phenomena of the cosmos are separated from us by unimaginable distance.

But astronomy and cosmology have completely changed the way we understand our world.

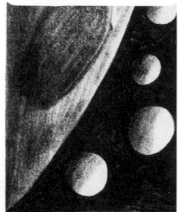

Think of Galileo discovering the four largest moons of Jupiter. Or Hubble, learning that the universe is expanding. Or the discovery of relic radiation from the Big Bang...

Another question! We're on a roll now. Yes?

But how is space like... relevant? To like... anything?

Well...

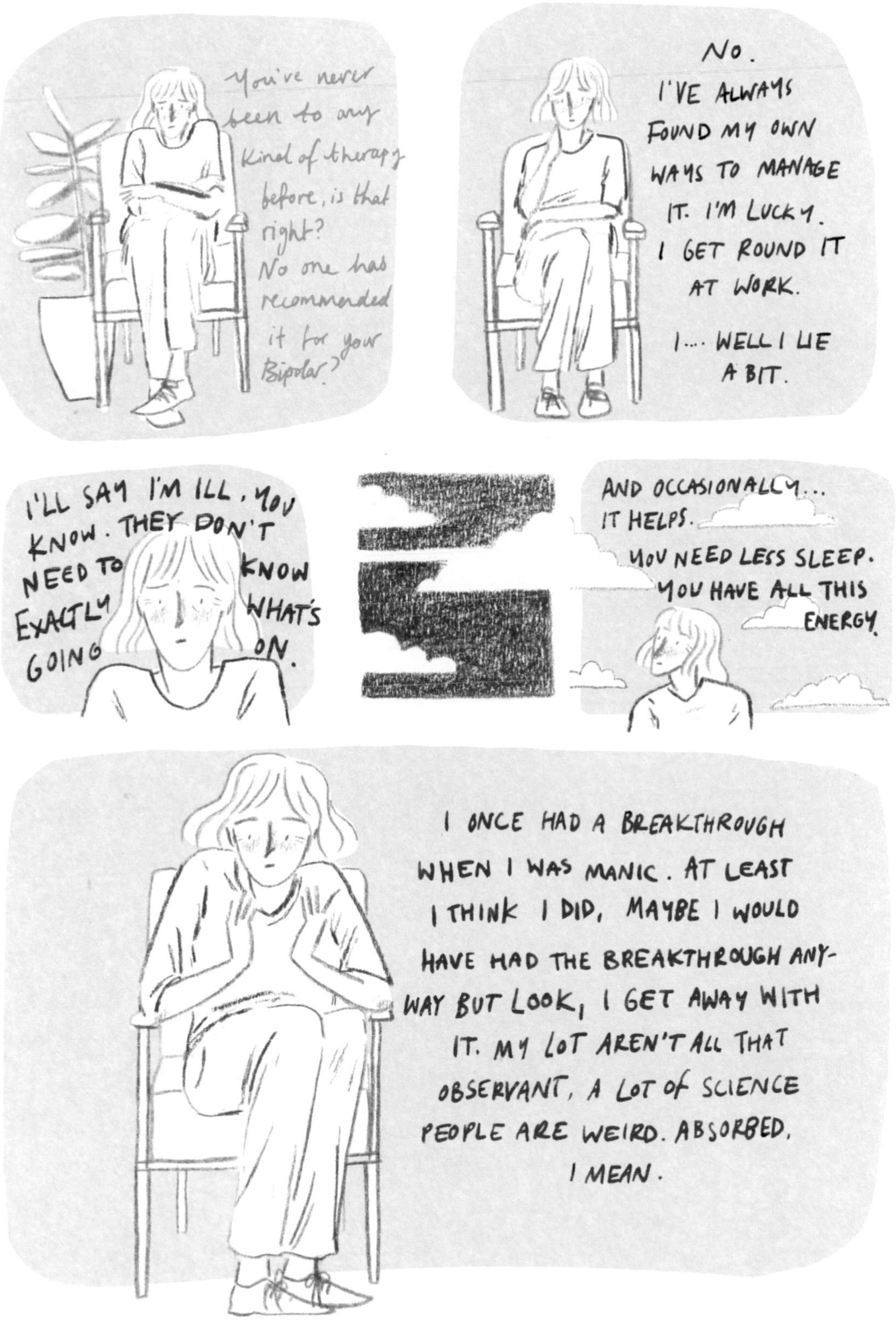
You've never been to any kind of therapy before, is that right? No one has recommended it for your Bipolar?
NO. I'VE ALWAYS FOUND MY OWN WAYS TO MANAGE IT. I'M LUCKY. I GET ROUND IT AT WORK.
I.... WELL I LIE A BIT.
I'LL SAY I'M ILL, YOU KNOW. THEY DON'T NEED TO KNOW EXACTLY WHAT'S GOING ON.
AND OCCASIONALLY... IT HELPS.
YOU NEED LESS SLEEP. YOU HAVE ALL THIS ENERGY.
I ONCE HAD A BREAKTHROUGH WHEN I WAS MANIC. AT LEAST I THINK I DID, MAYBE I WOULD HAVE HAD THE BREAKTHROUGH ANY-WAY BUT LOOK, I GET AWAY WITH IT. MY LOT AREN'T ALL THAT OBSERVANT, A LOT OF SCIENCE PEOPLE ARE WEIRD. ABSORBED, I MEAN.

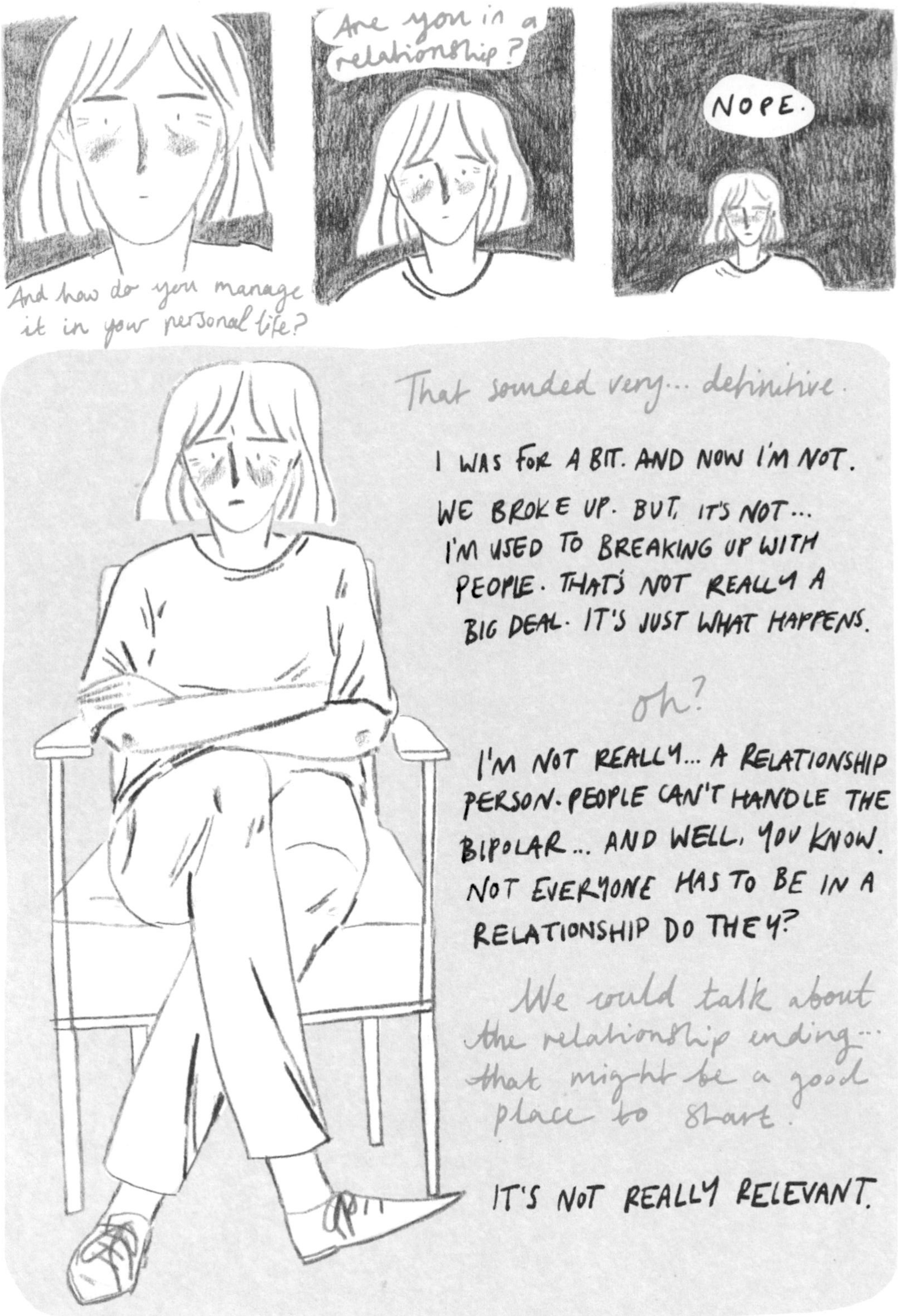
And how do you manage it in your personal life?
Are you in a relationship?
NOPE.
That sounded very... definitive.
I WAS FOR A BIT. AND NOW I'M NOT.
WE BROKE UP. BUT, IT'S NOT... I'M USED TO BREAKING UP WITH PEOPLE. THAT'S NOT REALLY A BIG DEAL. IT'S JUST WHAT HAPPENS.
Oh?
I'M NOT REALLY... A RELATIONSHIP PERSON. PEOPLE CAN'T HANDLE THE BIPOLAR... AND WELL, YOU KNOW. NOT EVERYONE HAS TO BE IN A RELATIONSHIP DO THEY?
We could talk about the relationship ending... that might be a good place to start.
IT'S NOT REALLY RELEVANT.

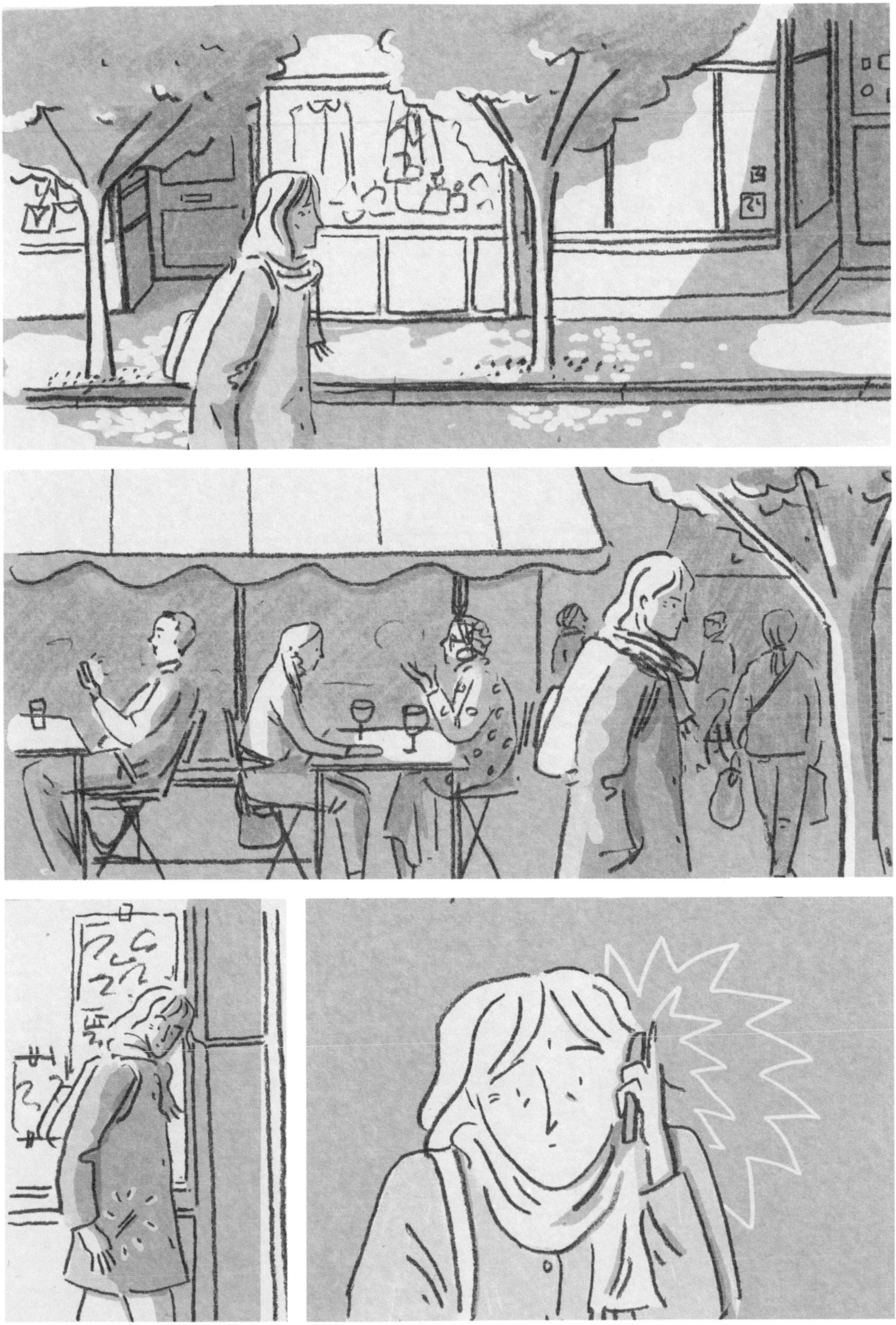

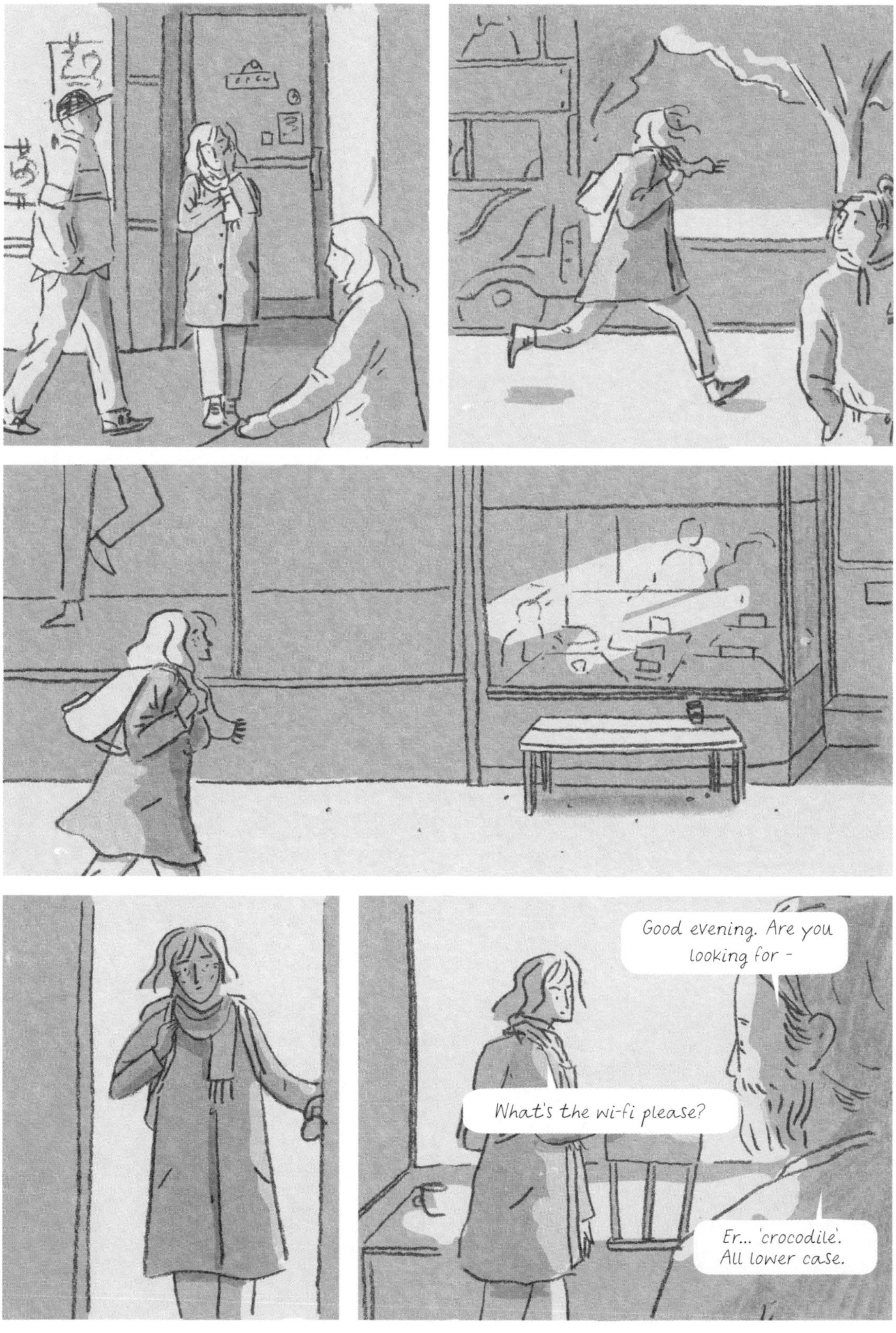
Good evening. Are you looking for -
What's the wi-fi please?
Er... 'crocodile'. All lower case.

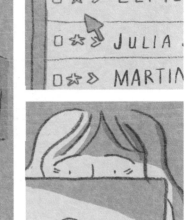

O ☆ ≫ ELPIS
O ☆ ≫ JULIA.
O ☆ ≫ MARTIN

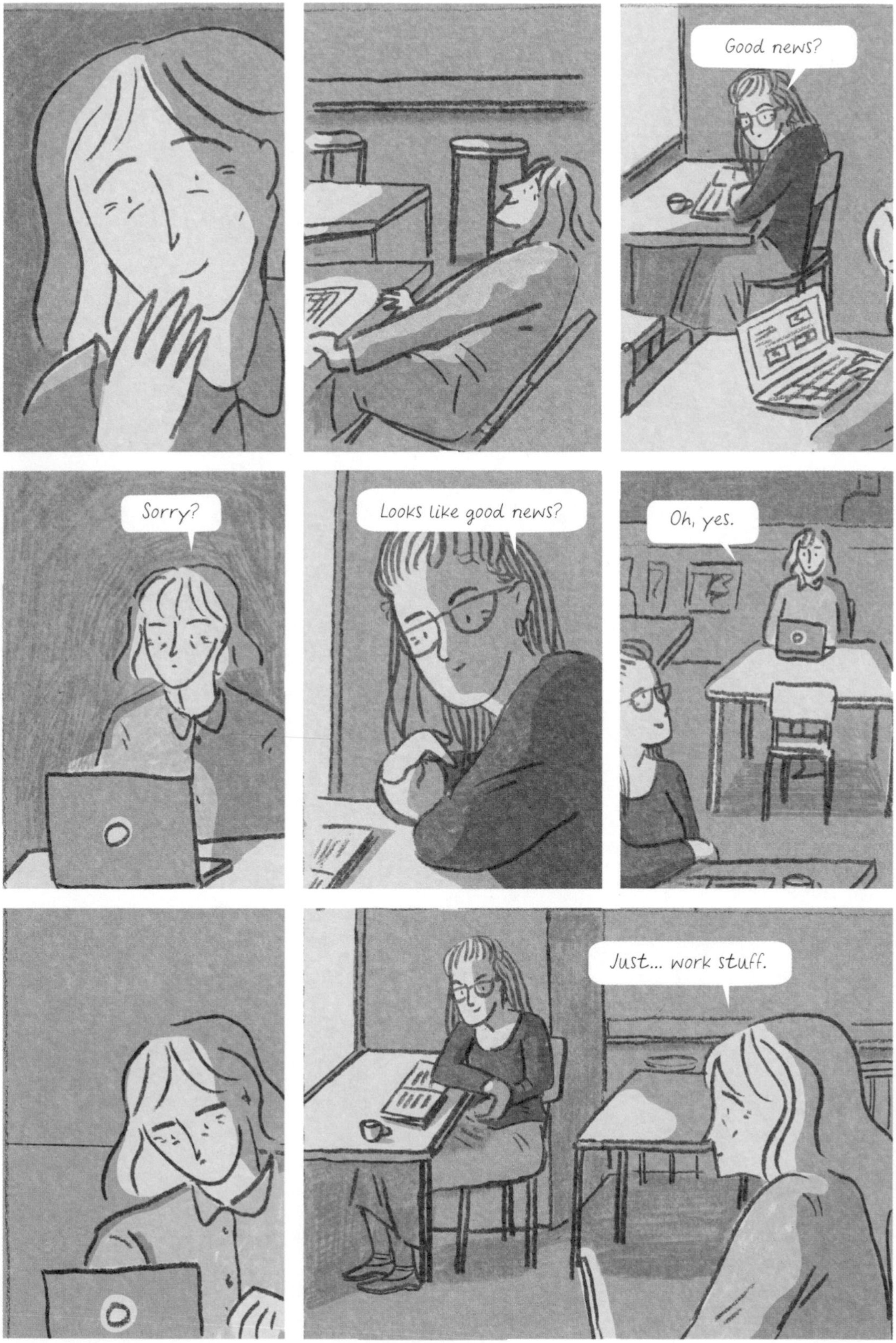
Good news?
Sorry?
Looks like good news?
Oh, yes.
Just... work stuff.

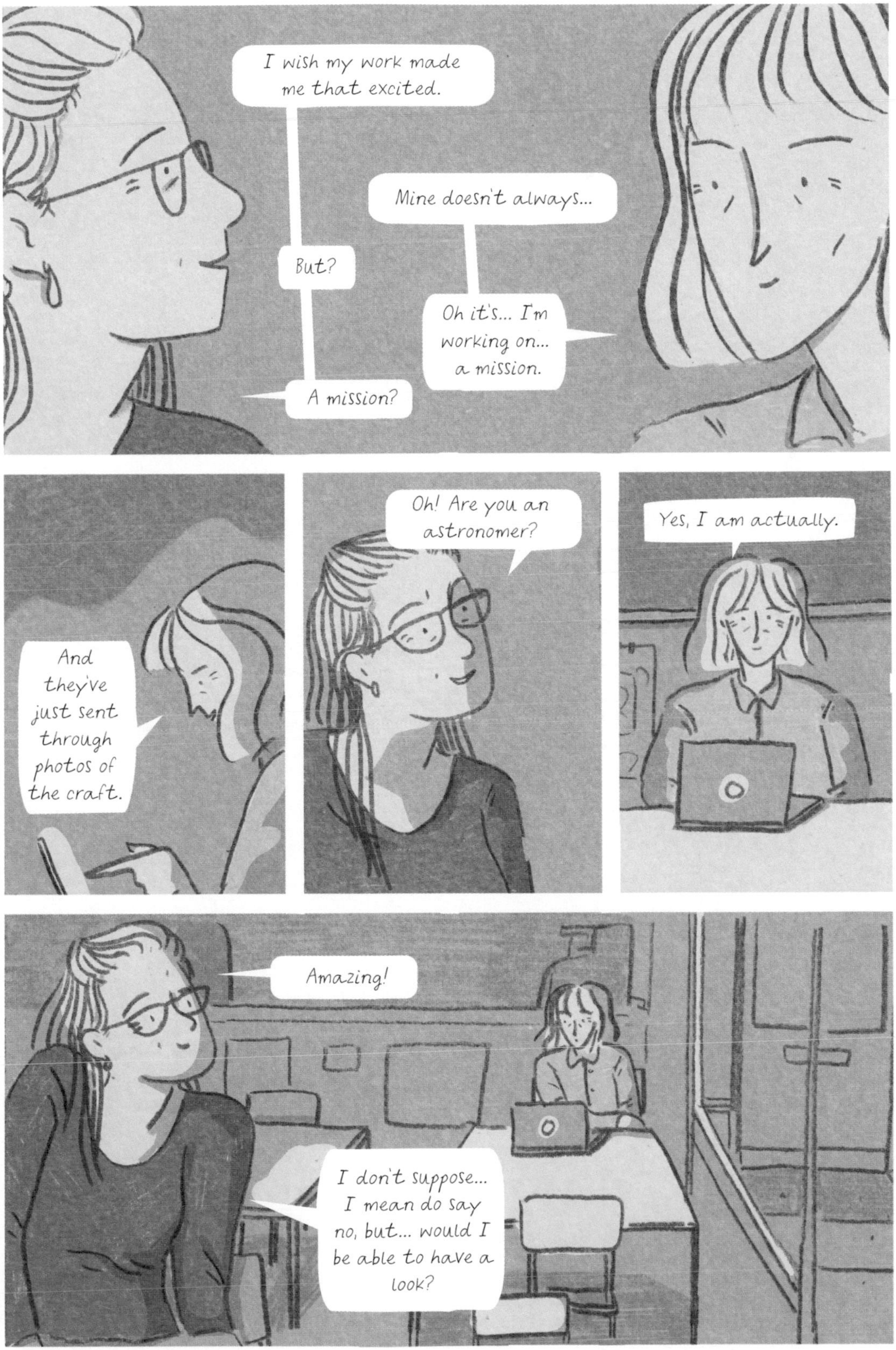
I wish my work made me that excited.
Mine doesn't always...
But?
Oh it's... I'm working on... a mission.
A mission?
And they've just sent through photos of the craft.
Oh! Are you an astronomer?
Yes, I am actually.
Amazing!
I don't suppose... I mean do say no, but... would I be able to have a look?

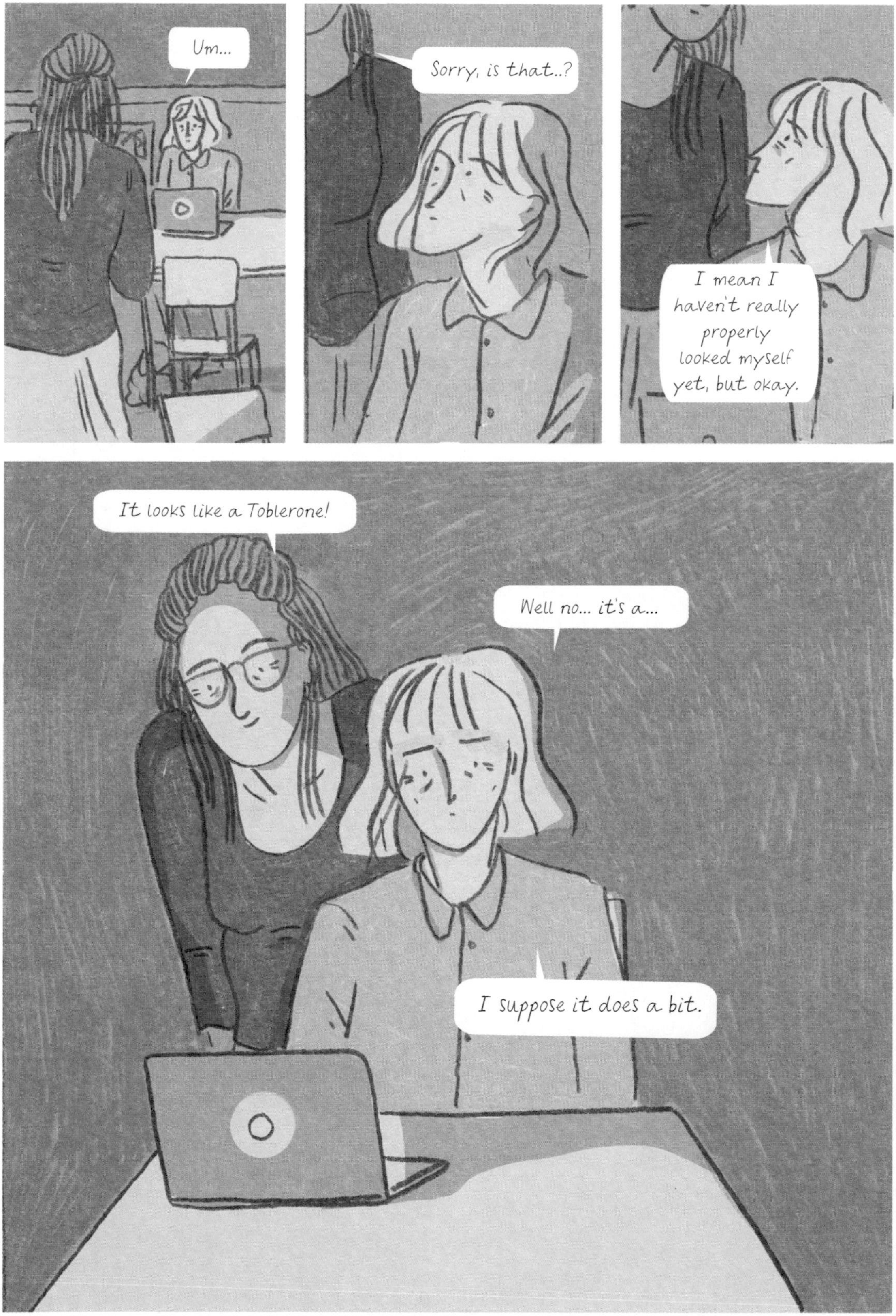
Um...
Sorry, is that..?
I mean I haven't really properly looked myself yet, but okay.
It looks like a Toblerone!
Well no... it's a...
I suppose it does a bit.

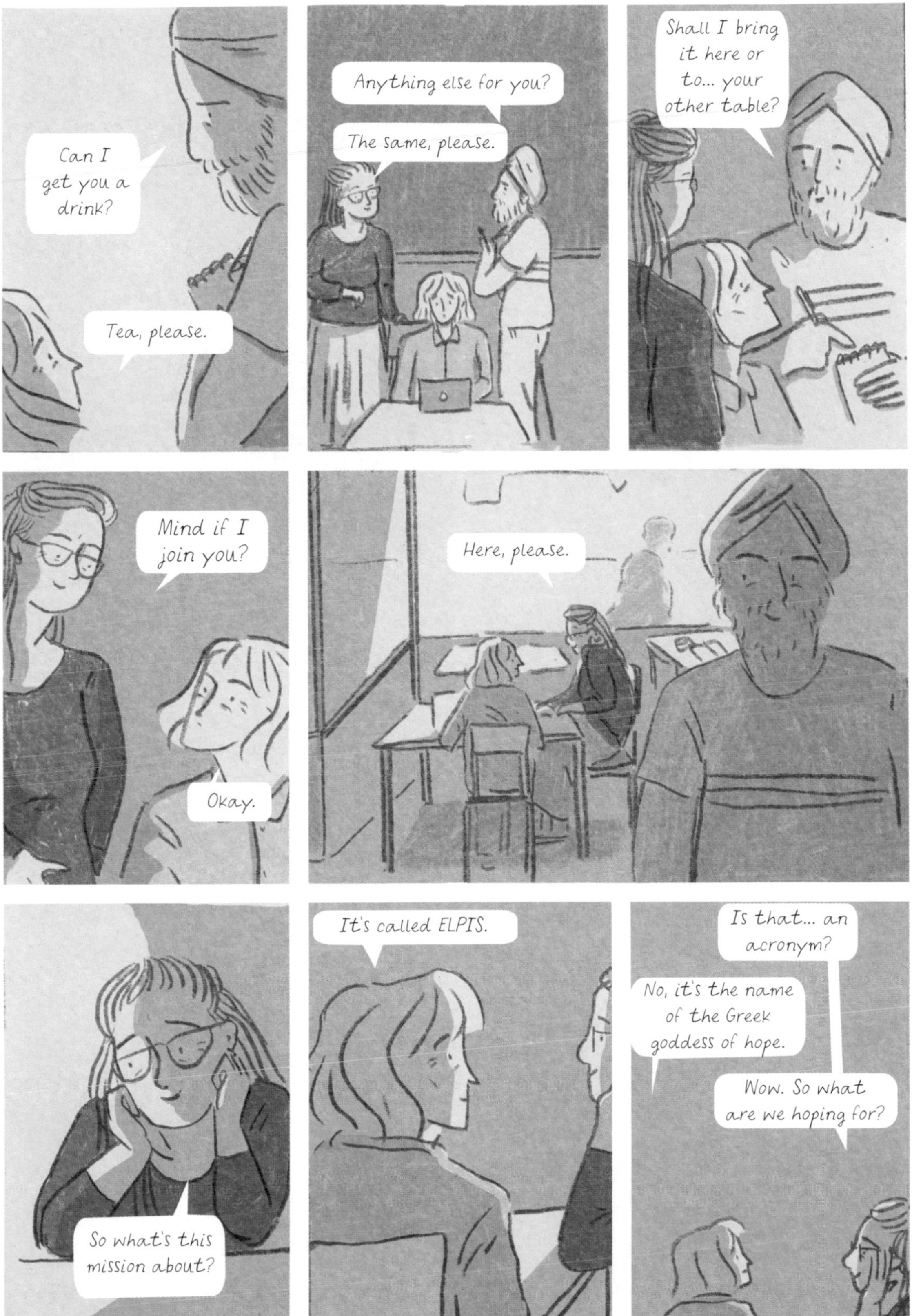
Can I get you a drink?
Tea, please.
Anything else for you?
The same, please.
Shall I bring it here or to... your other table?
Mind if I join you?
Okay.
Here, please.
So what's this mission about?
It's called ELPIS.
Is that... an acronym?
No, it's the name of the Greek goddess of hope.
Wow. So what are we hoping for?

It's a mission to find habitable exoplanets.
You've lost me already I'm afraid. What's an exoplanet?.
It's a planet outside of our solar system.
Right. Orbiting a different star?
Exactly.
Wow!
No one's done that yet, obviously, or you'd have heard about it. So these telescopes allow us to...

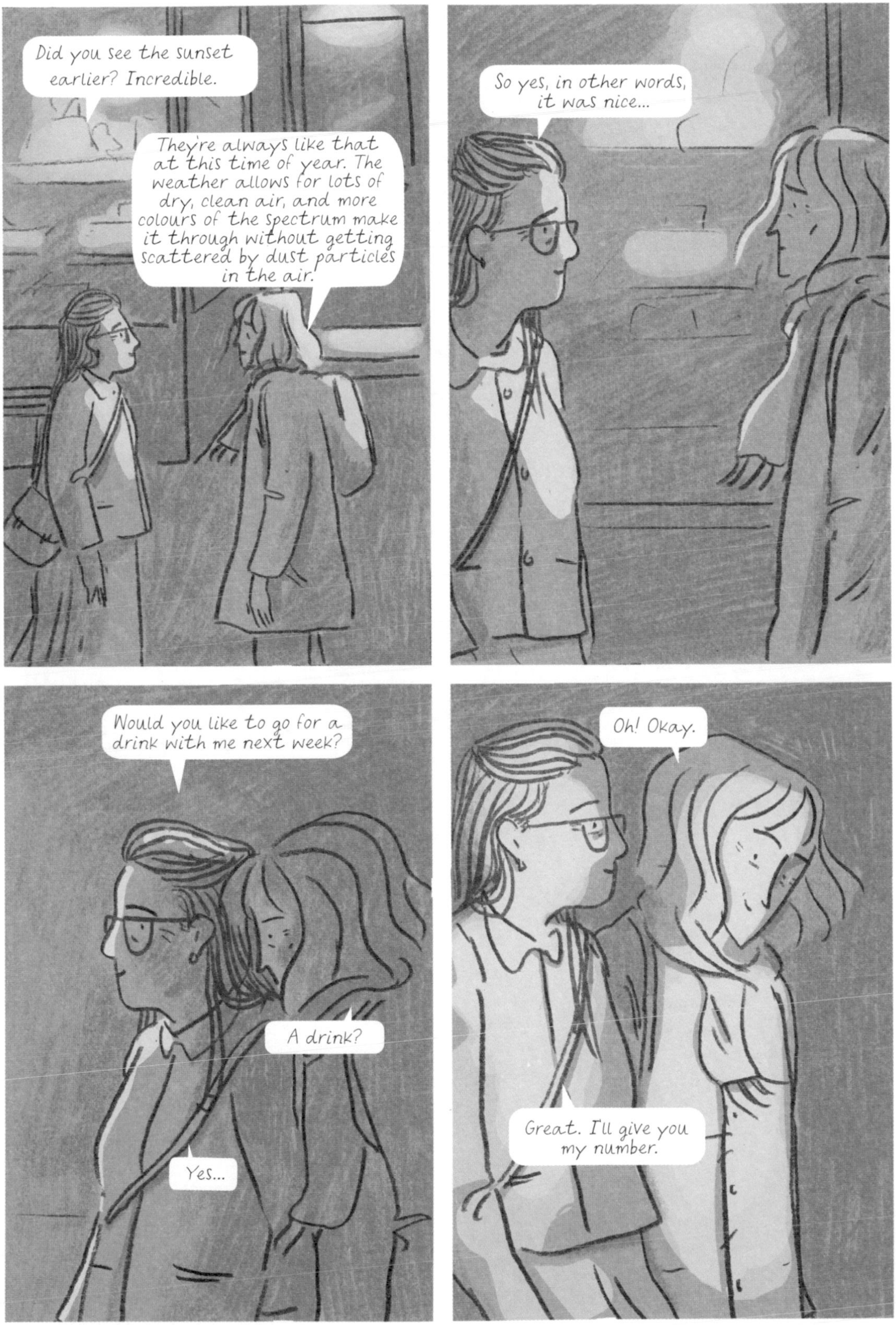
Did you see the sunset earlier? Incredible.
They're always like that at this time of year. The weather allows for lots of dry, clean air, and more colours of the spectrum make it through without getting scattered by dust particles in the air.
So yes, in other words, it was nice...
Would you like to go for a drink with me next week?
A drink?
Yes...
Oh! Okay.
Great. I'll give you my number.

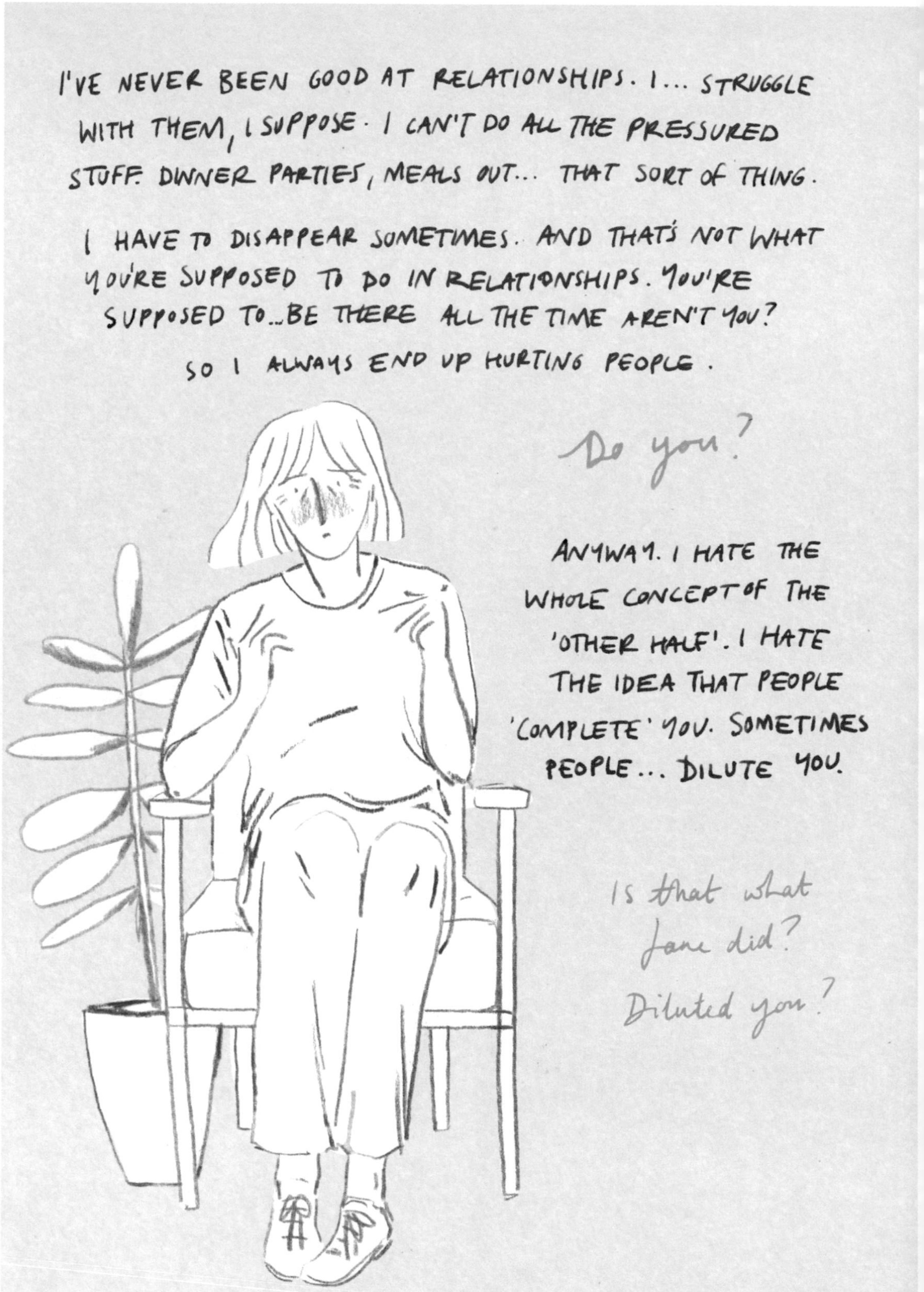

I'VE NEVER BEEN GOOD AT RELATIONSHIPS. I... STRUGGLE WITH THEM, I SUPPOSE. I CAN'T DO ALL THE PRESSURED STUFF. DINNER PARTIES, MEALS OUT... THAT SORT OF THING.

I HAVE TO DISAPPEAR SOMETIMES. AND THAT'S NOT WHAT YOU'RE SUPPOSED TO DO IN RELATIONSHIPS. YOU'RE SUPPOSED TO...BE THERE ALL THE TIME AREN'T YOU?

SO I ALWAYS END UP HURTING PEOPLE.

Do you?

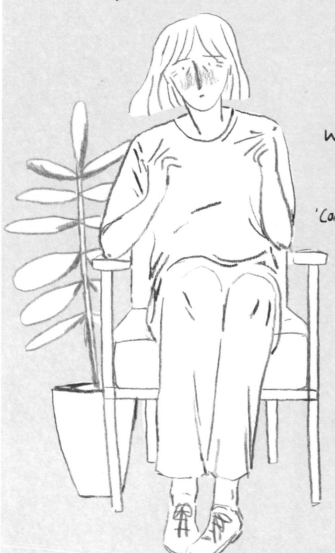

ANYWAY. I HATE THE WHOLE CONCEPT OF THE 'OTHER HALF'. I HATE THE IDEA THAT PEOPLE 'COMPLETE' YOU. SOMETIMES PEOPLE... DILUTE YOU.

Is that what Jane did? Diluted you?

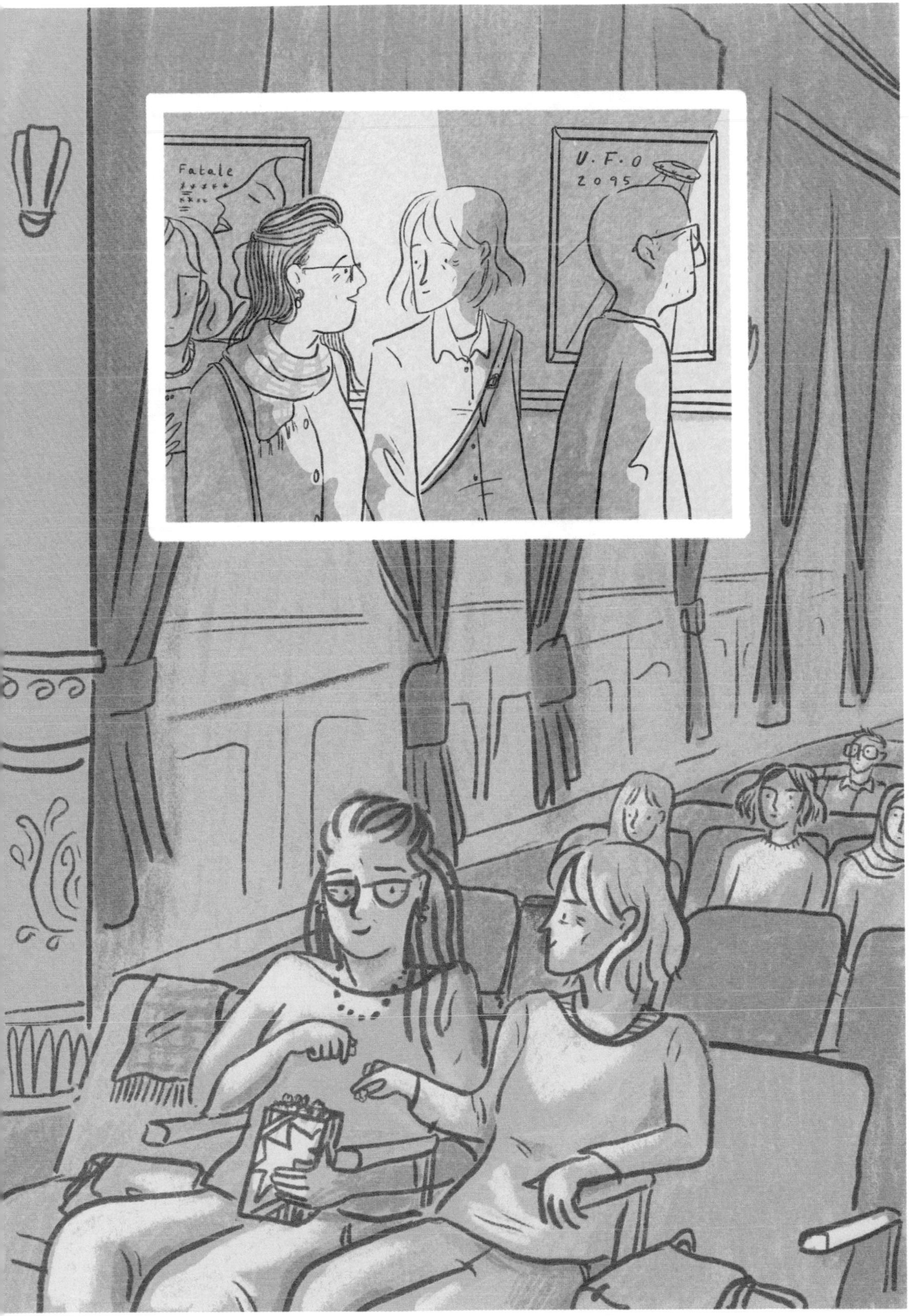
Fatale
U.F.O
2095

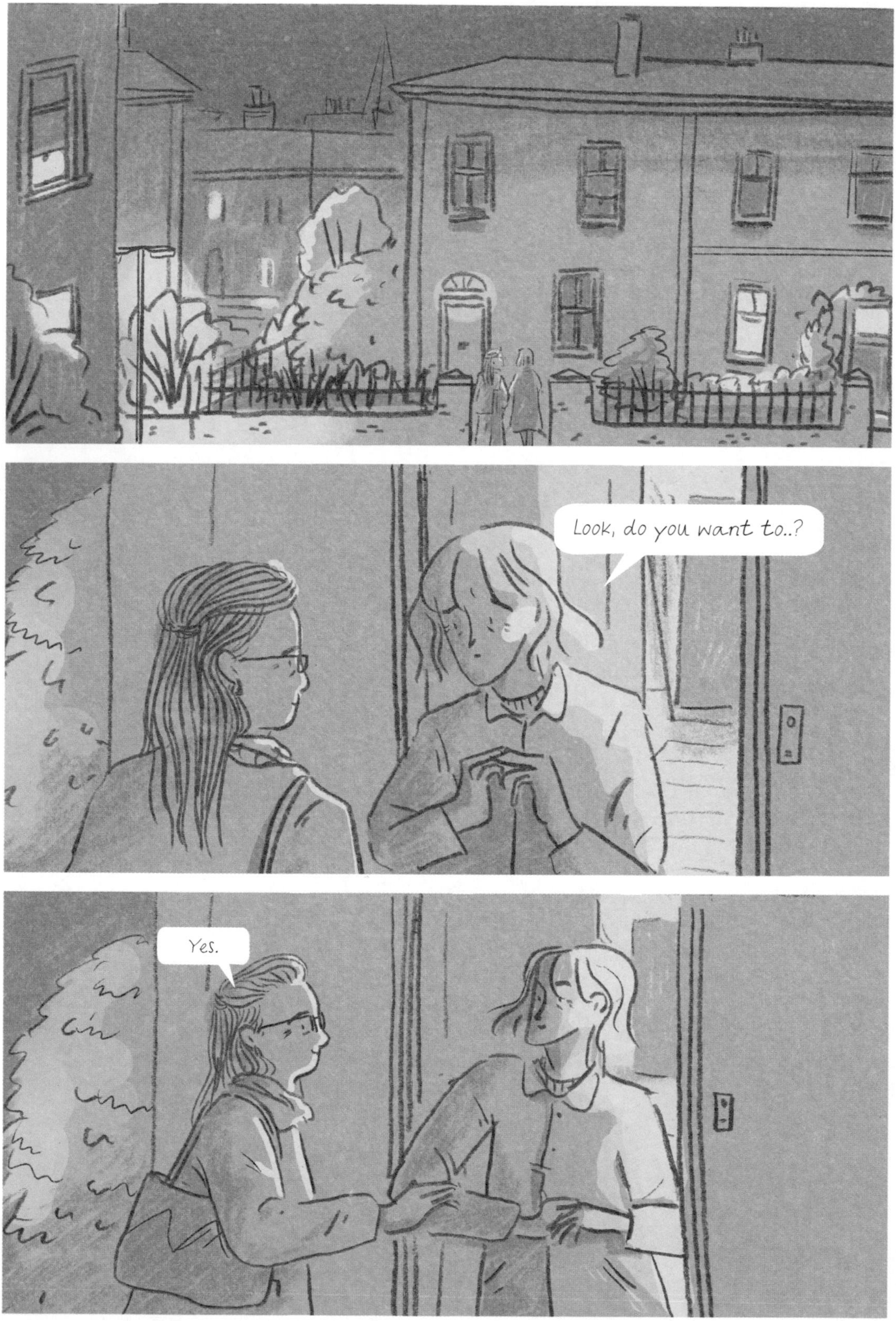
Look, do you want to..?
Yes.

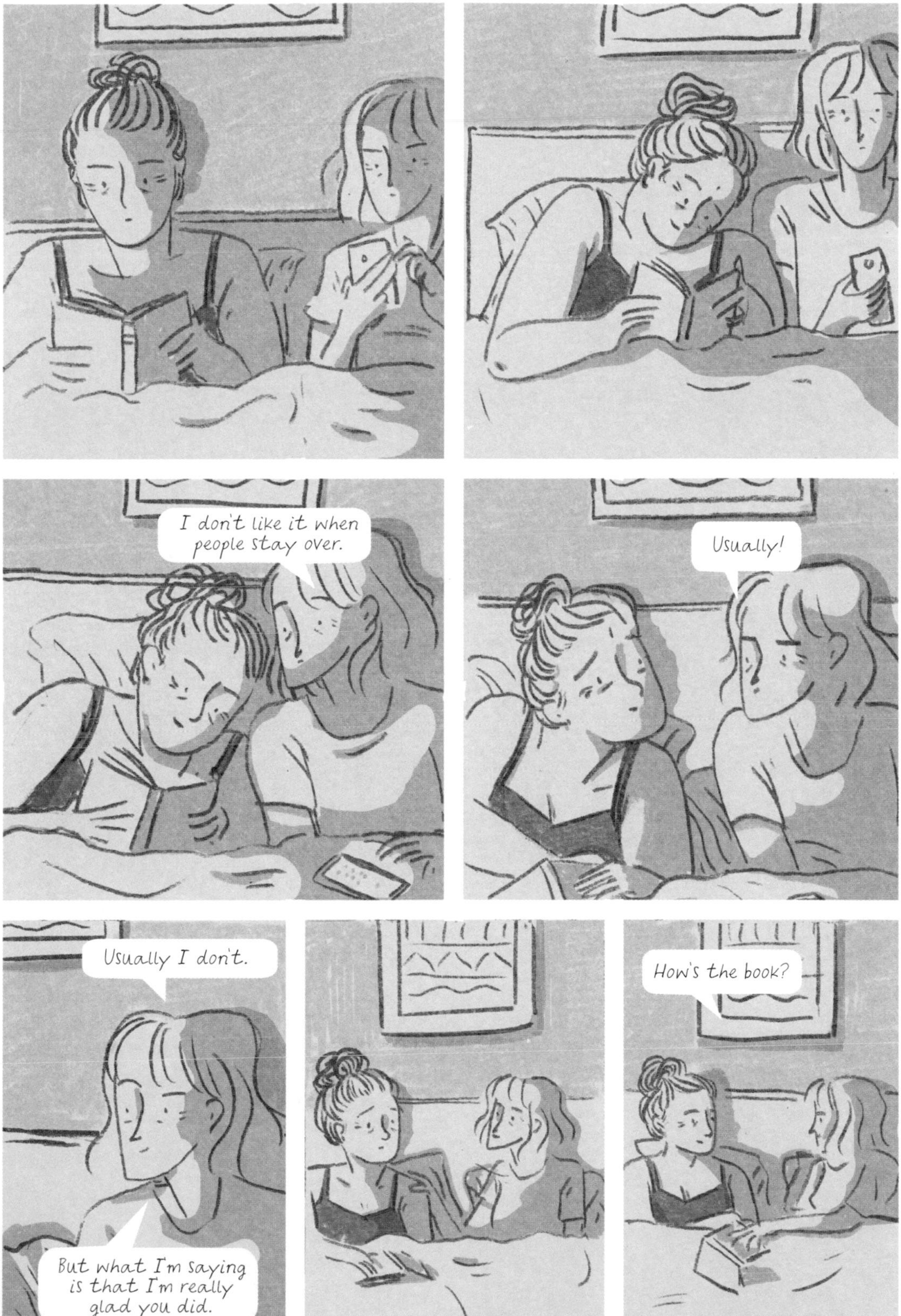
I don't like it when people stay over.
Usually!
Usually I don't.
But what I'm saying is that I'm really glad you did.
How's the book?

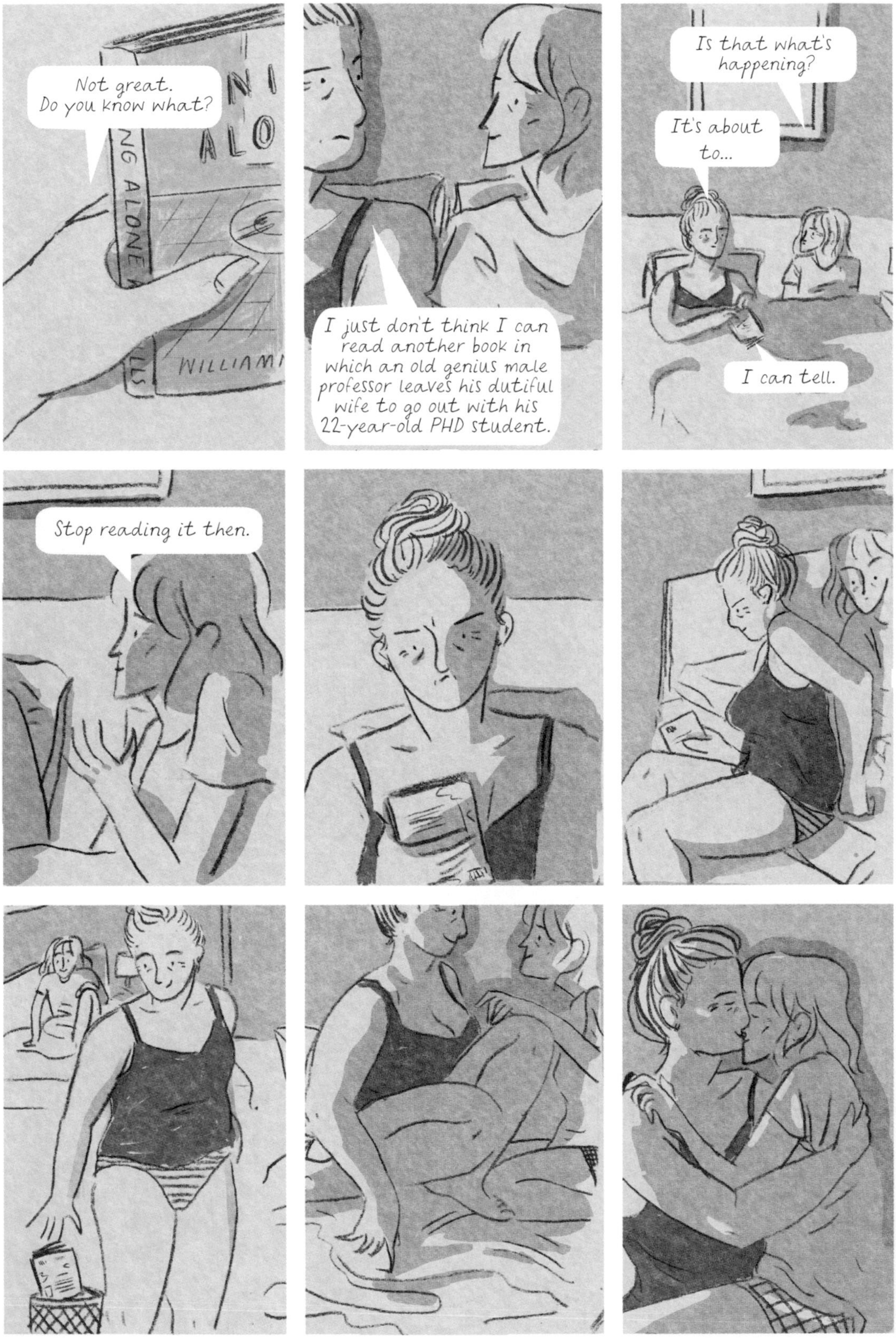
Not great.
Do you know what?
I just don't think I can read another book in which an old genius male professor leaves his dutiful wife to go out with his 22-year-old PHD student.
Is that what's happening?
It's about to...
I can tell.
Stop reading it then.

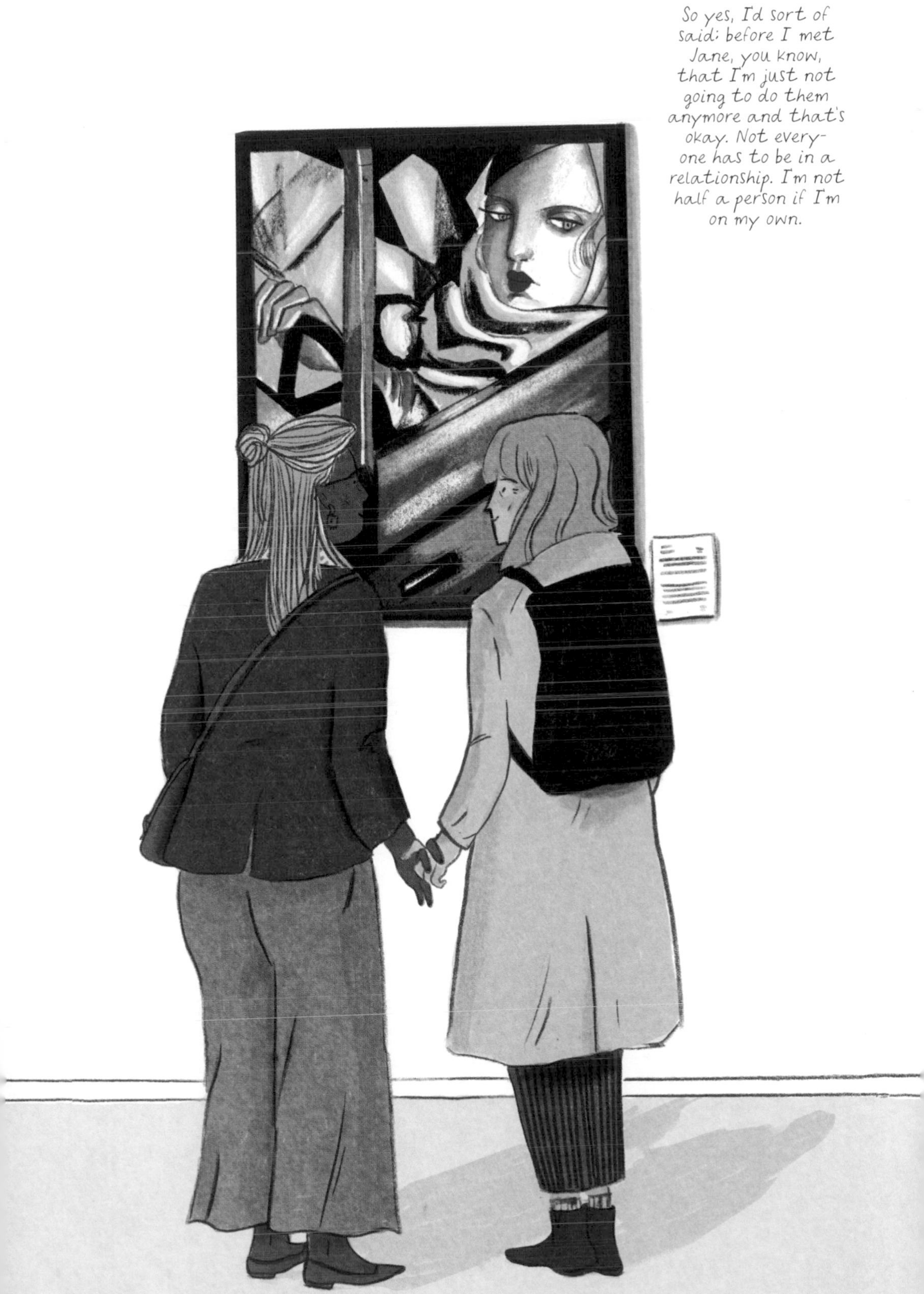
So yes, I'd sort of said; before I met Jane, you know, that I'm just not going to do them anymore and that's okay. Not every-one has to be in a relationship. I'm not half a person if I'm on my own.

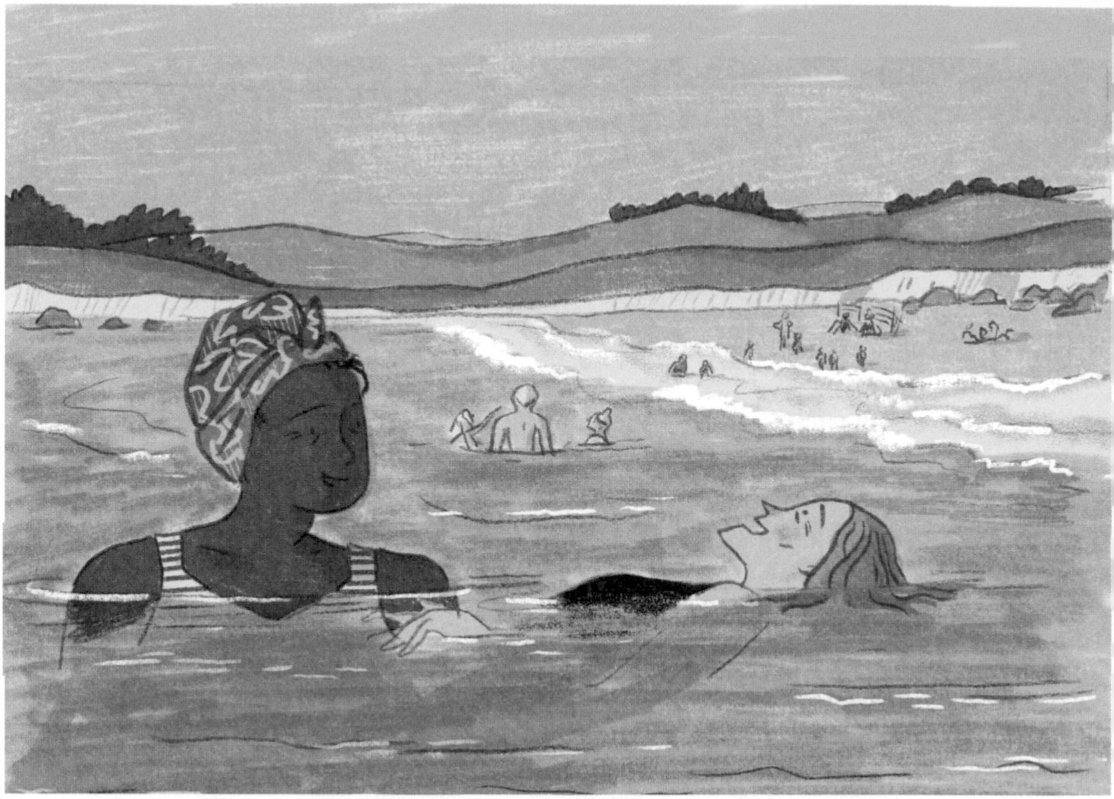

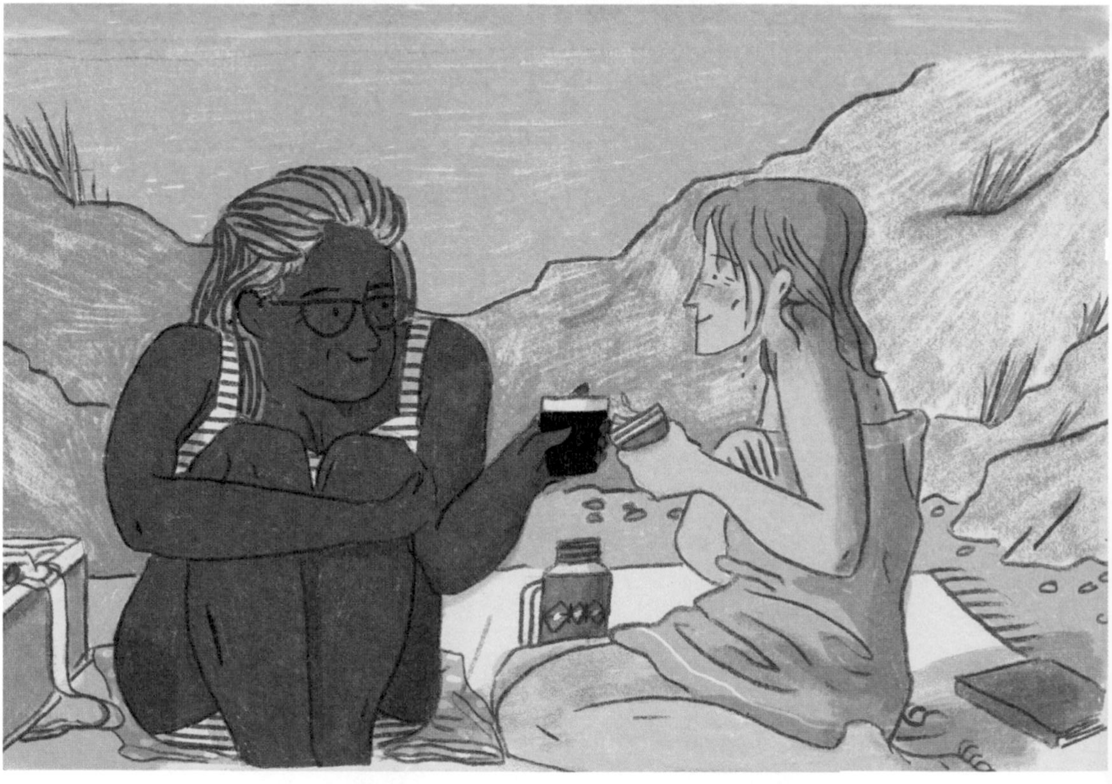

It was different with Jane. When I was with her I wasn't even thinking about breaking up with her. I normally spend the whole time worrying about when I'm going to have to do that... and trying to adhere to the campsite rule.

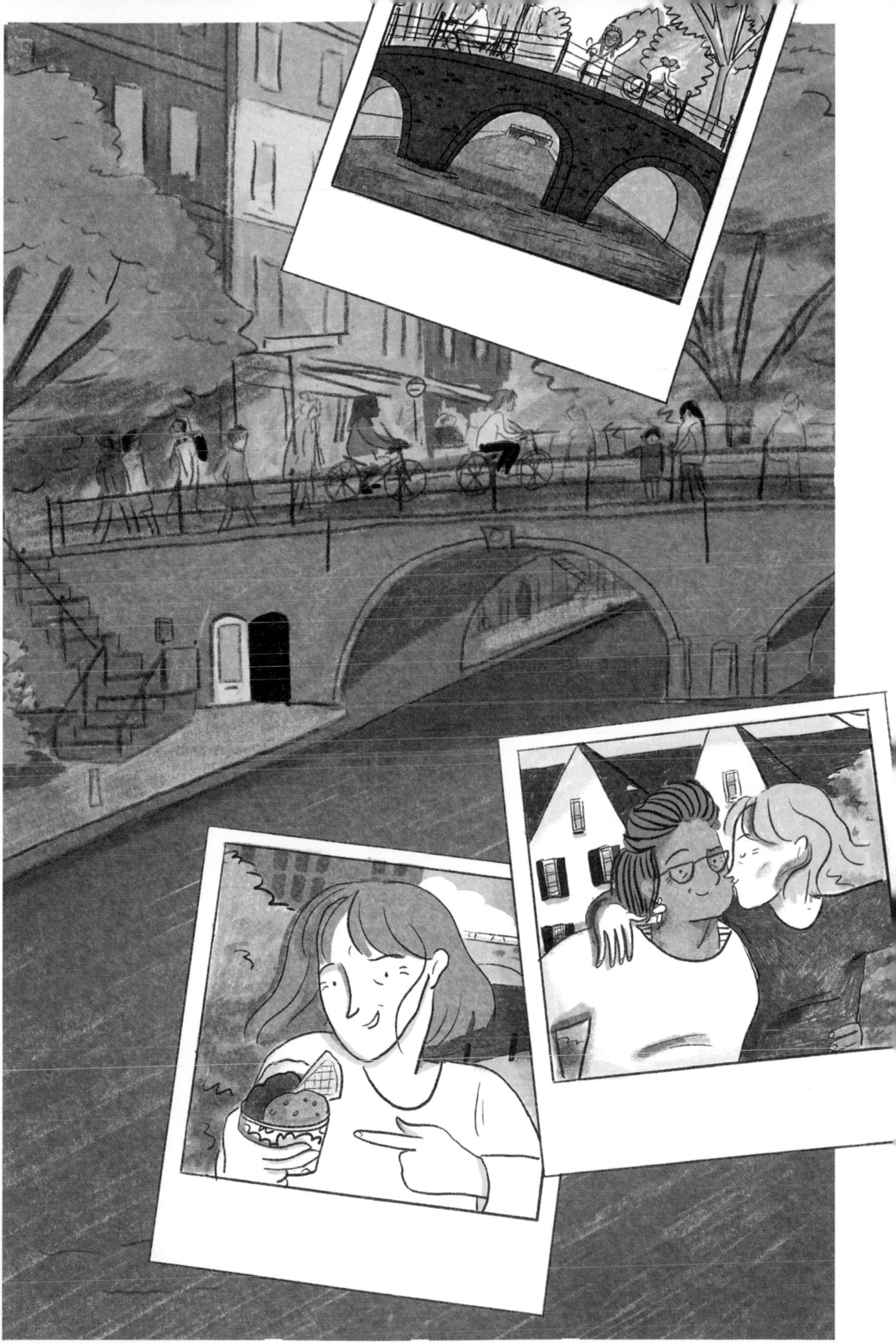

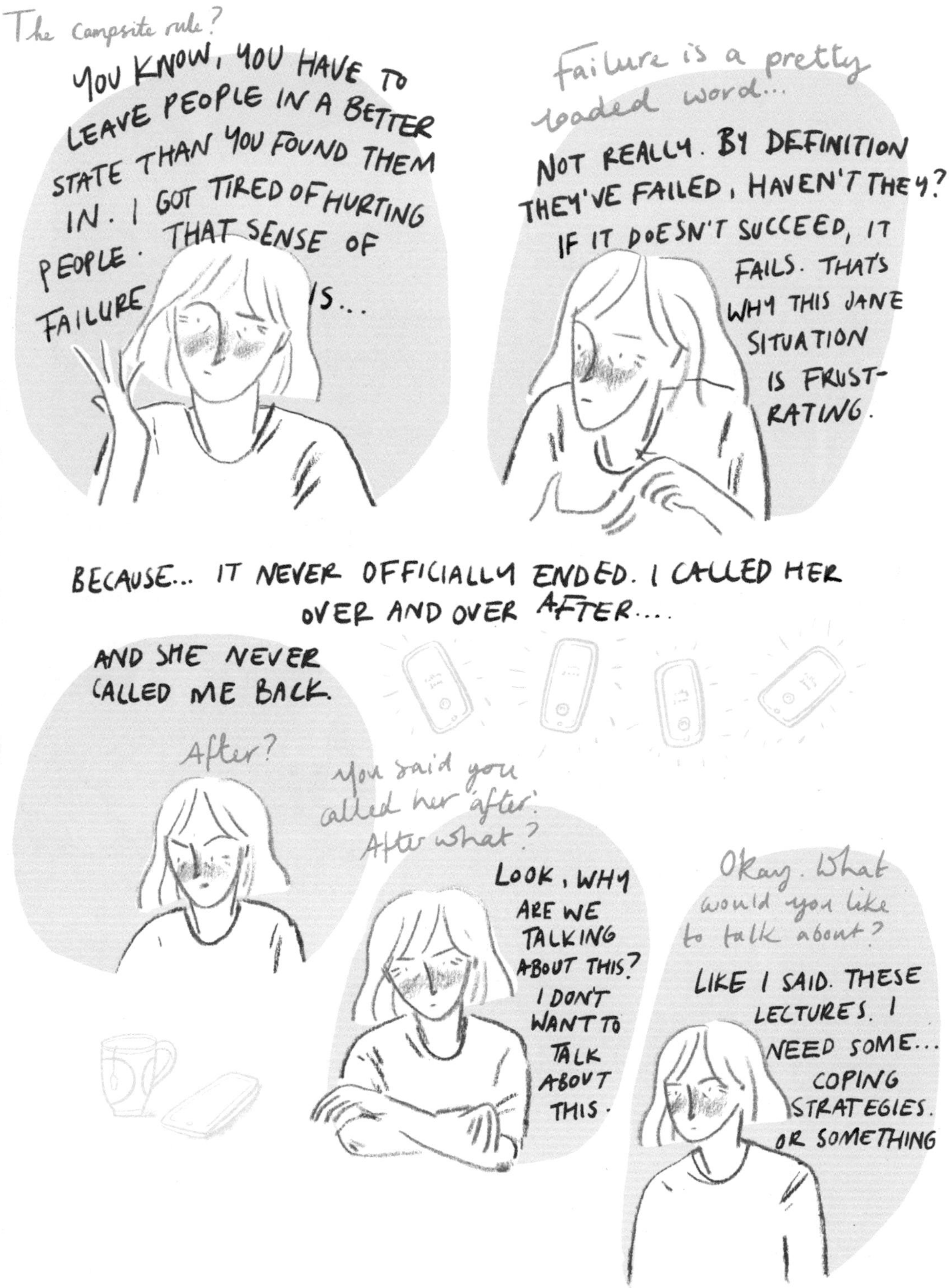
The campsite rule?
YOU KNOW, YOU HAVE TO LEAVE PEOPLE IN A BETTER STATE THAN YOU FOUND THEM IN. I GOT TIRED OF HURTING PEOPLE. THAT SENSE OF FAILURE IS...
Failure is a pretty loaded word...
NOT REALLY. BY DEFINITION THEY'VE FAILED, HAVEN'T THEY? IF IT DOESN'T SUCCEED, IT FAILS. THAT'S WHY THIS JANE SITUATION IS FRUSTRATING.
BECAUSE... IT NEVER OFFICIALLY ENDED. I CALLED HER OVER AND OVER AFTER....
AND SHE NEVER CALLED ME BACK.
After?
You said you called her 'after'. After what?
LOOK, WHY ARE WE TALKING ABOUT THIS? I DON'T WANT TO TALK ABOUT THIS.
Okay. What would you like to talk about?
LIKE I SAID. THESE LECTURES. I NEED SOME... COPING STRATEGIES. OR SOMETHING

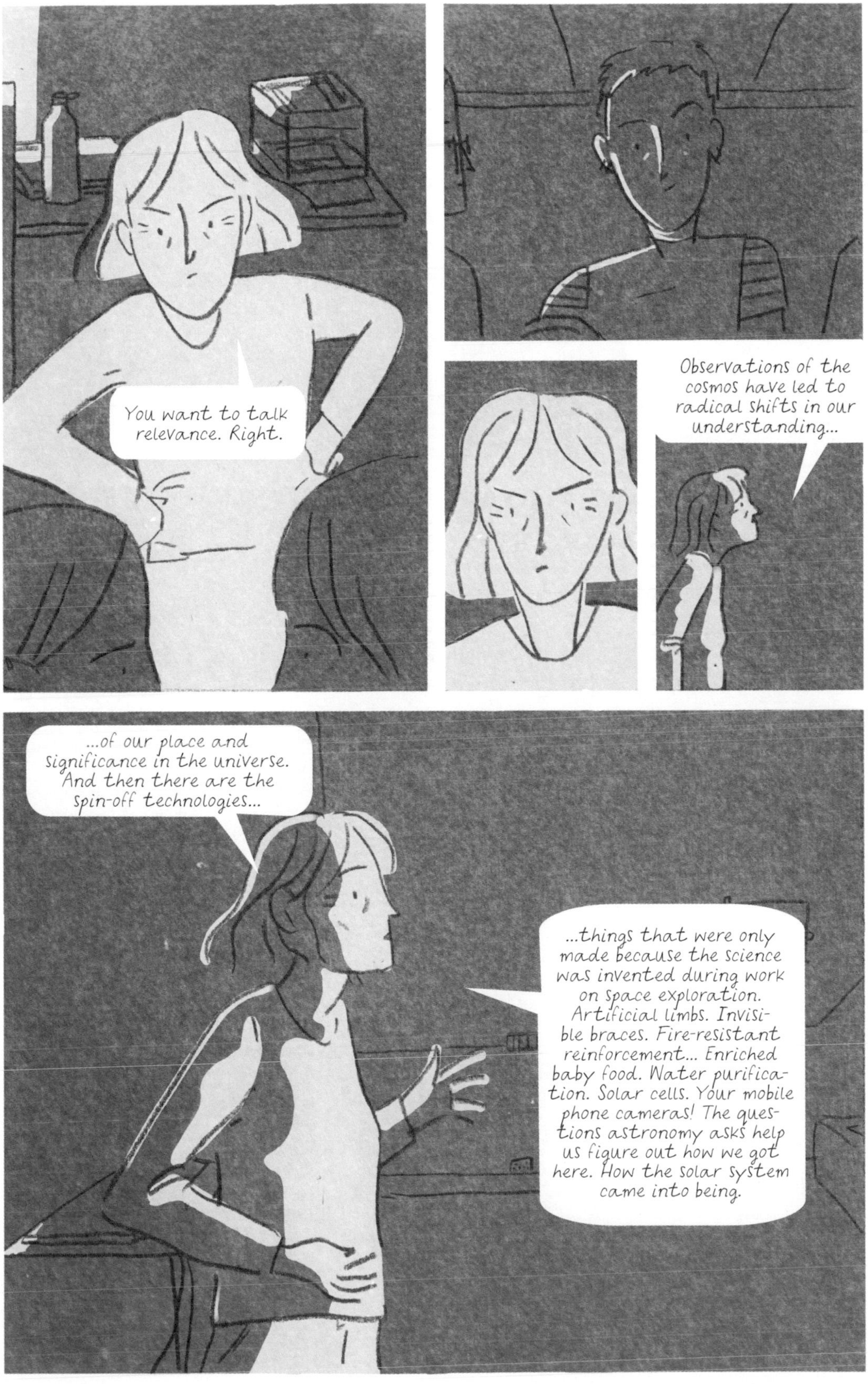
You want to talk relevance. Right.
Observations of the cosmos have led to radical shifts in our understanding...
...of our place and significance in the universe. And then there are the spin-off technologies...
...things that were only made because the science was invented during work on space exploration. Artificial limbs. Invisible braces. Fire-resistant reinforcement... Enriched baby food. Water purification. Solar cells. Your mobile phone cameras! The questions astronomy asks help us figure out how we got here. How the solar system came into being.

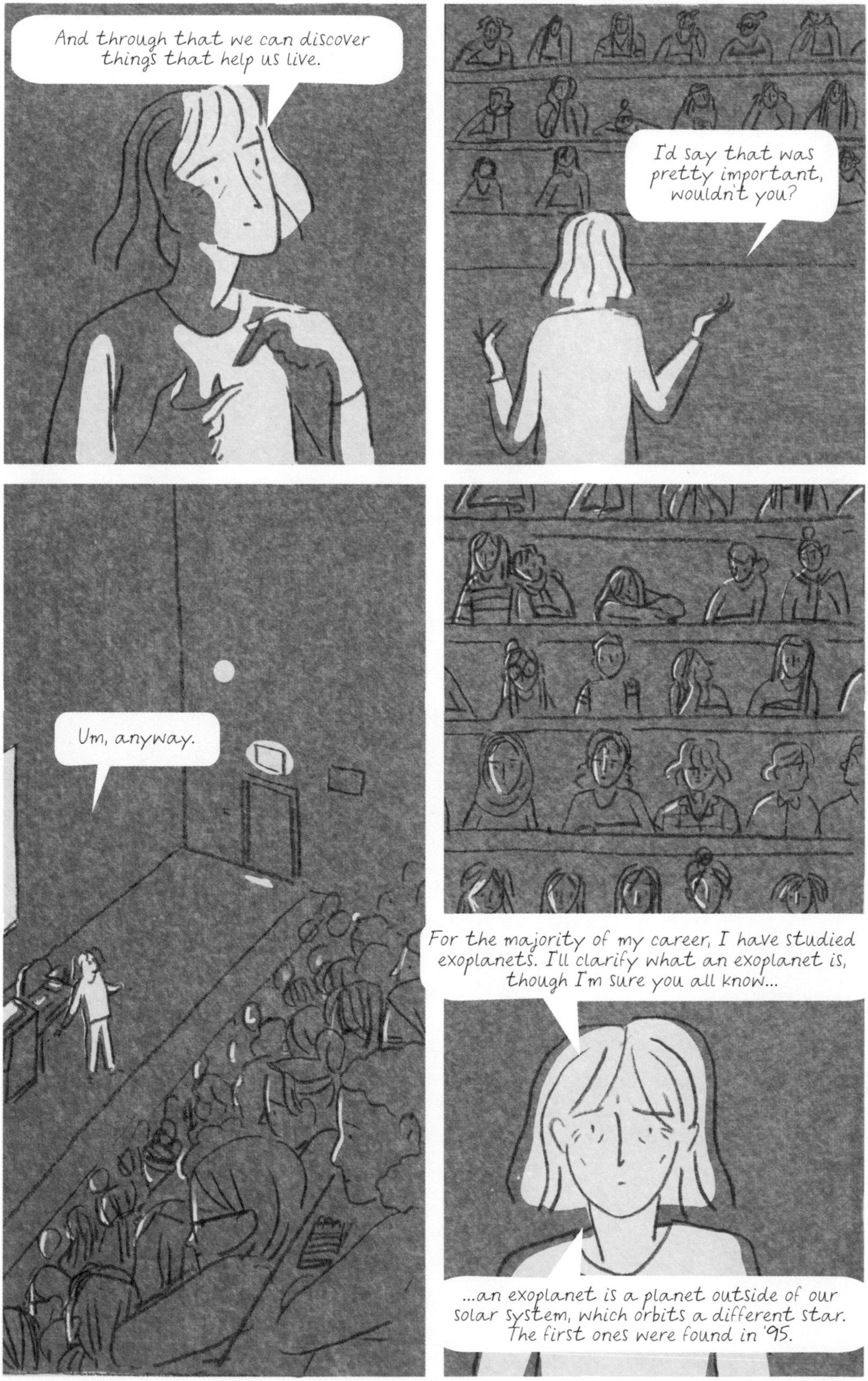
And through that we can discover things that help us live.
I'd say that was pretty important, wouldn't you?
Um, anyway.
For the majority of my career, I have studied exoplanets. I'll clarify what an exoplanet is, though I'm sure you all know...
...an exoplanet is a planet outside of our solar system, which orbits a different star. The first ones were found in '95.

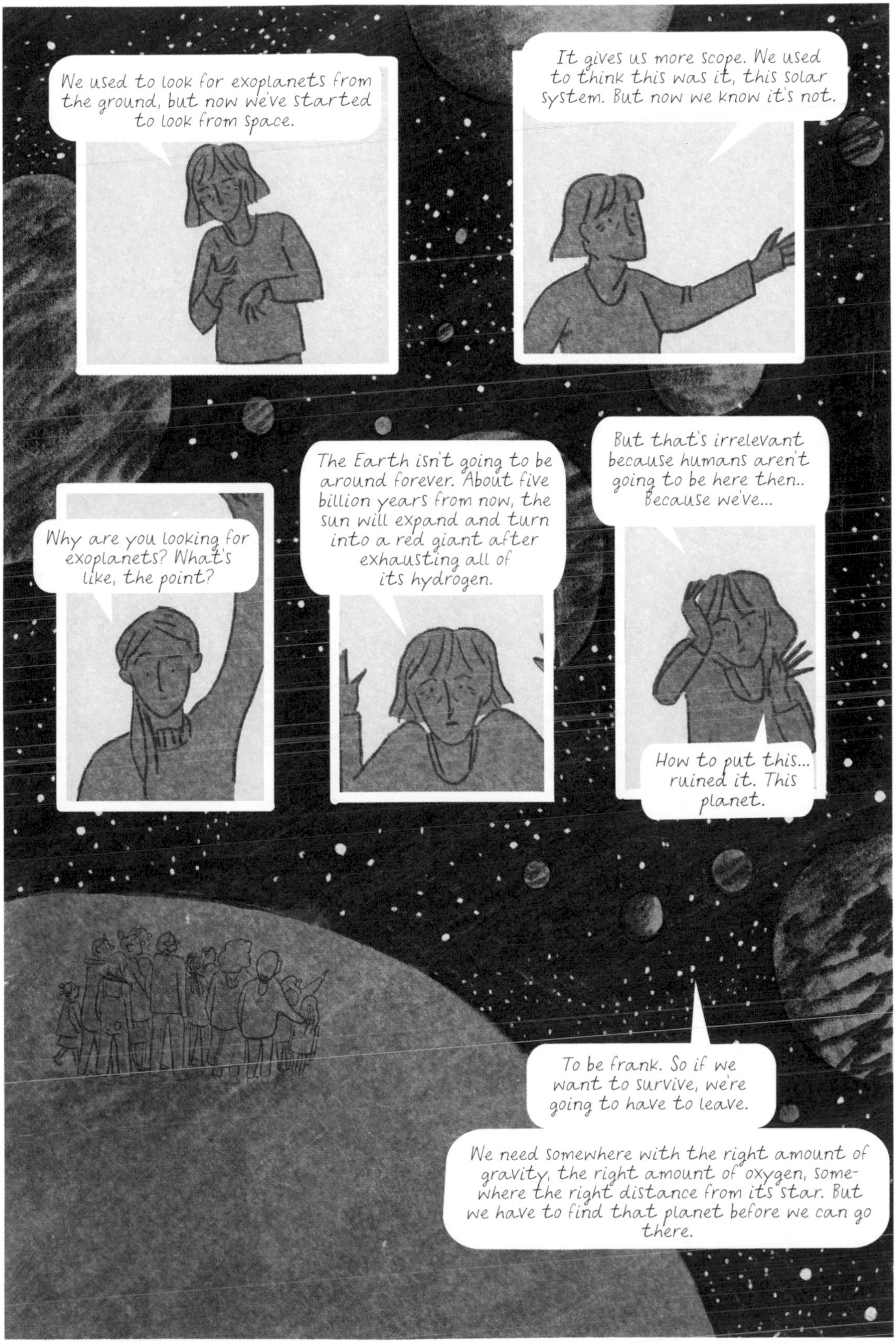

We used to look for exoplanets from the ground, but now we've started to look from space.
It gives us more scope. We used to think this was it, this solar system. But now we know it's not.
Why are you looking for exoplanets? What's like, the point?
The Earth isn't going to be around forever. About five billion years from now, the sun will expand and turn into a red giant after exhausting all of its hydrogen.
But that's irrelevant because humans aren't going to be here then.. Because we've...
How to put this... ruined it. This planet.
To be frank. So if we want to survive, we're going to have to leave.
We need somewhere with the right amount of gravity, the right amount of oxygen, somewhere the right distance from its star. But we have to find that planet before we can go there.

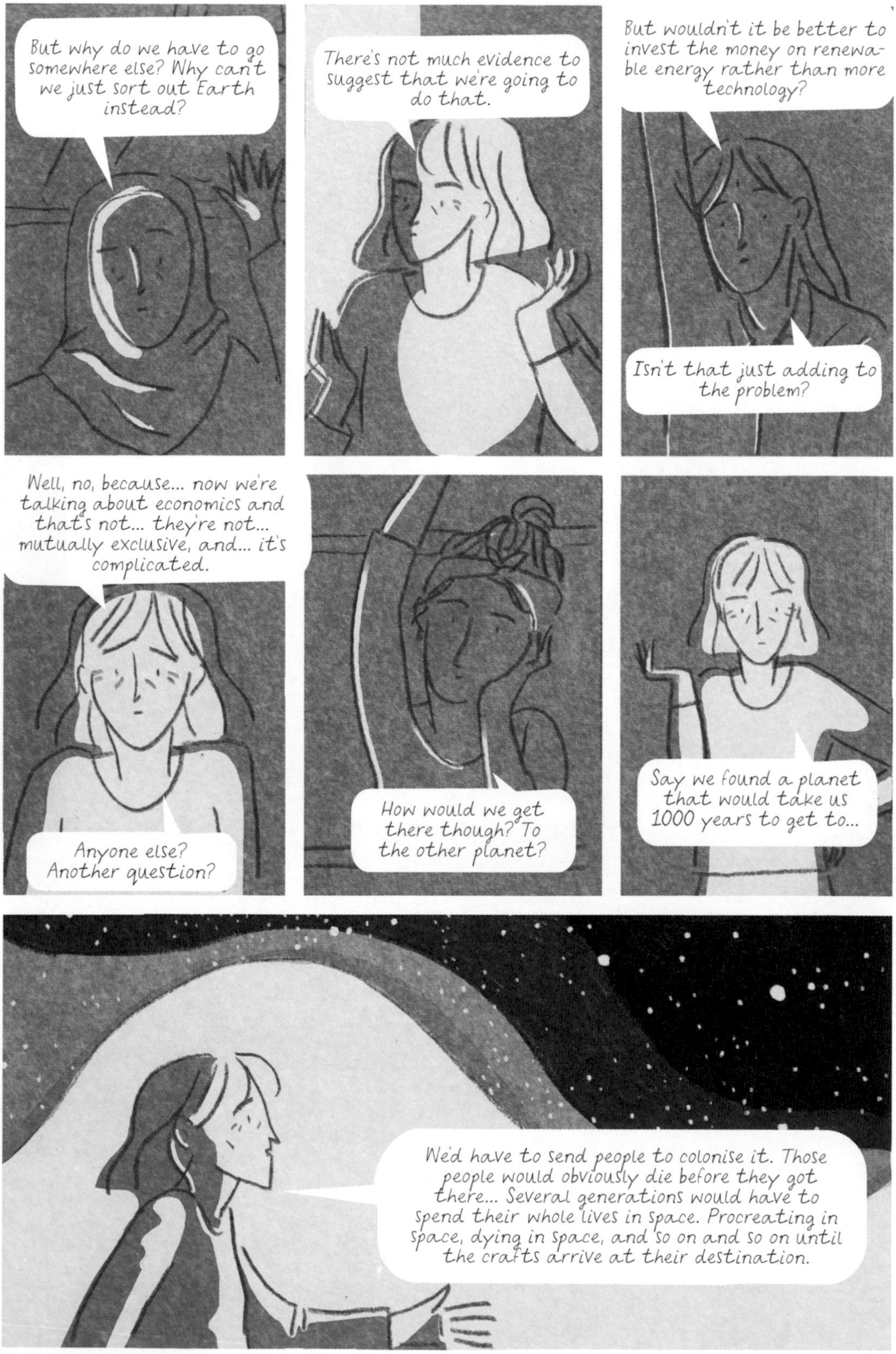
But why do we have to go somewhere else? Why can't we just sort out Earth instead?
There's not much evidence to suggest that we're going to do that.
But wouldn't it be better to invest the money on renewable energy rather than more technology?
Isn't that just adding to the problem?
Well, no, because... now we're talking about economics and that's not... they're not... mutually exclusive, and... it's complicated.
Anyone else? Another question?
How would we get there though? To the other planet?
Say we found a planet that would take us 1000 years to get to...
We'd have to send people to colonise it. Those people would obviously die before they got there... Several generations would have to spend their whole lives in space. Procreating in space, dying in space, and so on and so on until the crafts arrive at their destination.

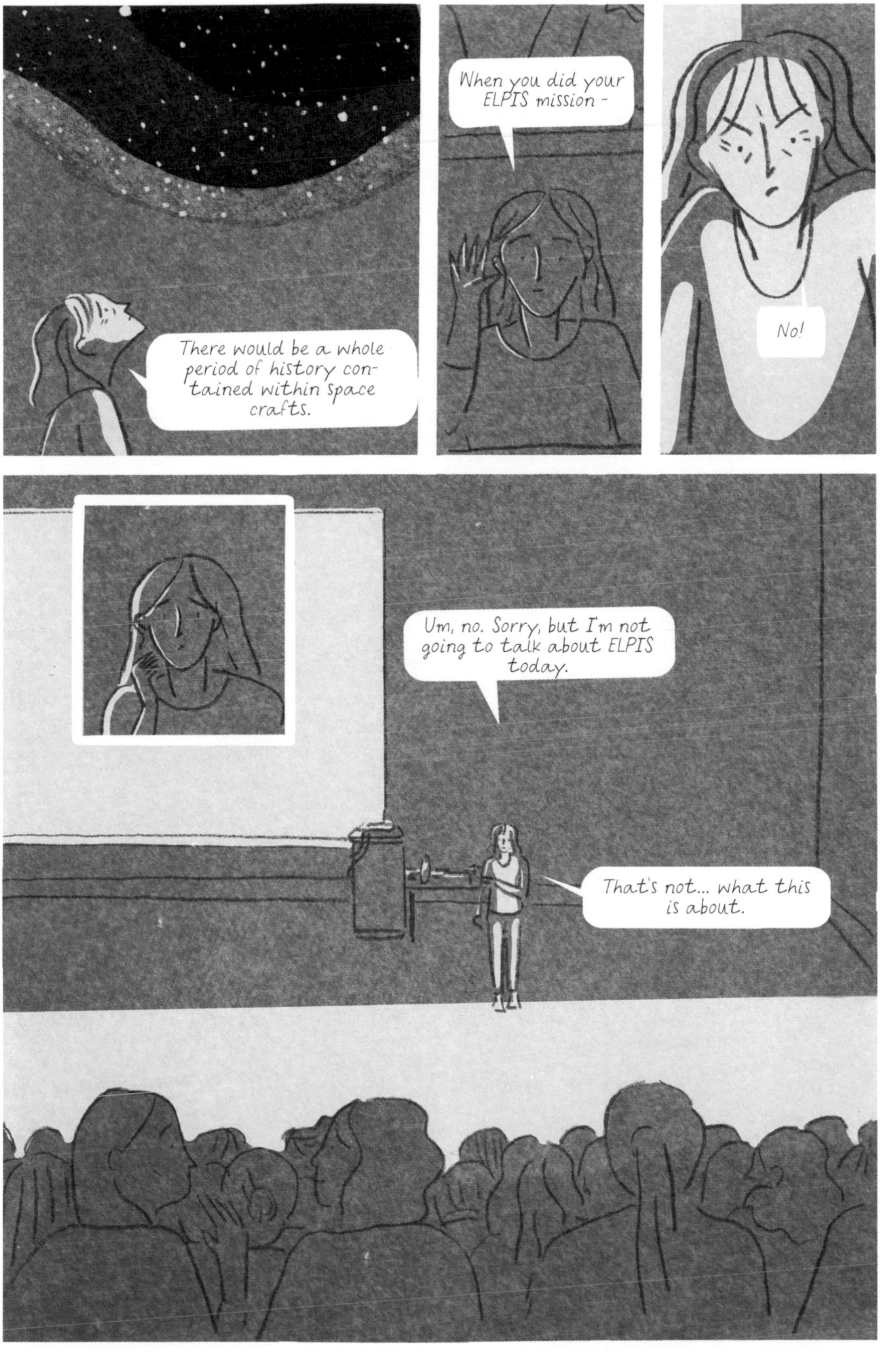
There would be a whole period of history contained within space crafts.
When you did your ELPIS mission -
No!
Um, no. Sorry, but I'm not going to talk about ELPIS today.
That's not... what this is about.

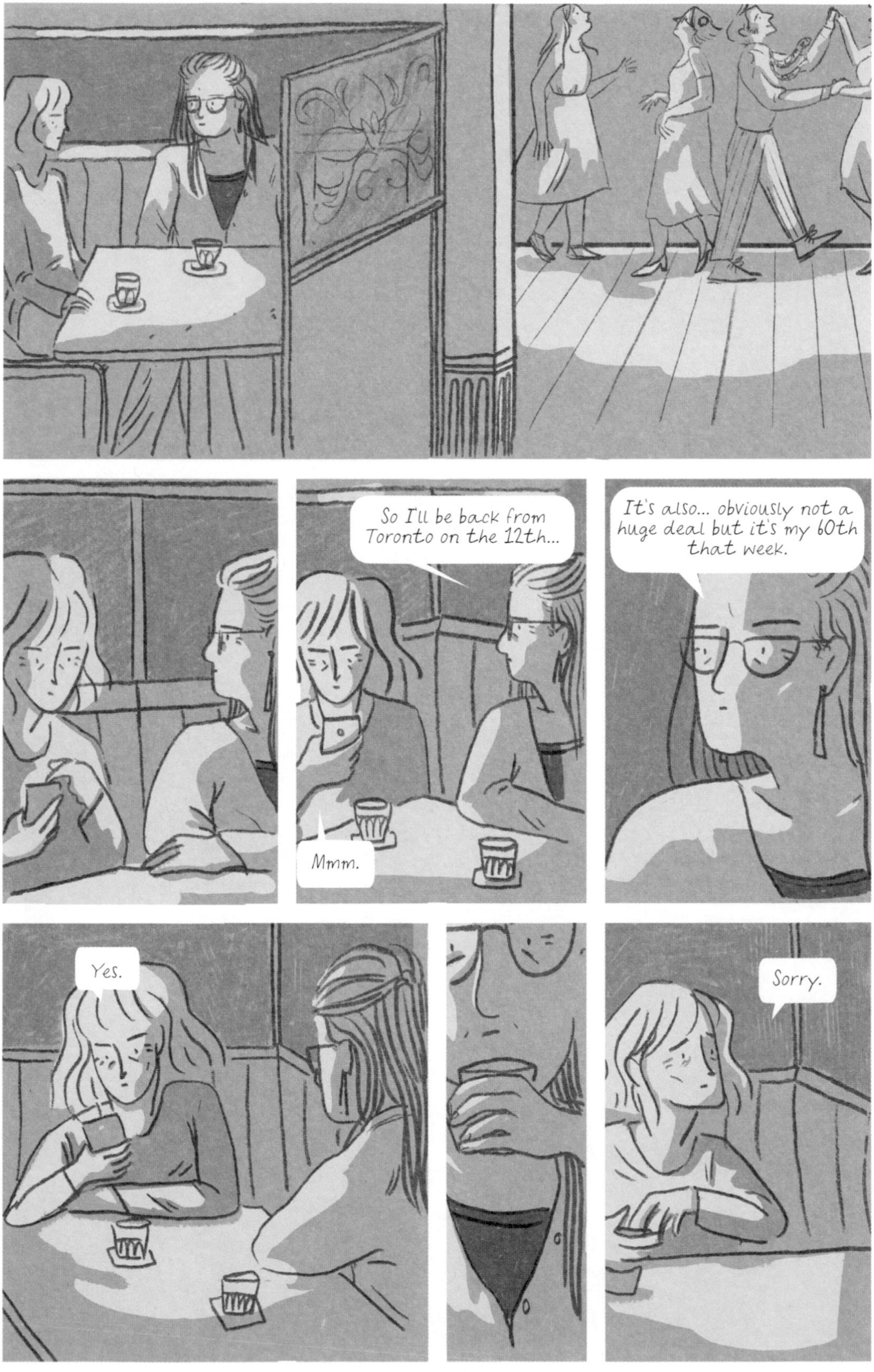
So I'll be back from Toronto on the 12th...
Mmm.
It's also... obviously not a huge deal but it's my 60th that week.
Yes.
Sorry.

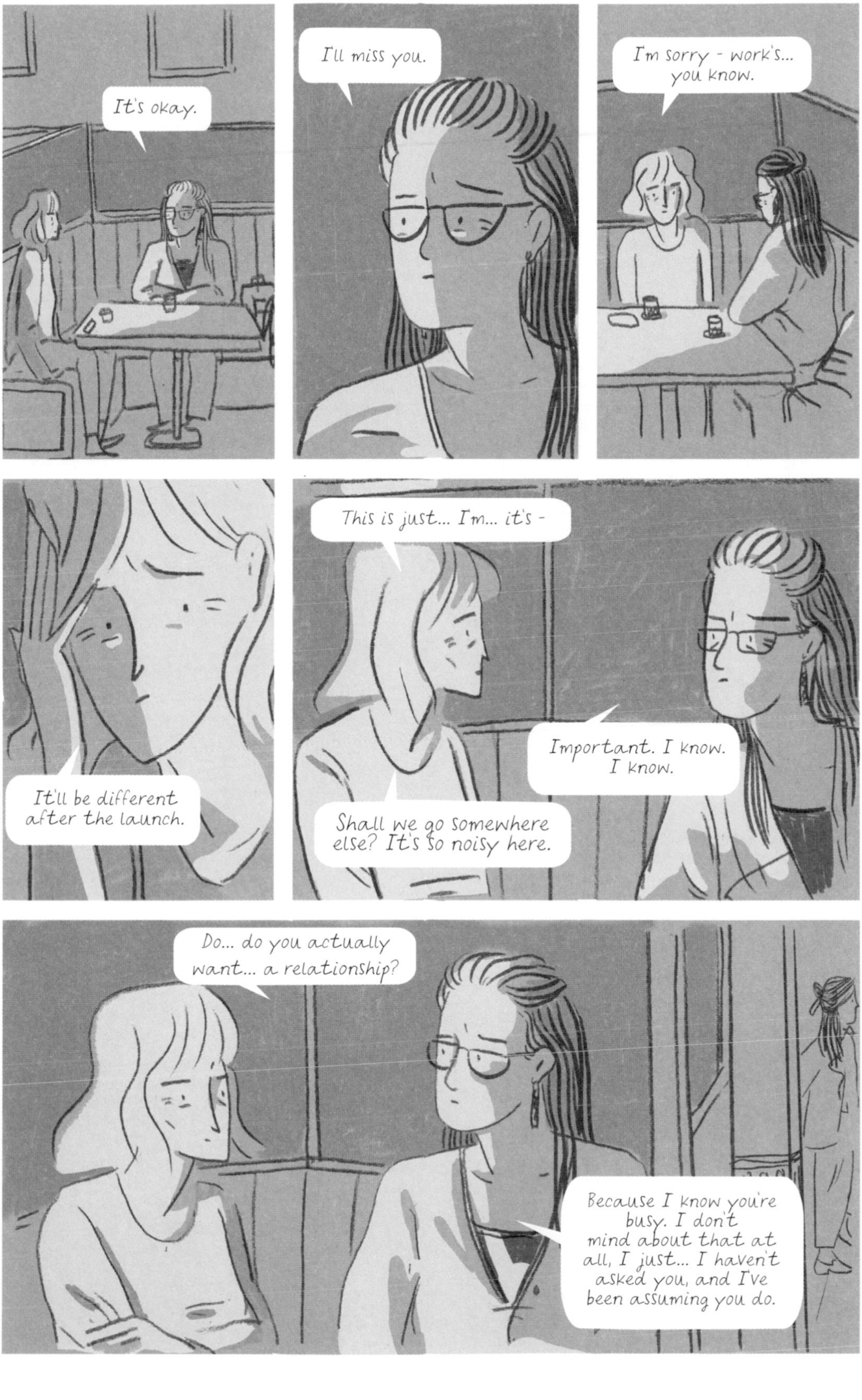
It's okay.
I'll miss you.
I'm sorry - work's... you know.
It'll be different after the launch.
This is just... I'm... it's -
Important. I know. I know.
Shall we go somewhere else? It's so noisy here.
Do... do you actually want... a relationship?
Because I know you're busy. I don't mind about that at all, I just... I haven't asked you, and I've been assuming you do.

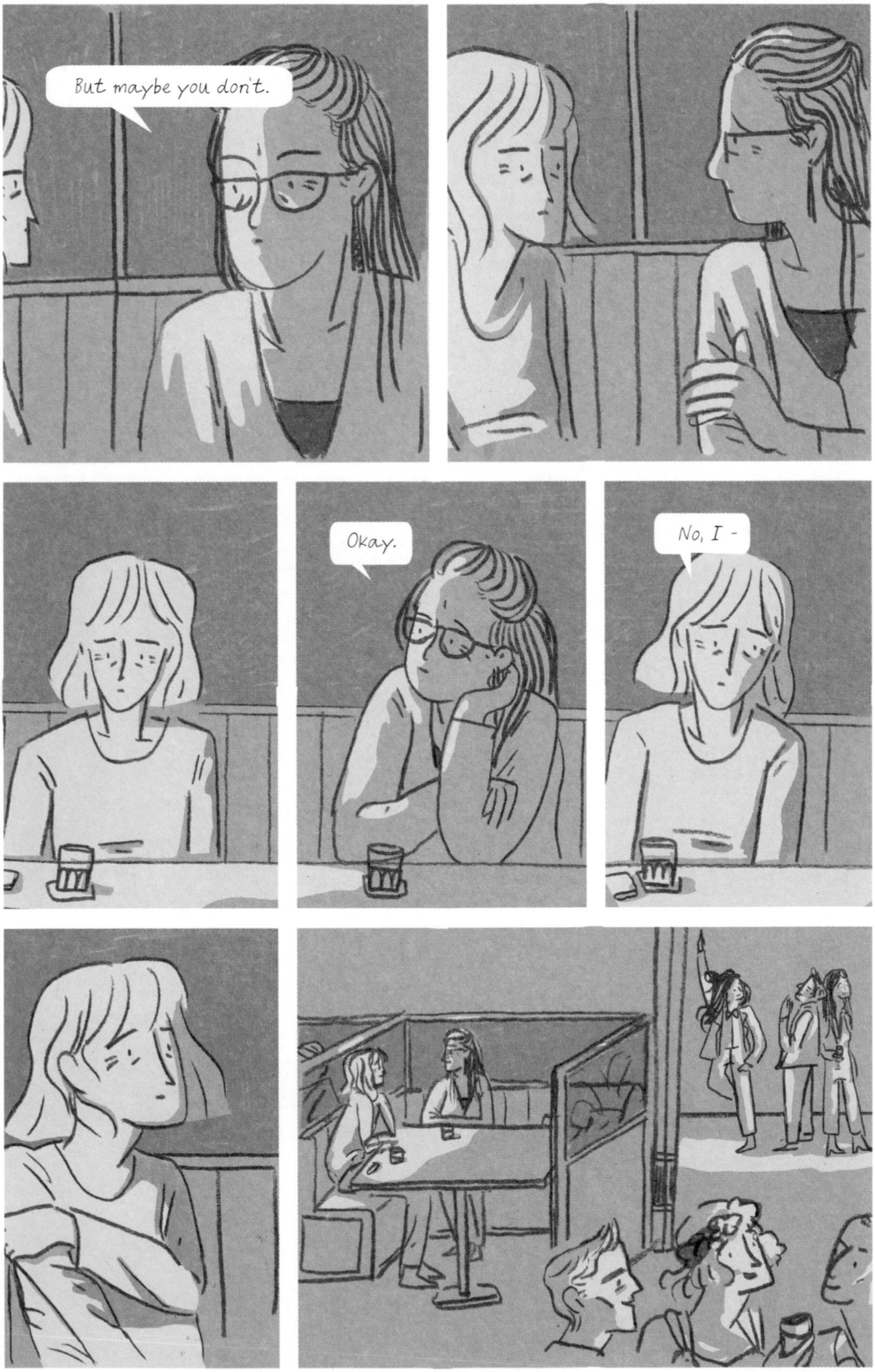
But maybe you don't.
Okay.
No, I -

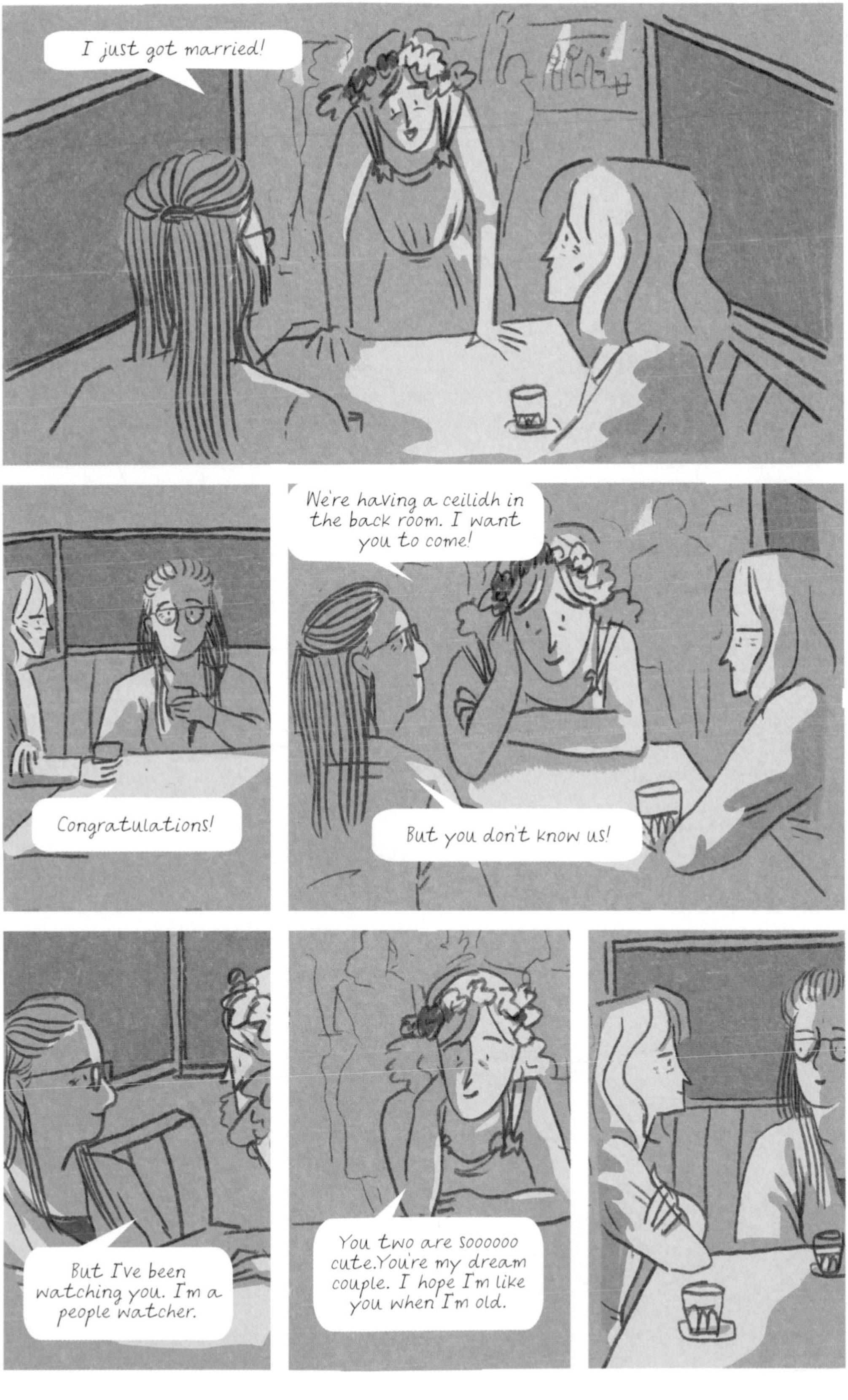
I just got married!
Congratulations!
We're having a ceilidh in the back room. I want you to come!
But you don't know us!
But I've been watching you. I'm a people watcher.
You two are soooooo cute.You're my dream couple. I hope I'm like you when I'm old.

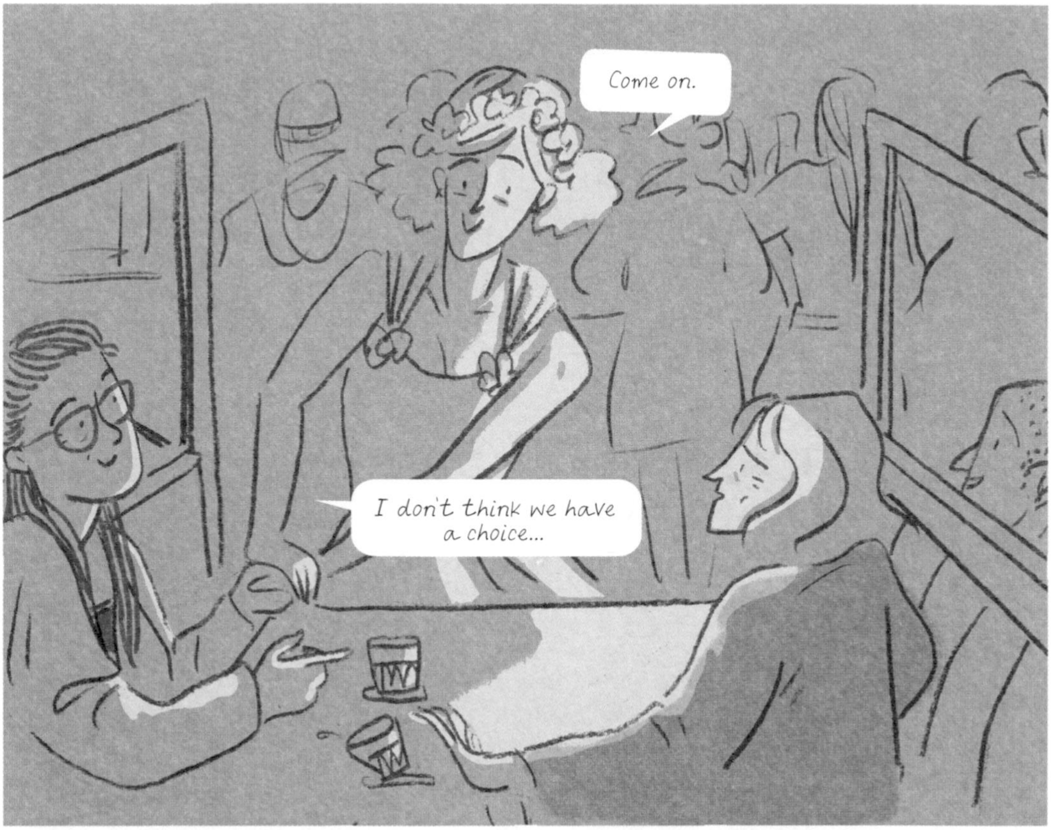
Come on.
I don't think we have a choice...

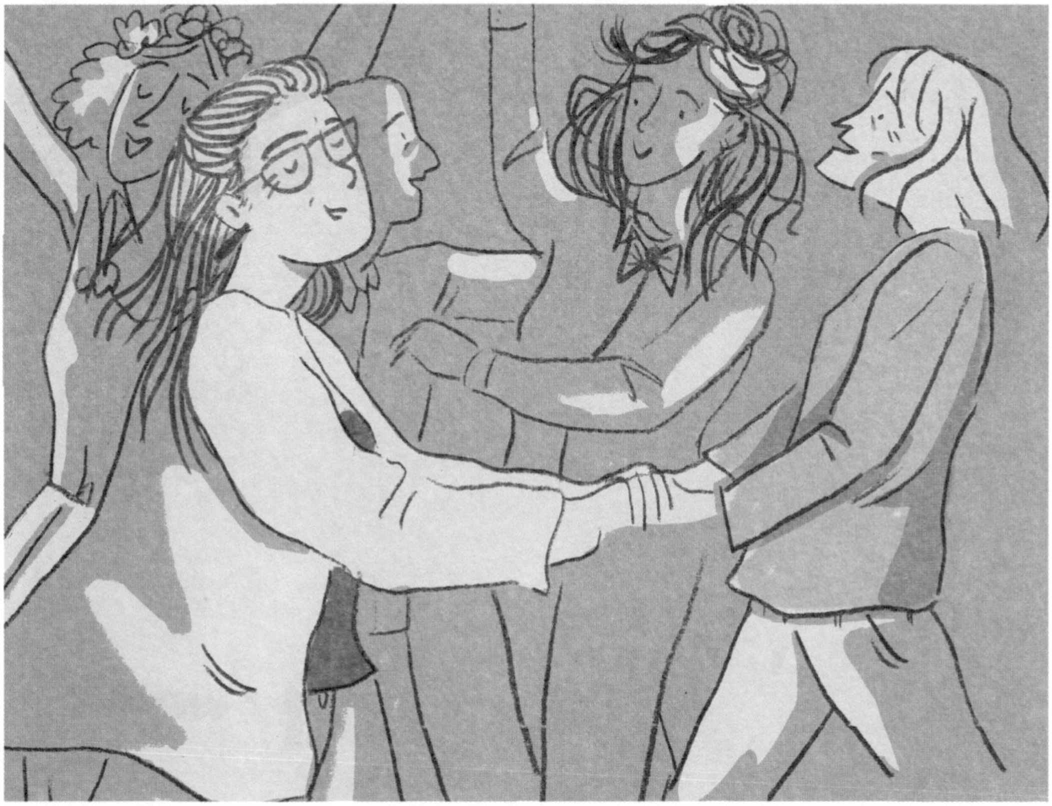

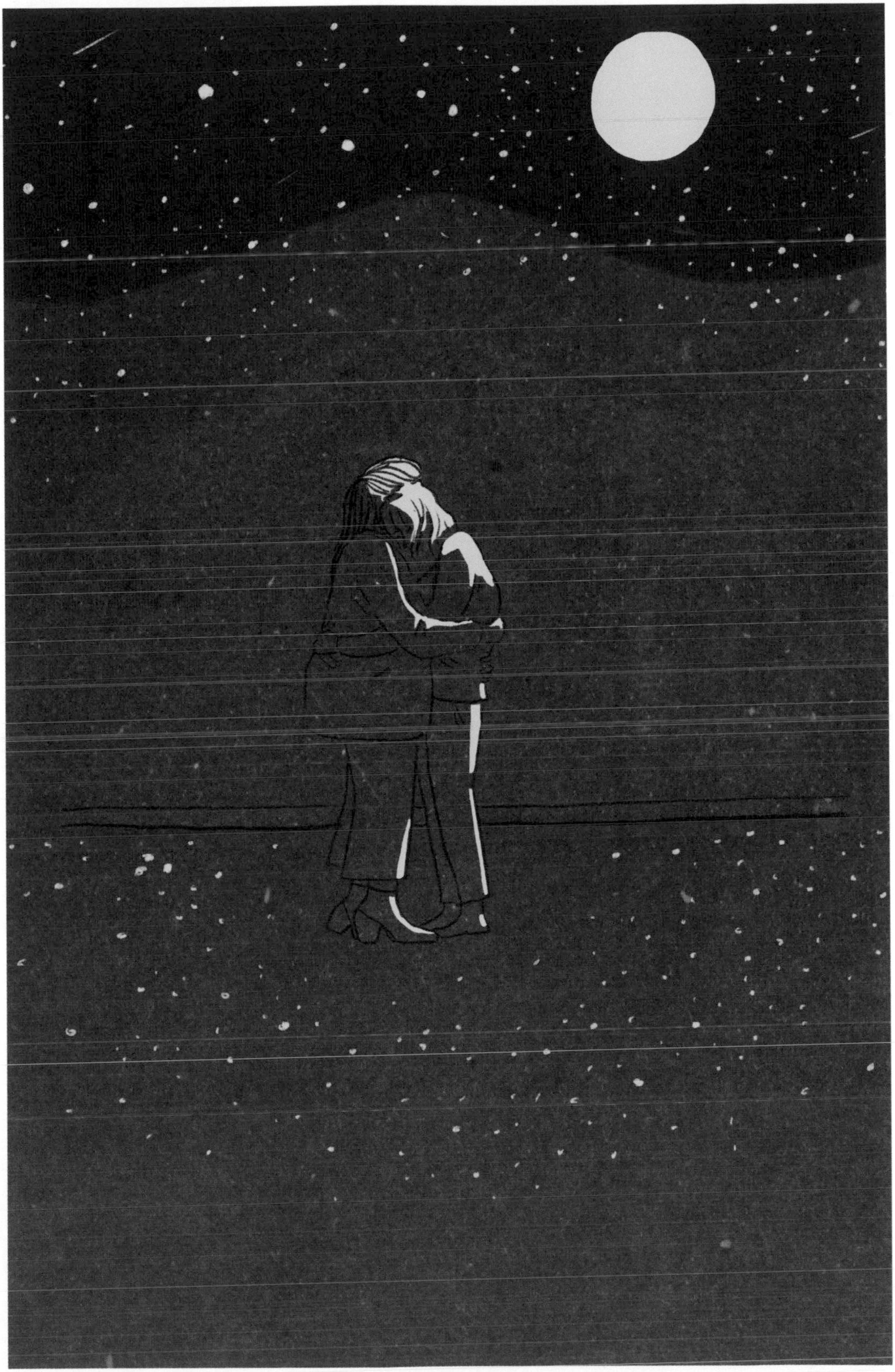

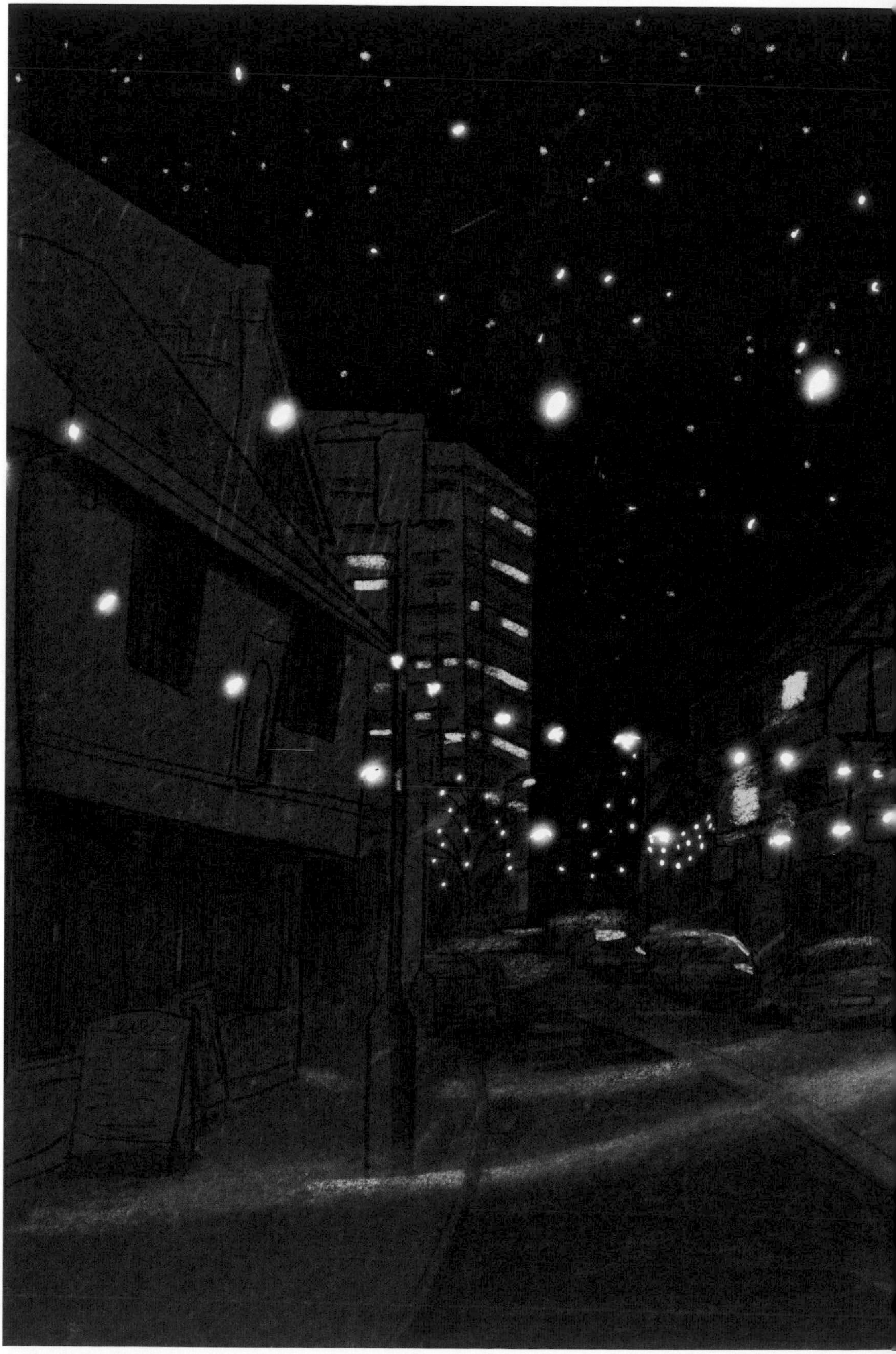

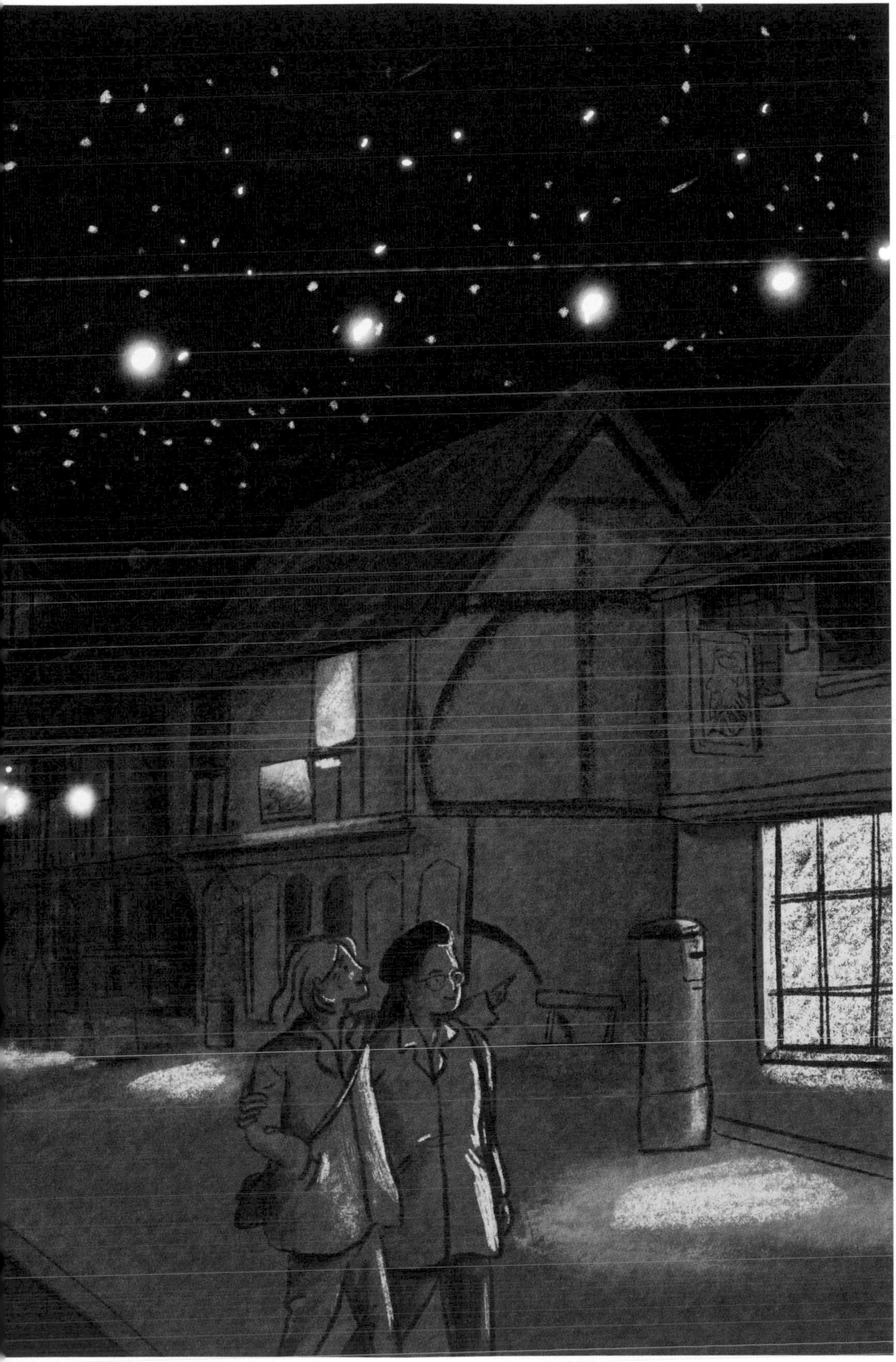

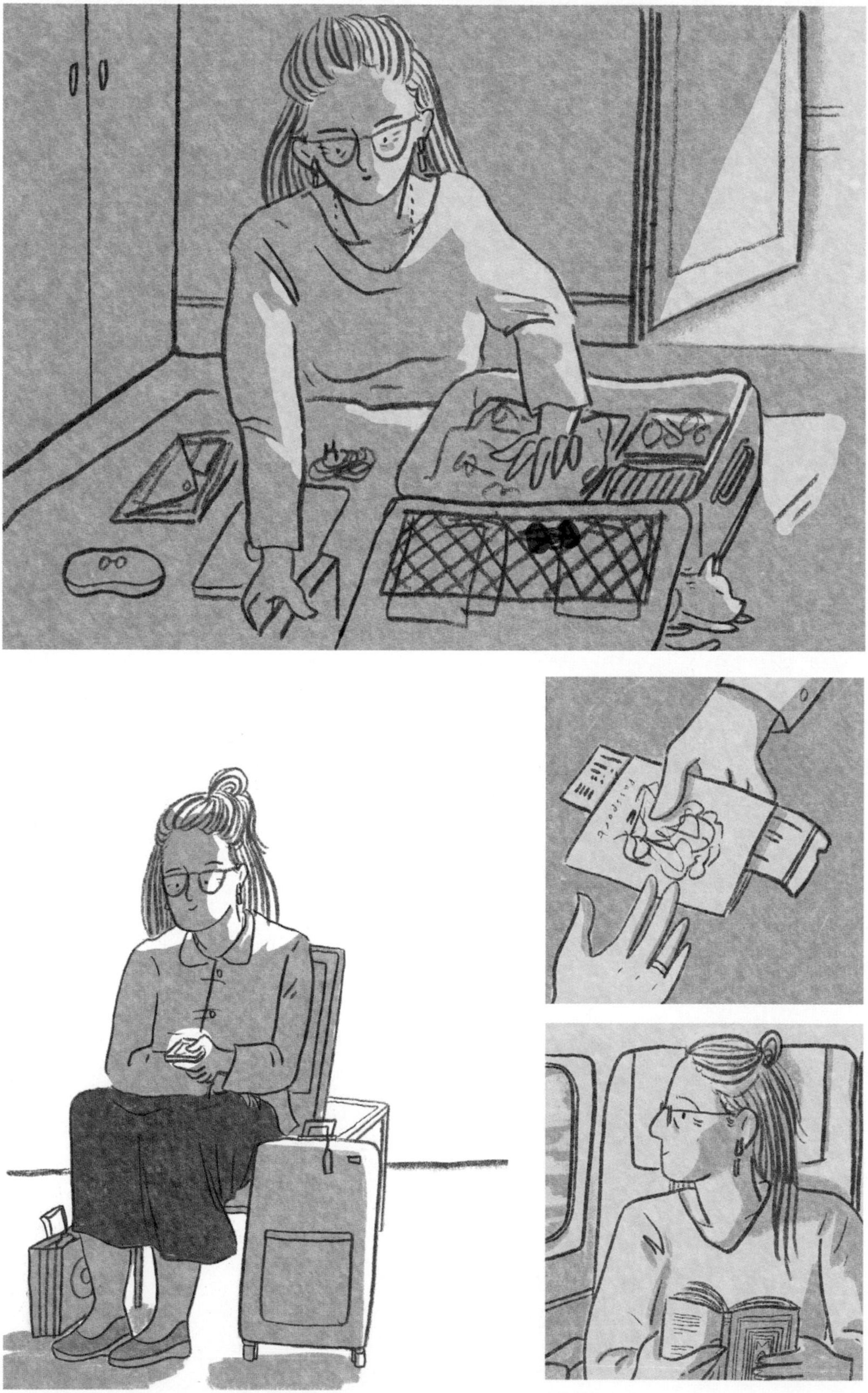
Passport

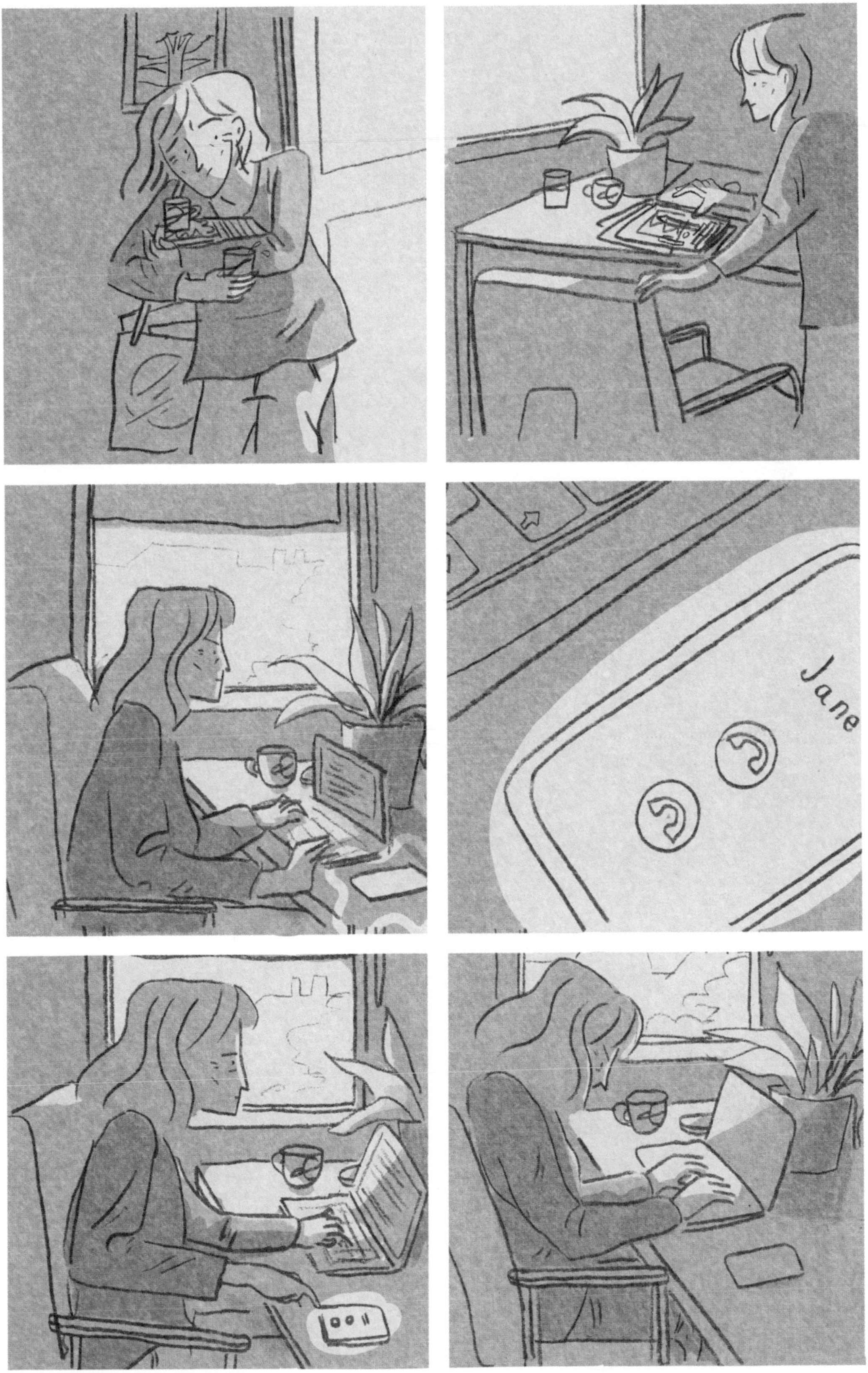
Jane

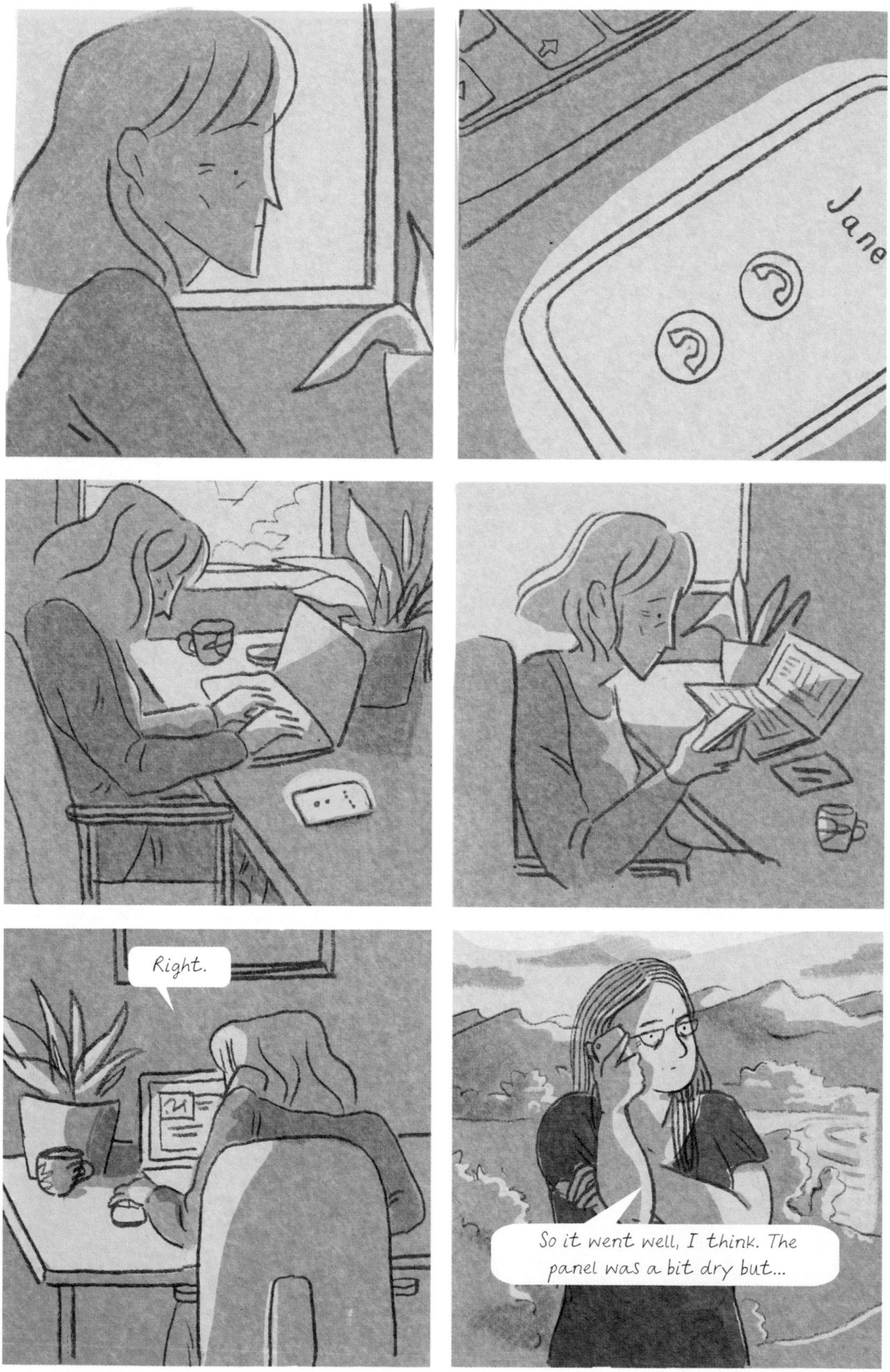
Jane
Right.
So it went well, I think. The panel was a bit dry but...

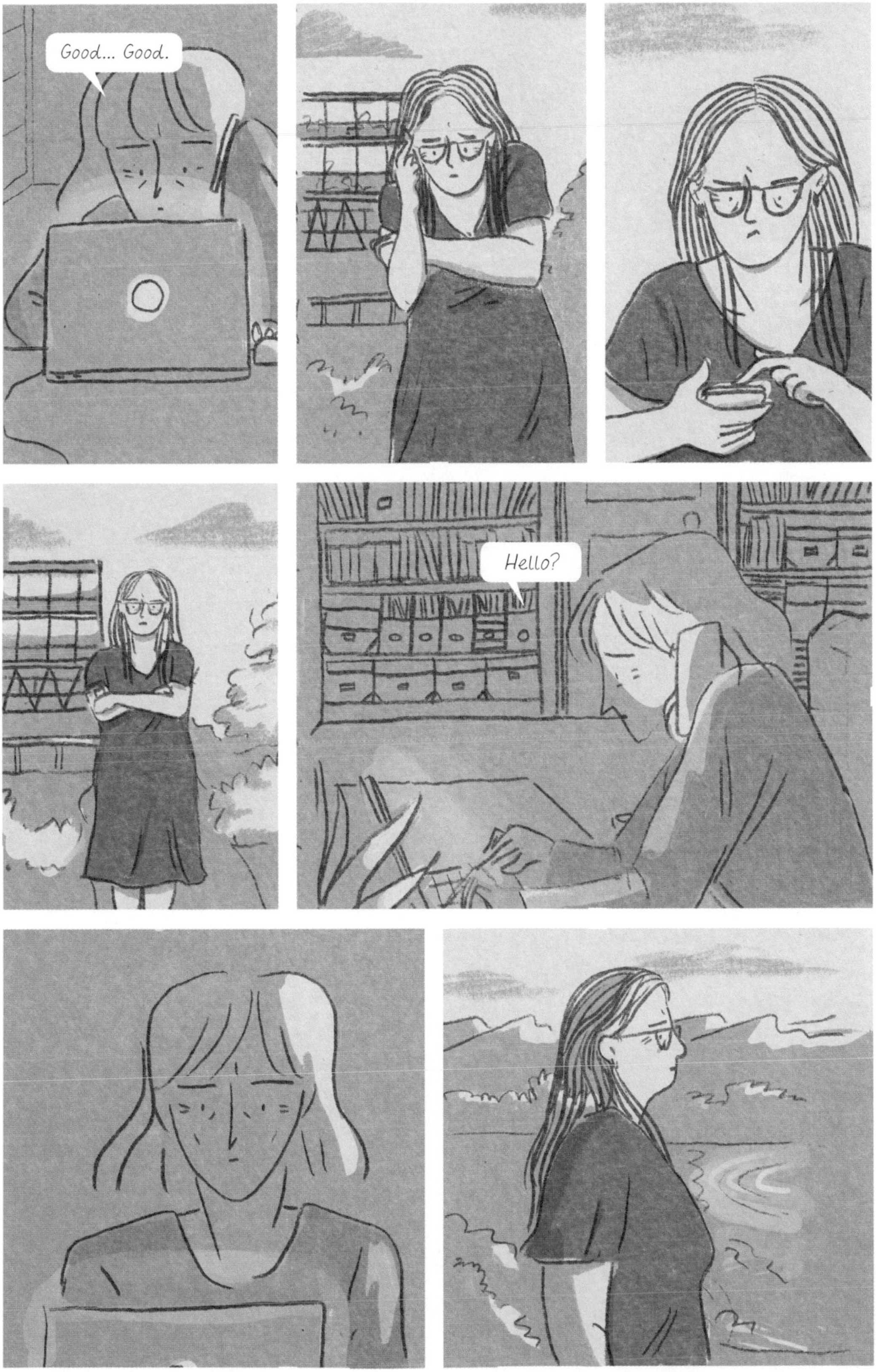
Good... Good.
Hello?

I'm not going to talk about that because I'm talking more about...

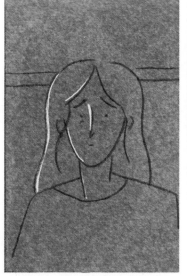

What this area of science is doing... more generally.

There's so much to... we've come so far, in terms of our knowledge of space...

Think what else we might one day be able to comprehend?

I read that Kepler recently found habitable planets.

Did you? You've certainly done your homework you lot!

Well that's... well no, not really. Kepler found planets but they're not... Basically what we're all looking for is another Earth. Okay? Earth 2. No one's found that yet.

Oh, it's you, no –

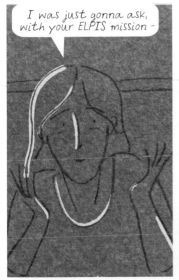

I was just gonna ask, with your ELPIS mission –

No! Look, I just said! That's not what I'm talking about.

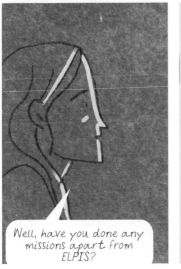

Well, have you done any missions apart from ELPIS?

Oh for God's sake! Um... well no, not... as such.

I've done lots of work with other people's projects and I was... d'you know what, no. The answer's no, okay?

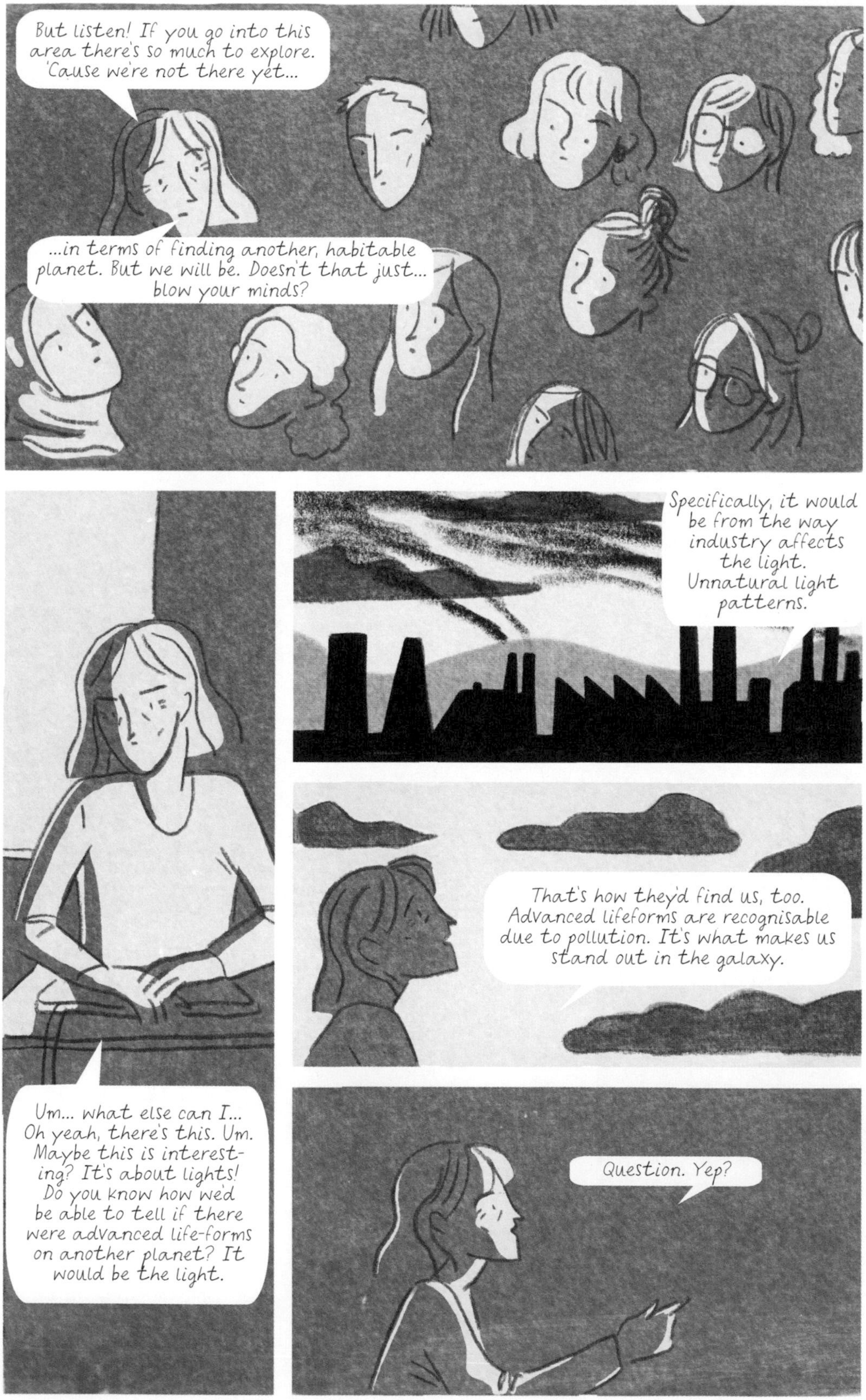
But listen! If you go into this area there's so much to explore. 'Cause we're not there yet...
...in terms of finding another, habitable planet. But we will be. Doesn't that just... blow your minds?
Um... what else can I... Oh yeah, there's this. Um. Maybe this is interesting? It's about lights! Do you know how we'd be able to tell if there were advanced life-forms on another planet? It would be the light.
Specifically, it would be from the way industry affects the light. Unnatural light patterns.
That's how they'd find us, too. Advanced lifeforms are recognisable due to pollution. It's what makes us stand out in the galaxy.
Question. Yep?

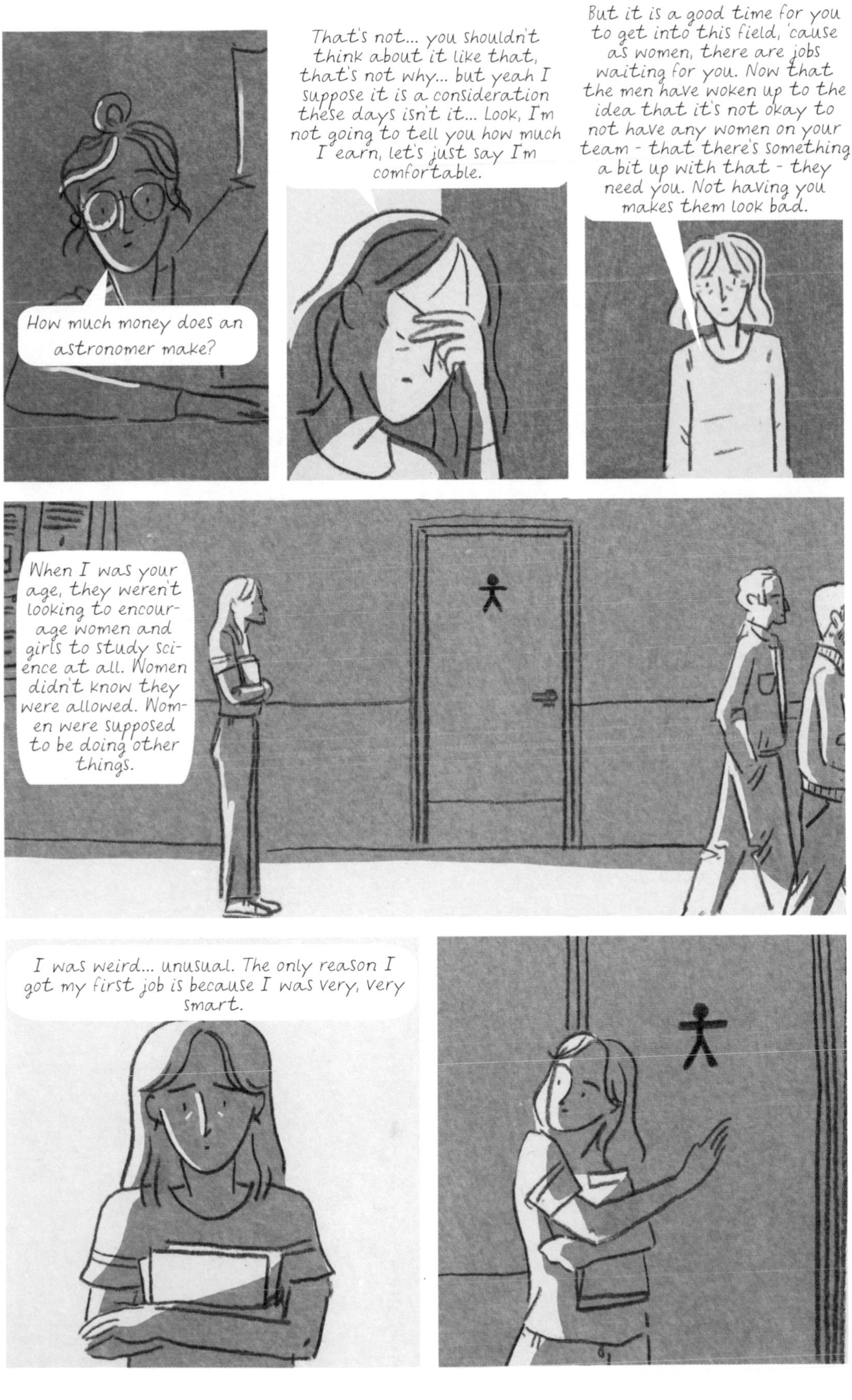
How much money does an astronomer make?
That's not... you shouldn't think about it like that, that's not why... but yeah I suppose it is a consideration these days isn't it... Look, I'm not going to tell you how much I earn, let's just say I'm comfortable.
But it is a good time for you to get into this field, 'cause as women, there are jobs waiting for you. Now that the men have woken up to the idea that it's not okay to not have any women on your team - that there's something a bit up with that - they need you. Not having you makes them look bad.
When I was your age, they weren't looking to encourage women and girls to study science at all. Women didn't know they were allowed. Women were supposed to be doing other things.
I was weird... unusual. The only reason I got my first job is because I was very, very smart.

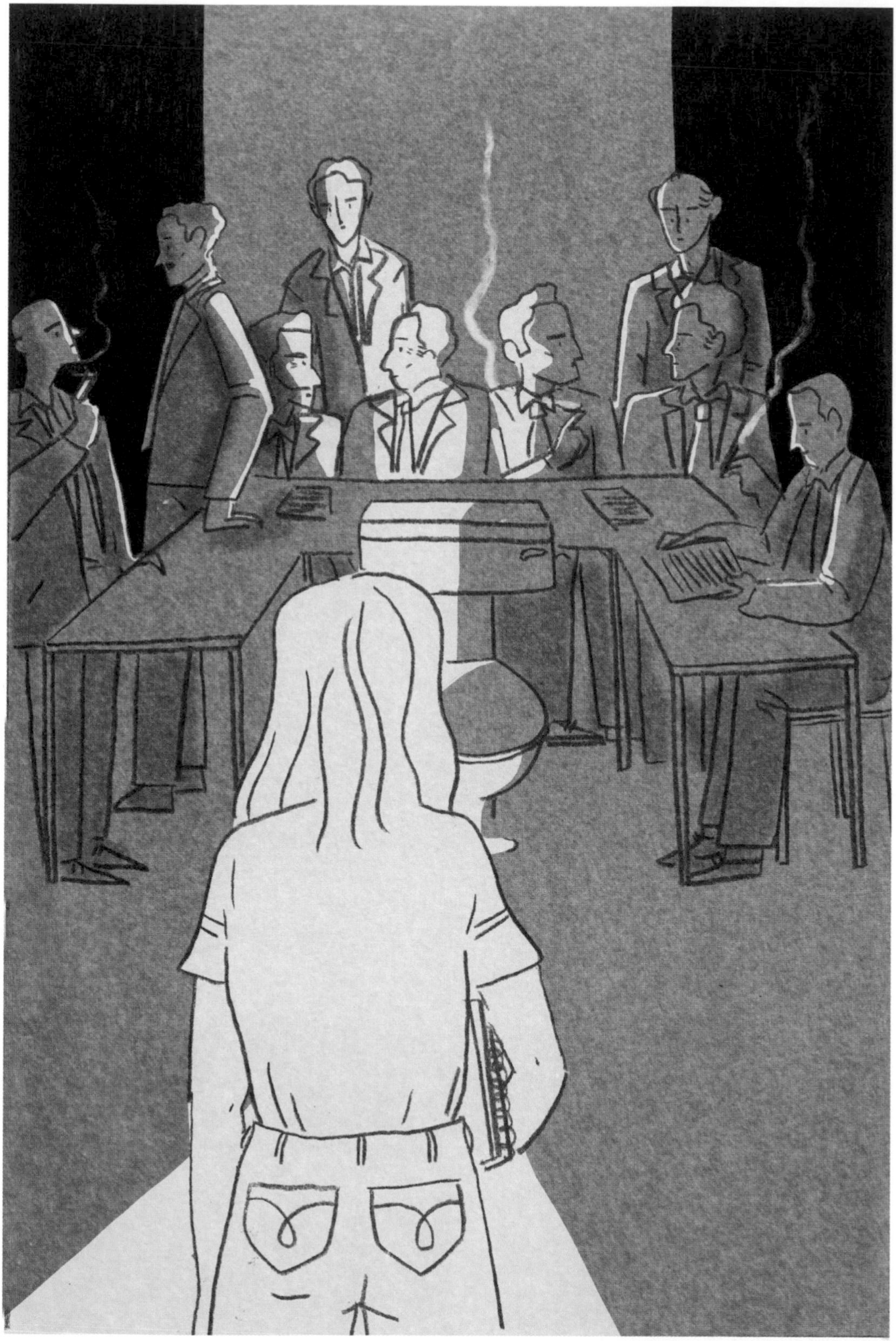

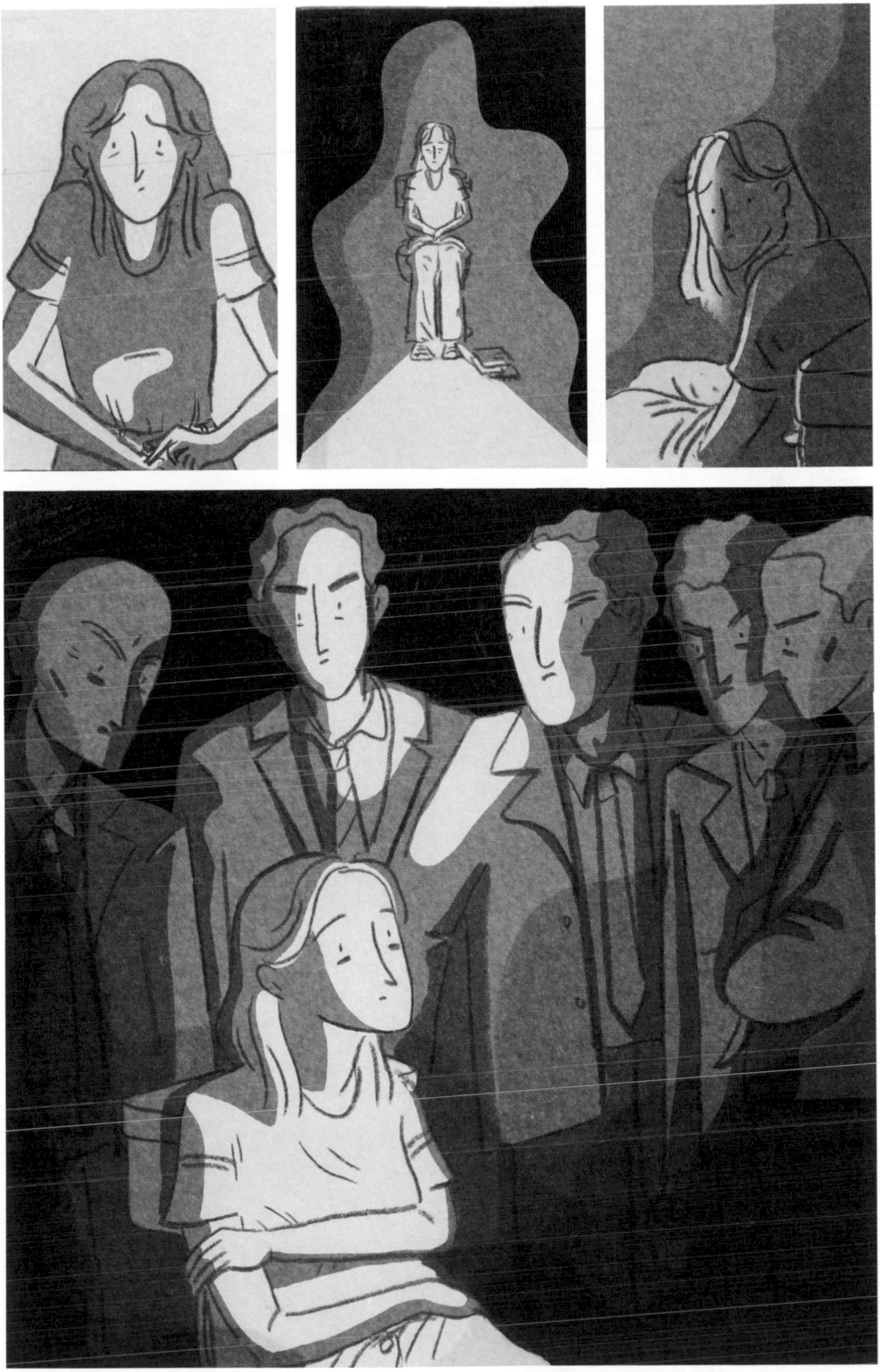

Yep, question?
What if you're not smart? What if you're stupid?
Well, I'm sure you're not... don't let what I said put you off! 'Cause I know that's not fair. Women shouldn't have to be geniuses all the time.
Not every man working at NASA is a genius... I want you to know that you're allowed...
You've got a question? Is it about ELPIS?
Yeah...
Well I've said. Quite a few times now. That I don't want to talk about ELPIS. And you keep asking. Which is really rude. So we're going to move on. Another question. Come on, another question. A better question!
Sorry, but what even is ELPIS?
You're really pushing it, you lot!.

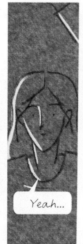

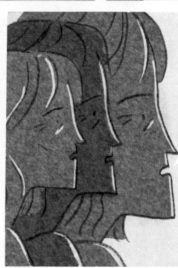

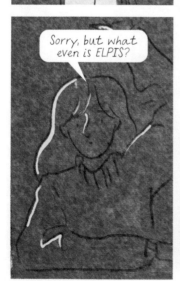

THE FIRST LECTURE'S IN A FEW WEEKS AND AT THE MOMENT I CAN'T SEE HOW I'M GOING TO...
They sound like they're very important to you.
YOU ALREADY SAID THAT!
Why do you think that is?
IS THIS WHAT THERAPY IS? JUST... VAGUE QUESTIONS. I ALWAYS THOUGHT IT MIGHT BE LIKE THIS.
JANE ALWAYS SAID I SHOULD GO BUT I SAID TO HER, IT'S JUST VAGUE QUESTIONS THAT DON'T GO ANY-WHERE.
Is that why you came? Jane suggested it?
NO.
Why do you think Jane thought you should have therapy?
OH. SHE THOUGHT I WAS 'EMOTIONALLY UNAVAILABLE'.
JUST... STUFF LIKE... I NEVER TOLD HER I MISSED HER. SHE WORKED AWAY A LOT, AND SHE'D SAY 'I'LL MISS YOU', AND THEN LEAVE THIS GAP. I KNEW I WAS SUPPOSED TO SAY IT BACK. IN THE GAP. BUT I DIDN'T.
Did you? Miss her?
YOU KNOW. IF I'M DEPRESSED, I CAN'T BE TELLING SOMEONE I MISS THEM.
And what about when you weren't depressed? Did you say it then?

Did Jane find your Bipolar difficult?
YES. WELL... I MEAN, NOT EXACTLY. BECAUSE... SHE DIDN'T KNOW. OBVIOUSLY. I DONT TELL PEOPLE.
But you said that people can't handle it?
YES. THAT'S WHY I DON'T TELL THEM.
So... How'd you know they can't handle it?
BECAUSE... OBVIOUSLY THEY COULDN'T. SO HOW COULD I TELL THEM? I'VE DONE ...YOU KNOW... REALLY BAD THINGS.
You've done things you feel ashamed of?
YES.
Can you say more about that?
I HATE THIS!
Sorry.

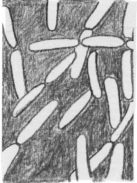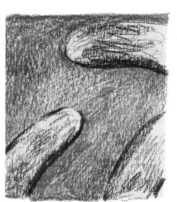

IT'S JUST... LOOK THE REASON I'VE NEVER WANTED TO COME TO ANYTHING LIKE THIS IS BECAUSE THIS ISN'T... SCIENCE. OR IT'S A BIT SCIENCE BUT NOT ENOUGH FOR ME. THERE'S NOT ENOUGH EVIDENCE THAT IT WORKS. SCIENCE INVOLVES MEASURING WITH GREAT PRECISION... BIOLOGISTS PLACING CELLS UNDER MICROSCOPES... CHEMISTS MEASURING WHAT HAPPENS TO MOLECULES WHEN EXPOSED TO HEAT. ASTROPHYSICISTS MEASURING THE EXPANSION OF THE UNIVERSE! WE DO EXPERIMENTS! BUT YOU... YOU... IT'S JUST ASKING QUESTIONS. AND I COULD SAY ANYTHING!

It is a science. It's just, the things we're measuring are... human beings. And humans lie. And self-deceive. Psychology necessarily relies on indirect measurements. But this field is a science; even if we do put the word 'social' in front of it. I think that accuracy of measurement may not be the best criterion by which to judge what is and is not a science!

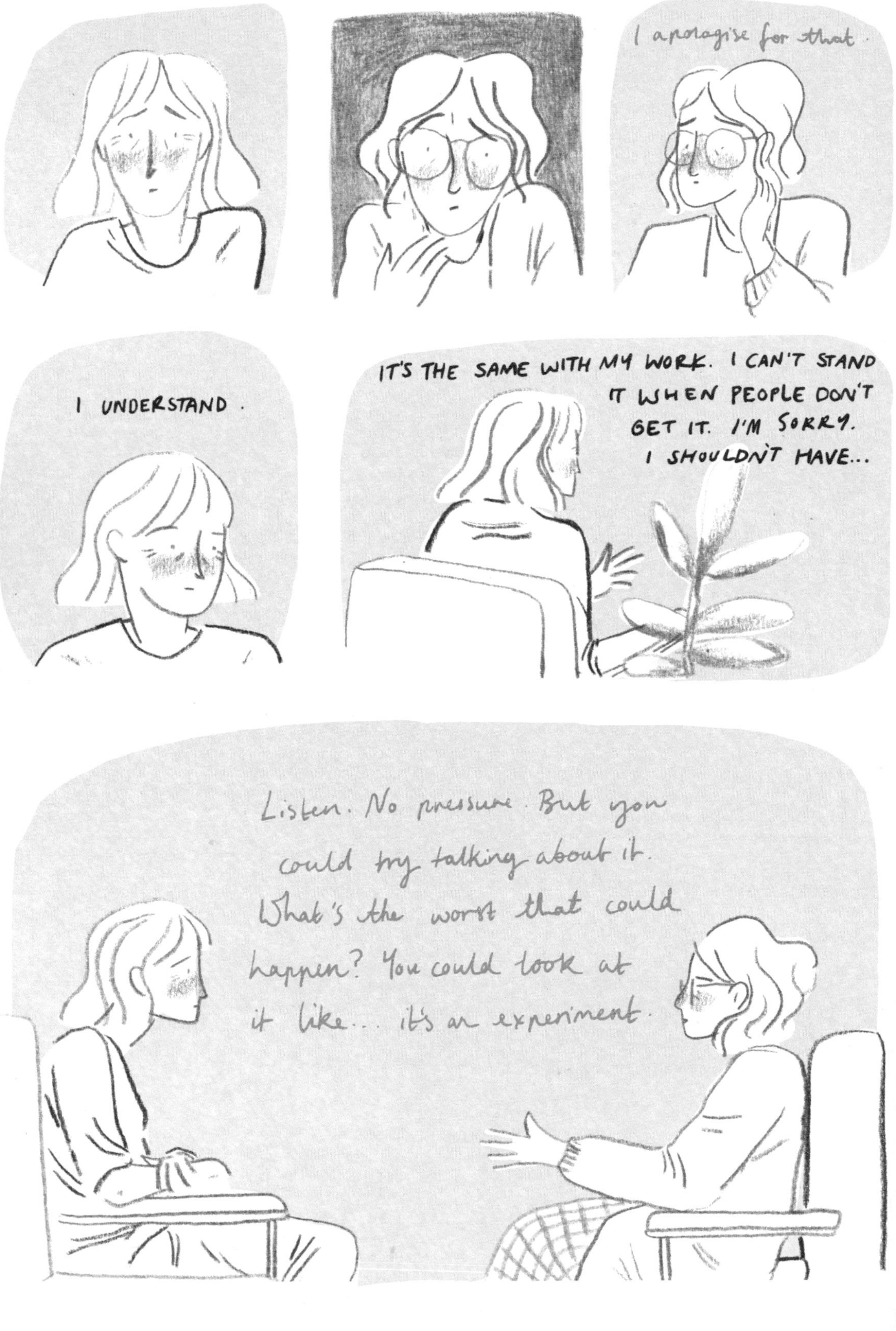
I apologise for that.
I UNDERSTAND.
IT'S THE SAME WITH MY WORK. I CAN'T STAND IT WHEN PEOPLE DON'T GET IT. I'M SORRY. I SHOULDN'T HAVE...
Listen. No pressure. But you could try talking about it. What's the worst that could happen? You could look at it like... it's an experiment.

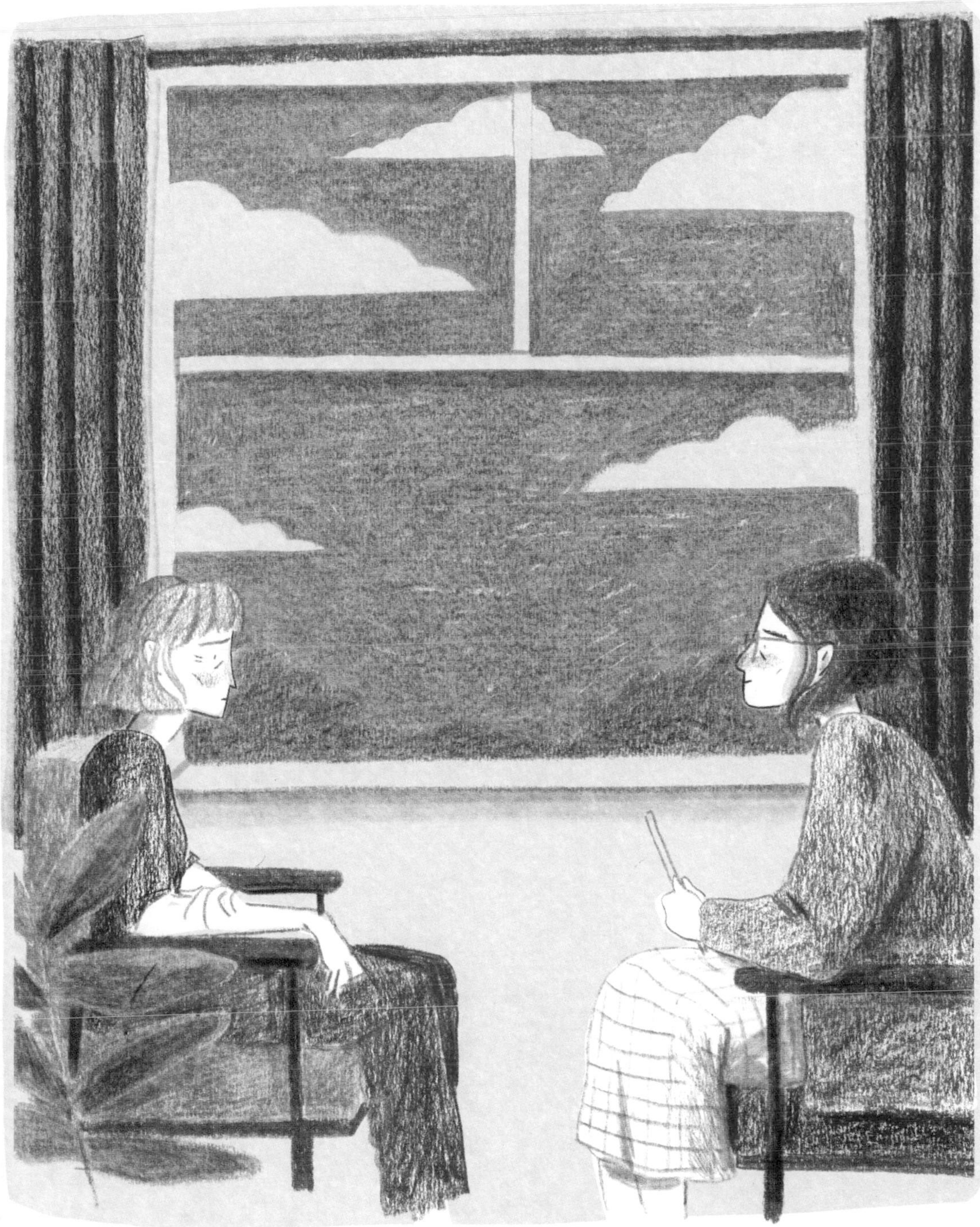

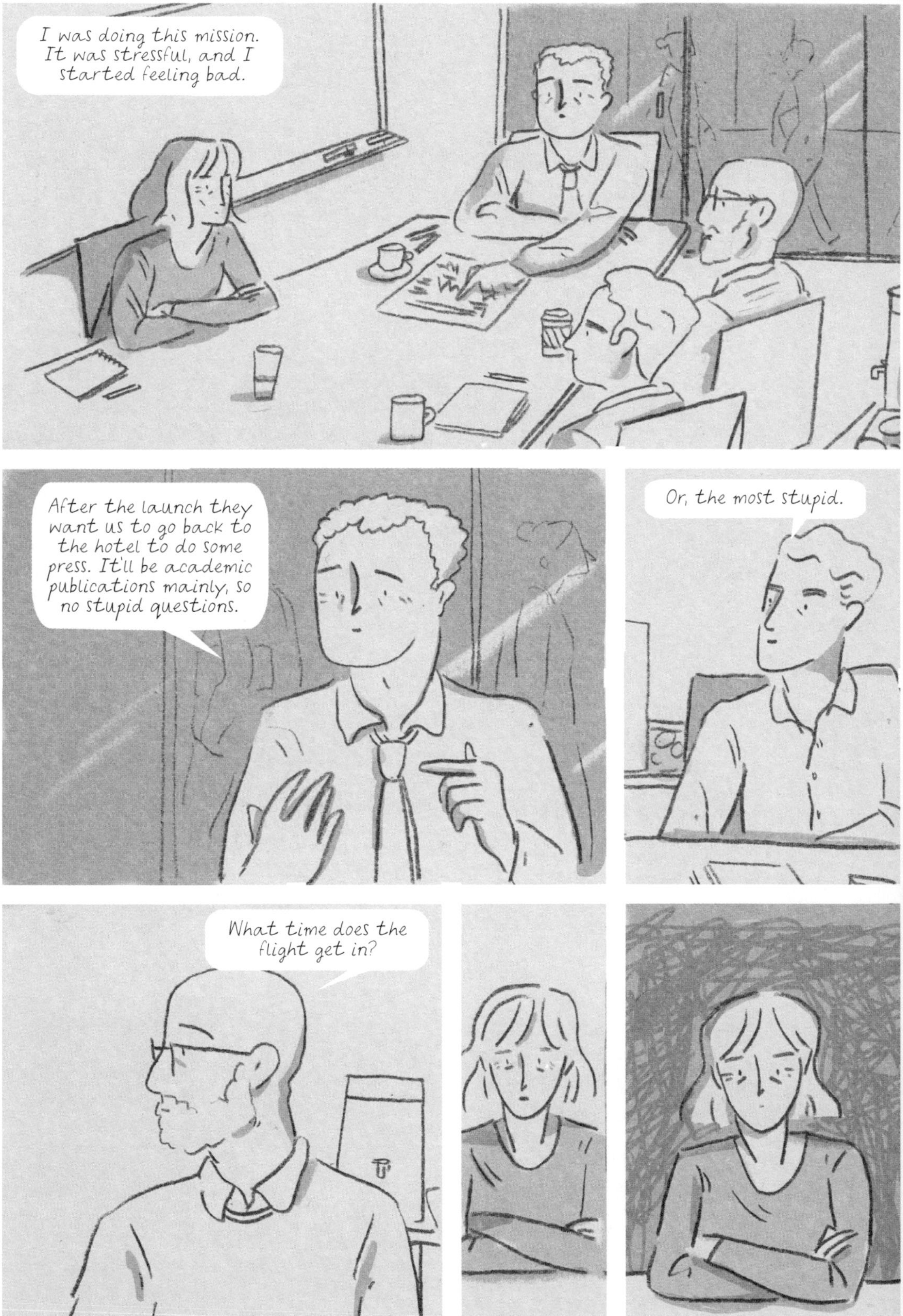
I was doing this mission. It was stressful, and I started feeling bad.
After the launch they want us to go back to the hotel to do some press. It'll be academic publications mainly, so no stupid questions.
Or, the most stupid.
What time does the flight get in?

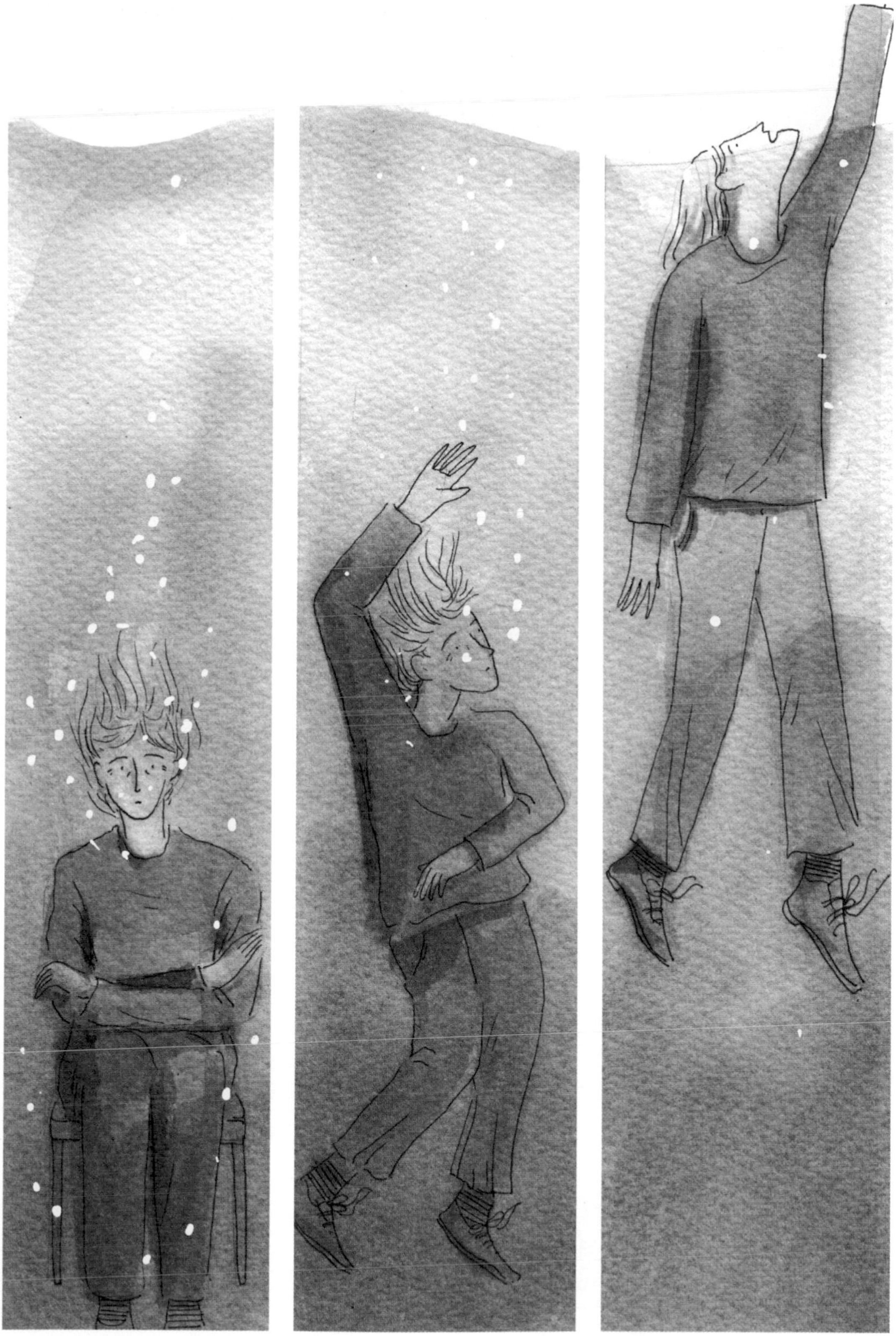

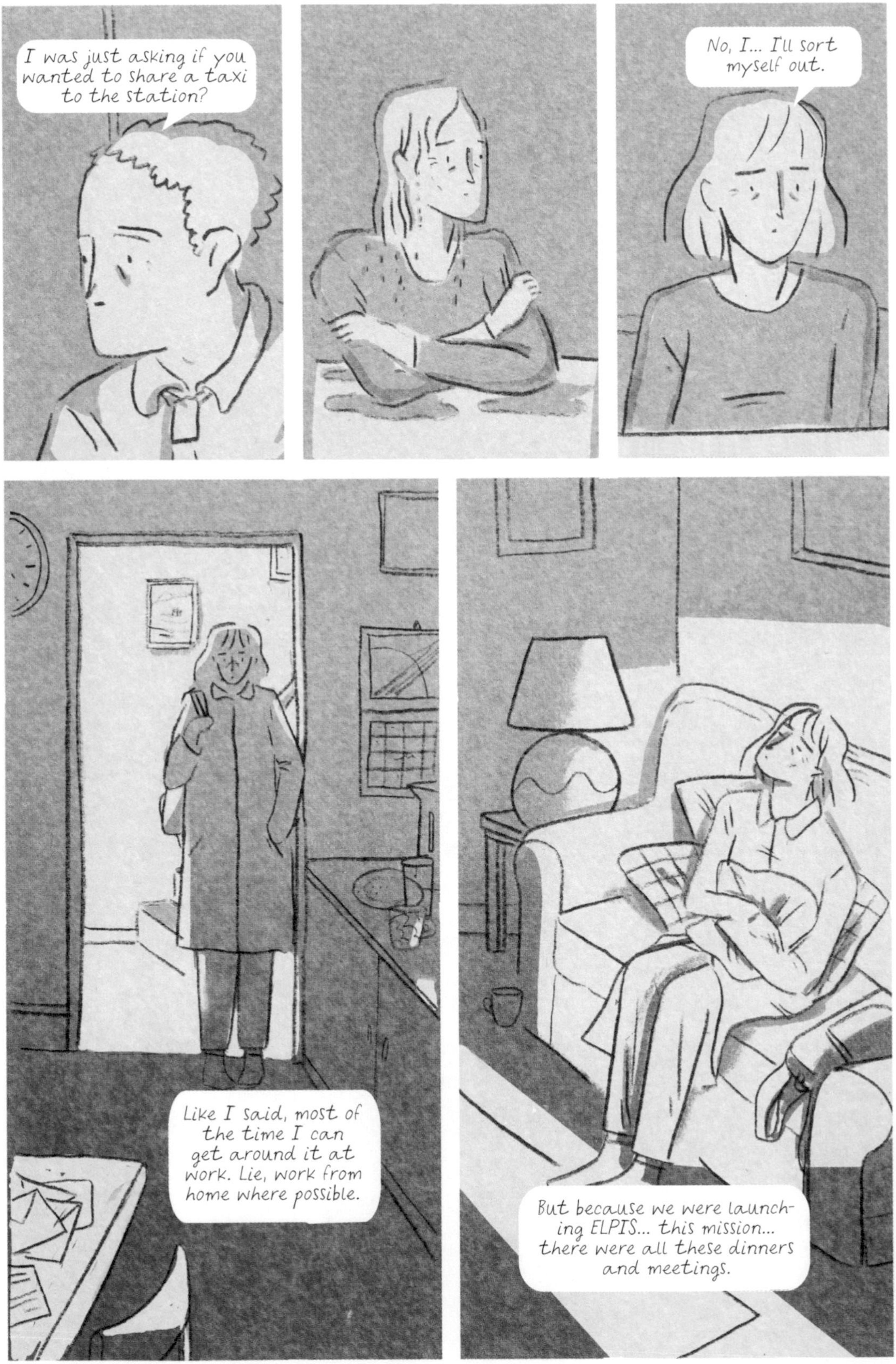
I was just asking if you wanted to share a taxi to the station?
No, I... I'll sort myself out.
Like I said, most of the time I can get around it at work. Lie, work from home where possible.
But because we were launching ELPIS... this mission... there were all these dinners and meetings.

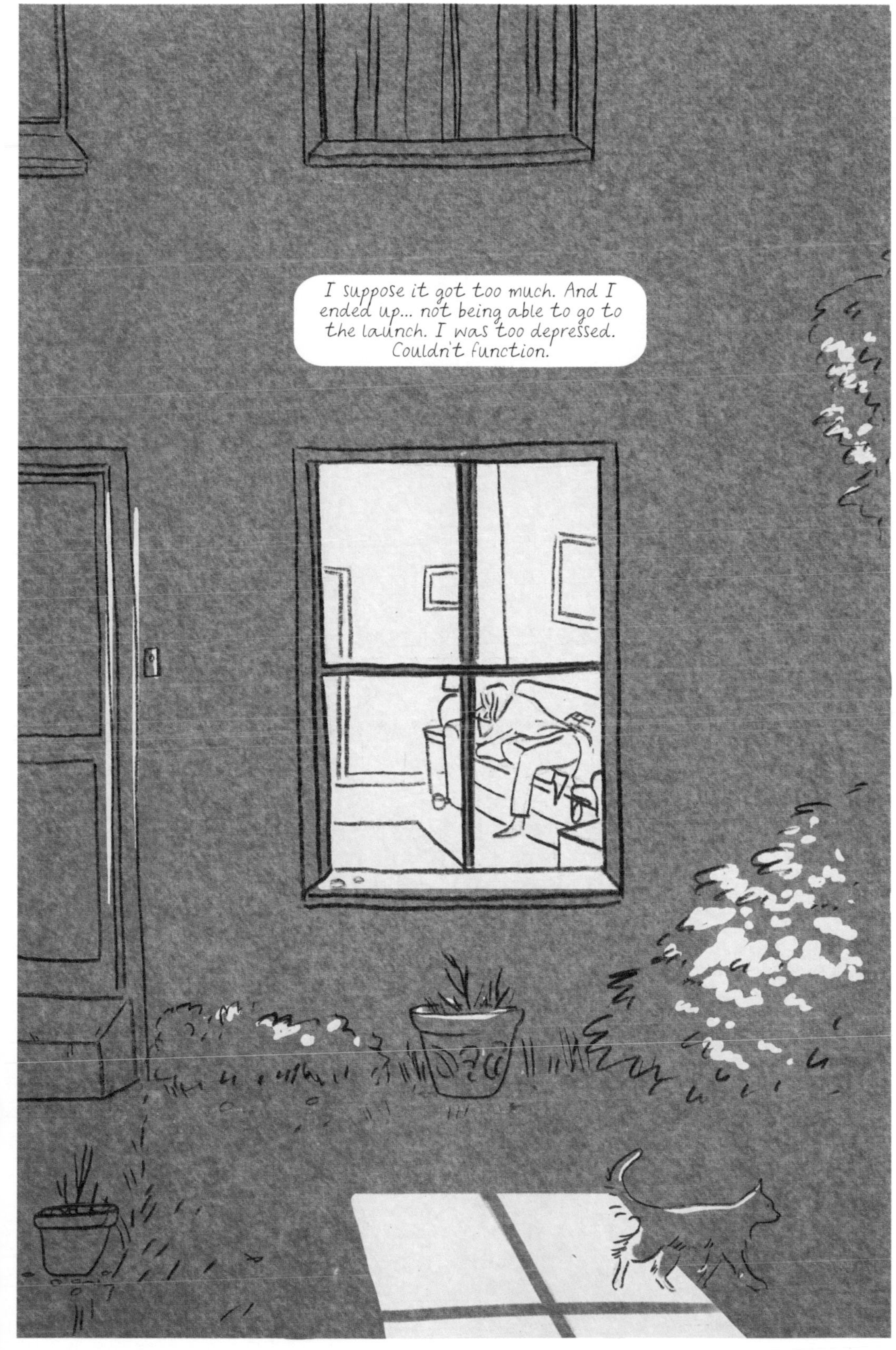
I suppose it got too much. And I ended up... not being able to go to the launch. I was too depressed. Couldn't function.

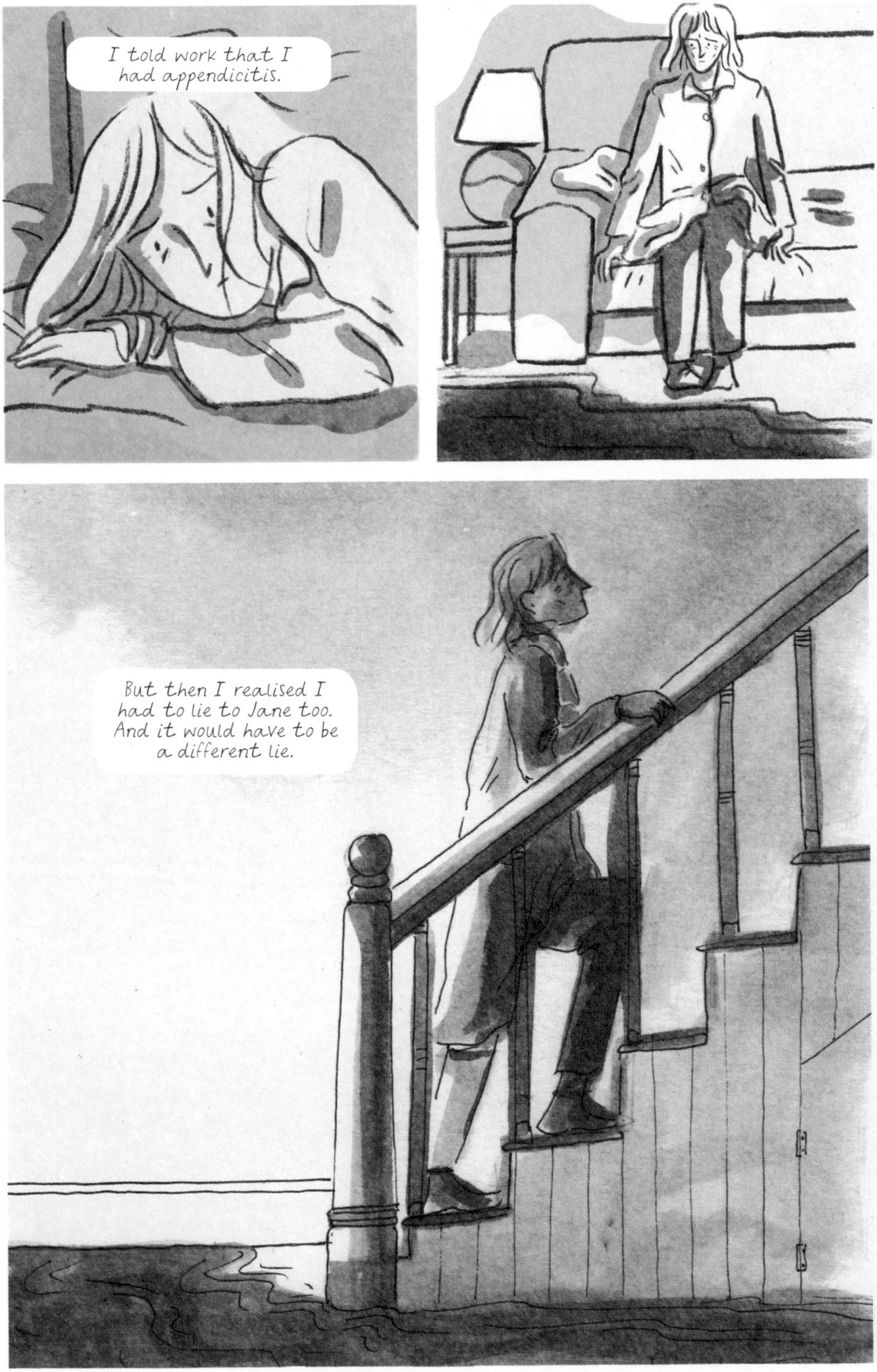
I told work that I had appendicitis.
But then I realised I had to lie to Jane too. And it would have to be a different lie.

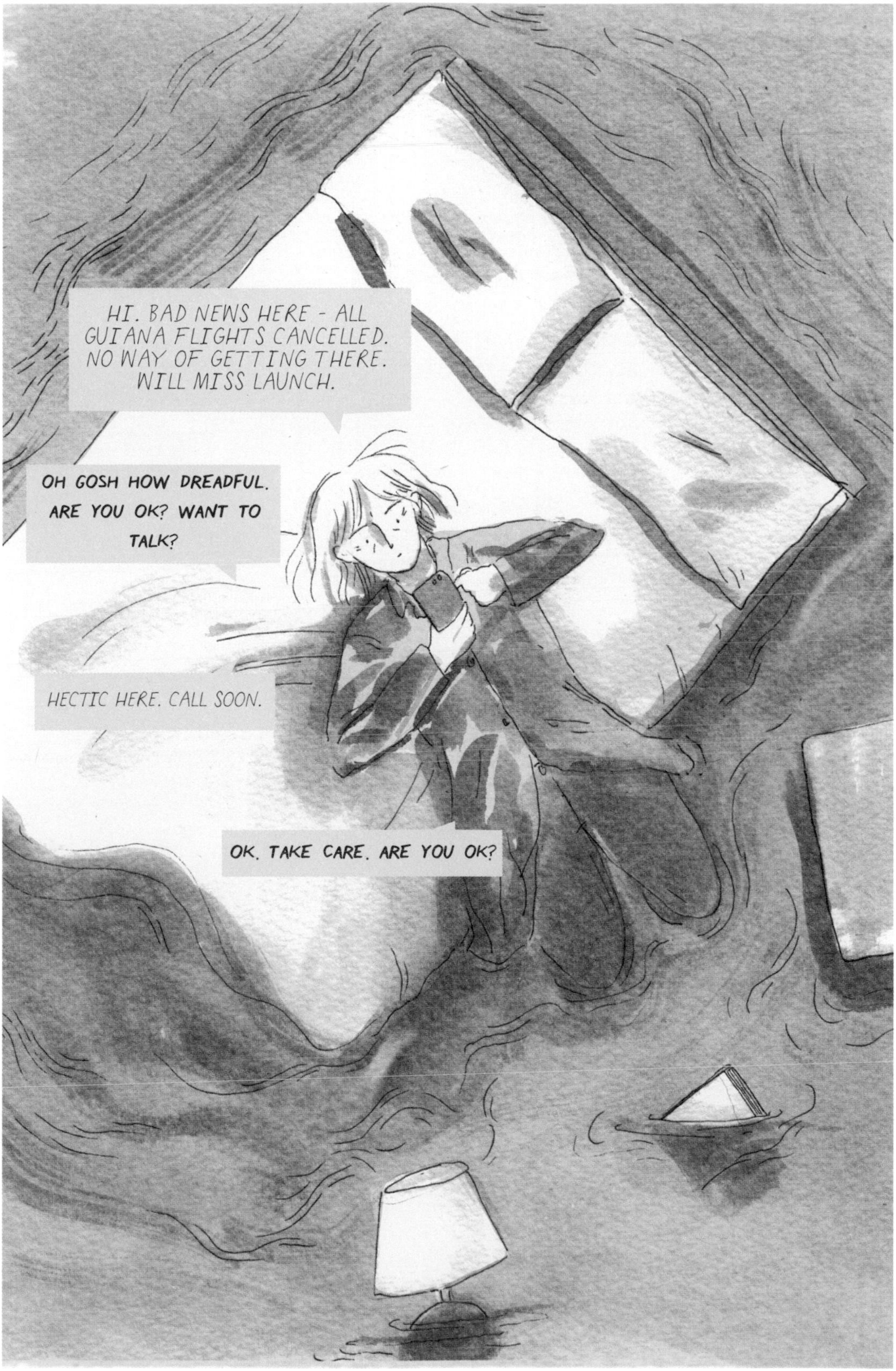
HI. BAD NEWS HERE - ALL GUIANA FLIGHTS CANCELLED. NO WAY OF GETTING THERE. WILL MISS LAUNCH.
OH GOSH HOW DREADFUL. ARE YOU OK? WANT TO TALK?
HECTIC HERE. CALL SOON.
OK. TAKE CARE. ARE YOU OK?

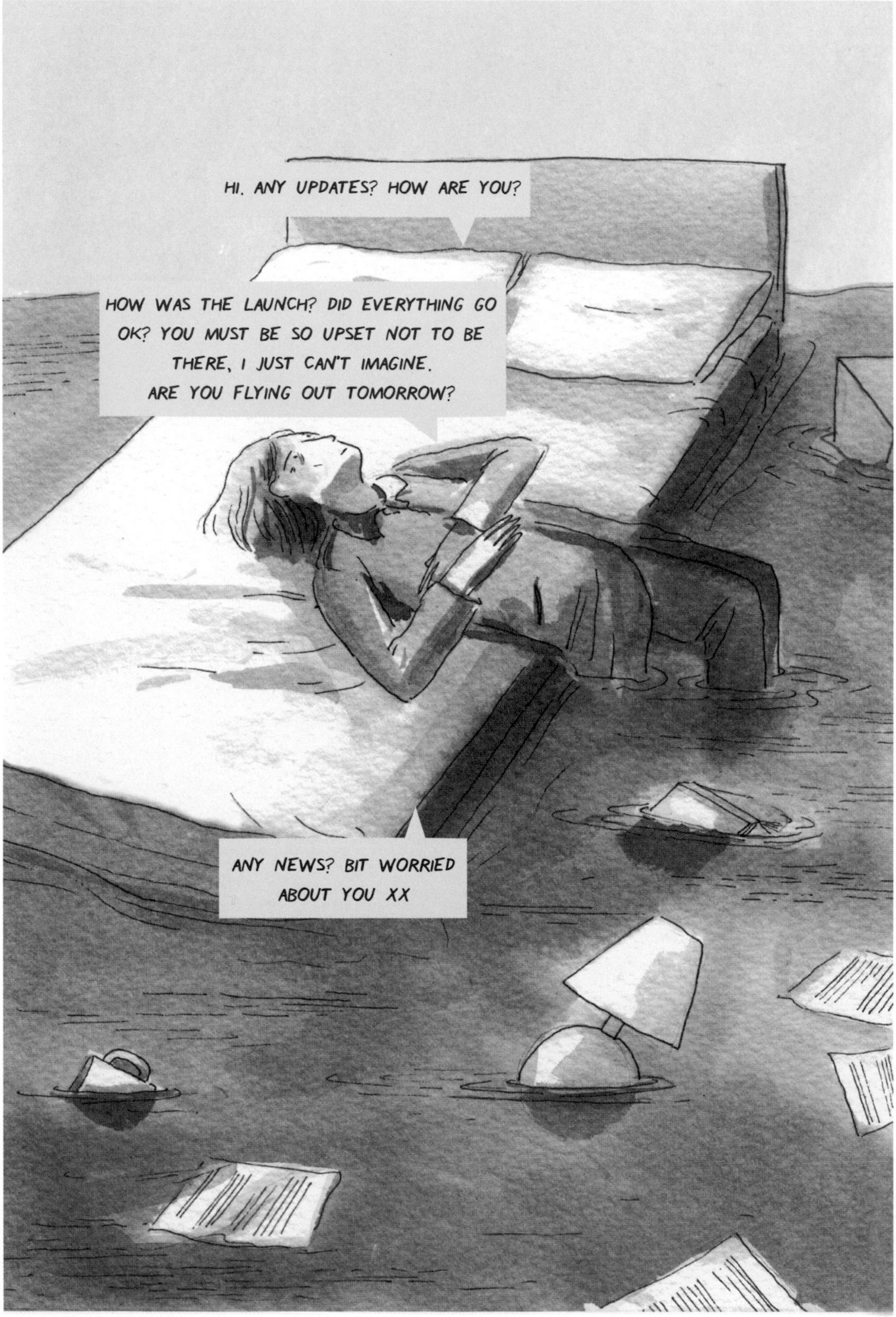
HI. ANY UPDATES? HOW ARE YOU?
HOW WAS THE LAUNCH? DID EVERYTHING GO OK? YOU MUST BE SO UPSET NOT TO BE THERE, I JUST CAN'T IMAGINE. ARE YOU FLYING OUT TOMORROW?
ANY NEWS? BIT WORRIED ABOUT YOU XX

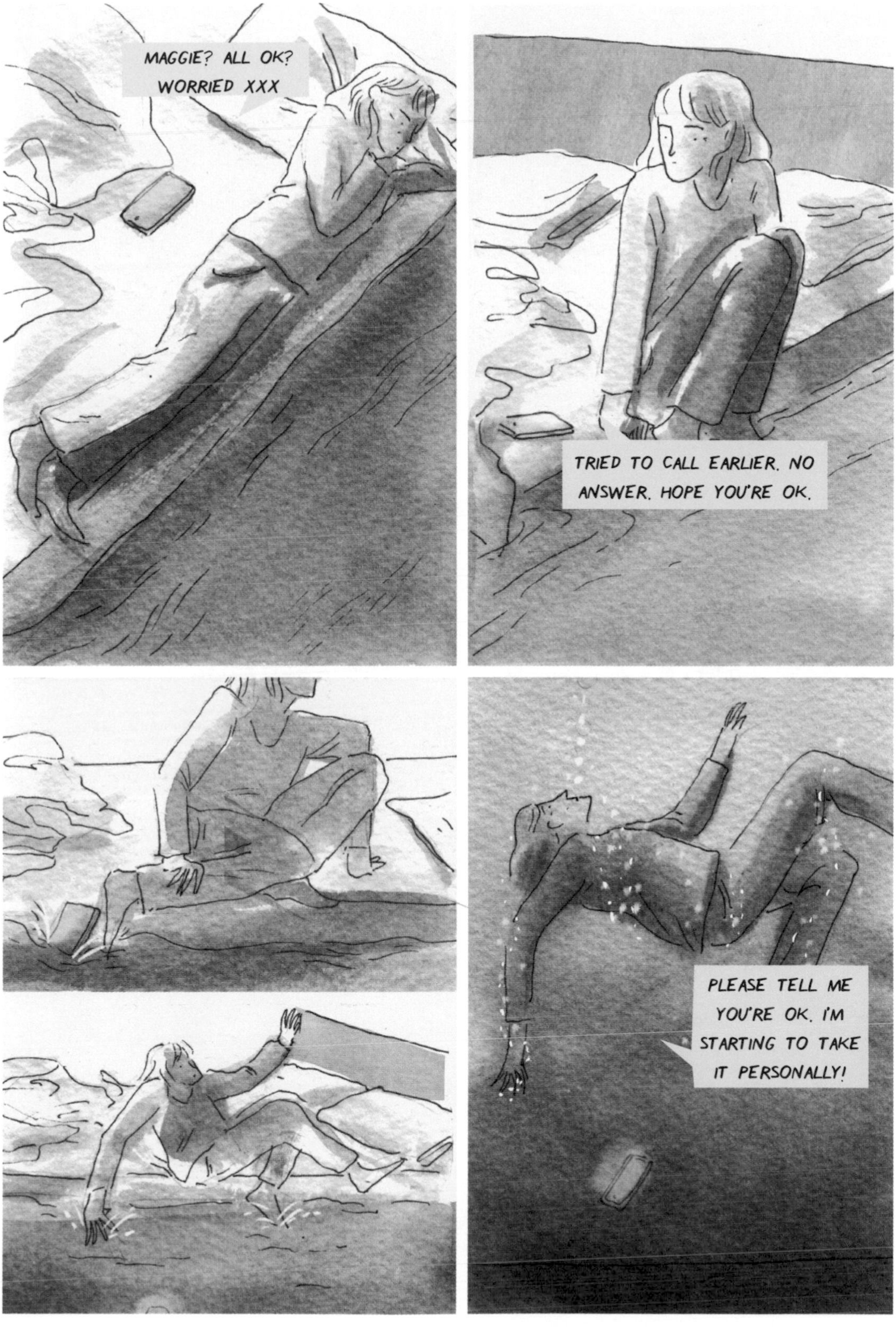
MAGGIE? ALL OK? WORRIED XXX
TRIED TO CALL EARLIER. NO ANSWER. HOPE YOU'RE OK.
PLEASE TELL ME YOU'RE OK. I'M STARTING TO TAKE IT PERSONALLY!

So I clocked out. The launch happened. It went well. I watched the livestream in bed. I slept and slept. After a fortnight or so, I felt pretty much normal again.

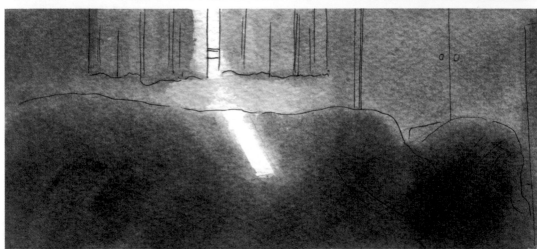

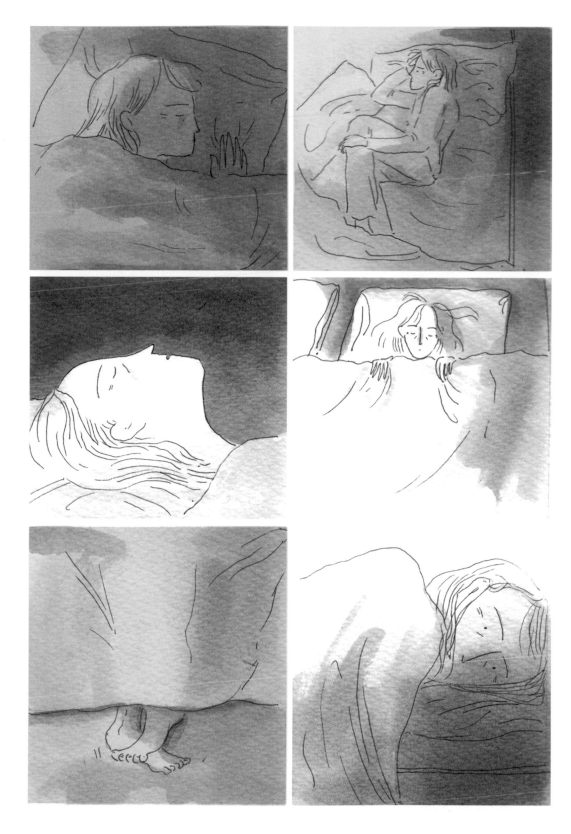

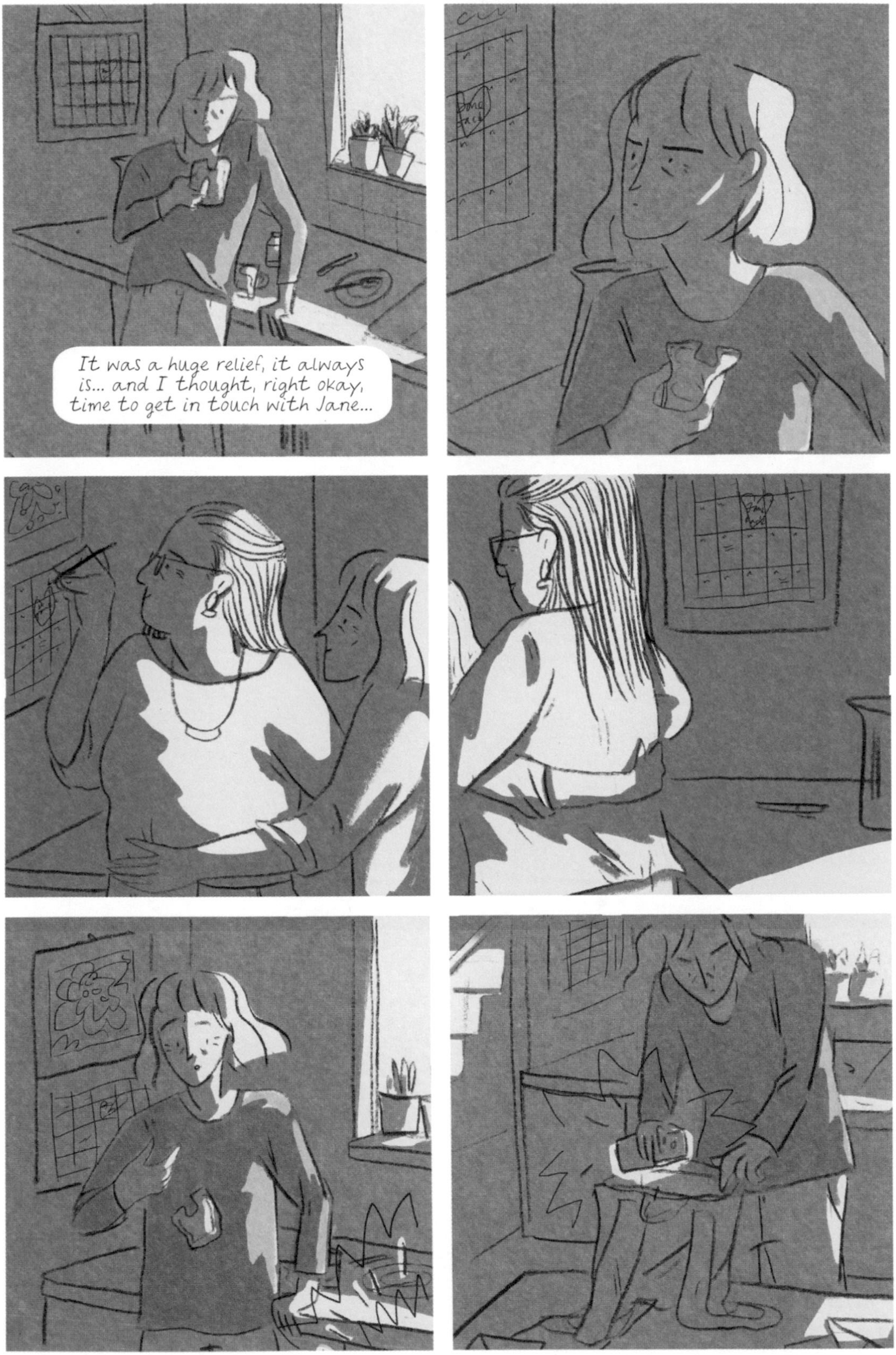
It was a huge relief, it always is... and I thought, right okay, time to get in touch with Jane...

Alarm:
Interview: 9.30am

Interview!

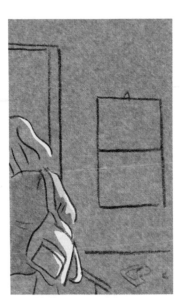

This mission is pretty much like, the pinnacle of your career, right?

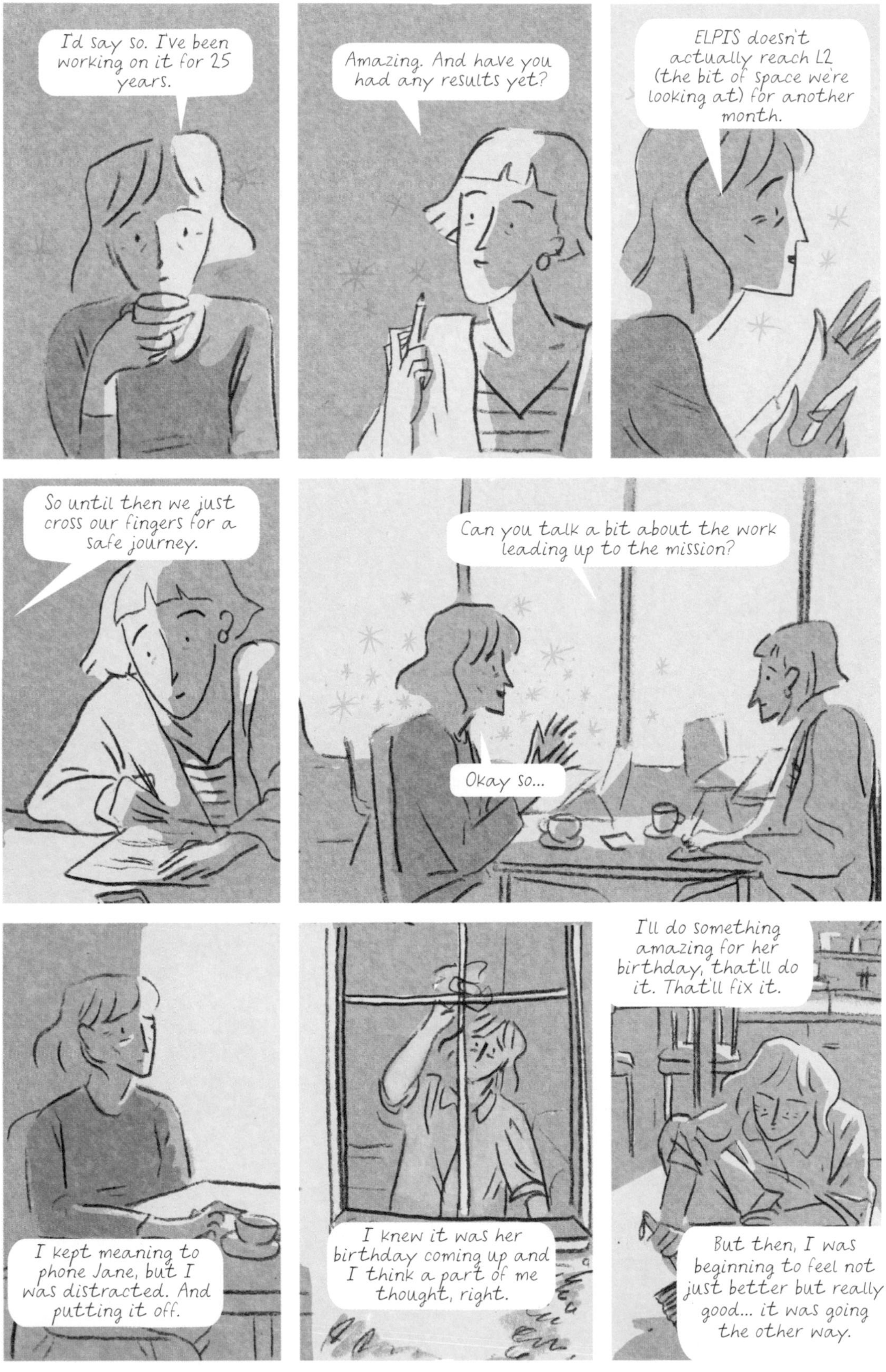
I'd say so. I've been working on it for 25 years.
Amazing. And have you had any results yet?
ELPIS doesn't actually reach L2 (the bit of space we're looking at) for another month.
So until then we just cross our fingers for a safe journey.
Can you talk a bit about the work leading up to the mission?
Okay so...
I kept meaning to phone Jane, but I was distracted. And putting it off.
I knew it was her birthday coming up and I think a part of me thought, right.
I'll do something amazing for her birthday, that'll do it. That'll fix it.
But then, I was beginning to feel not just better but really good... it was going the other way.

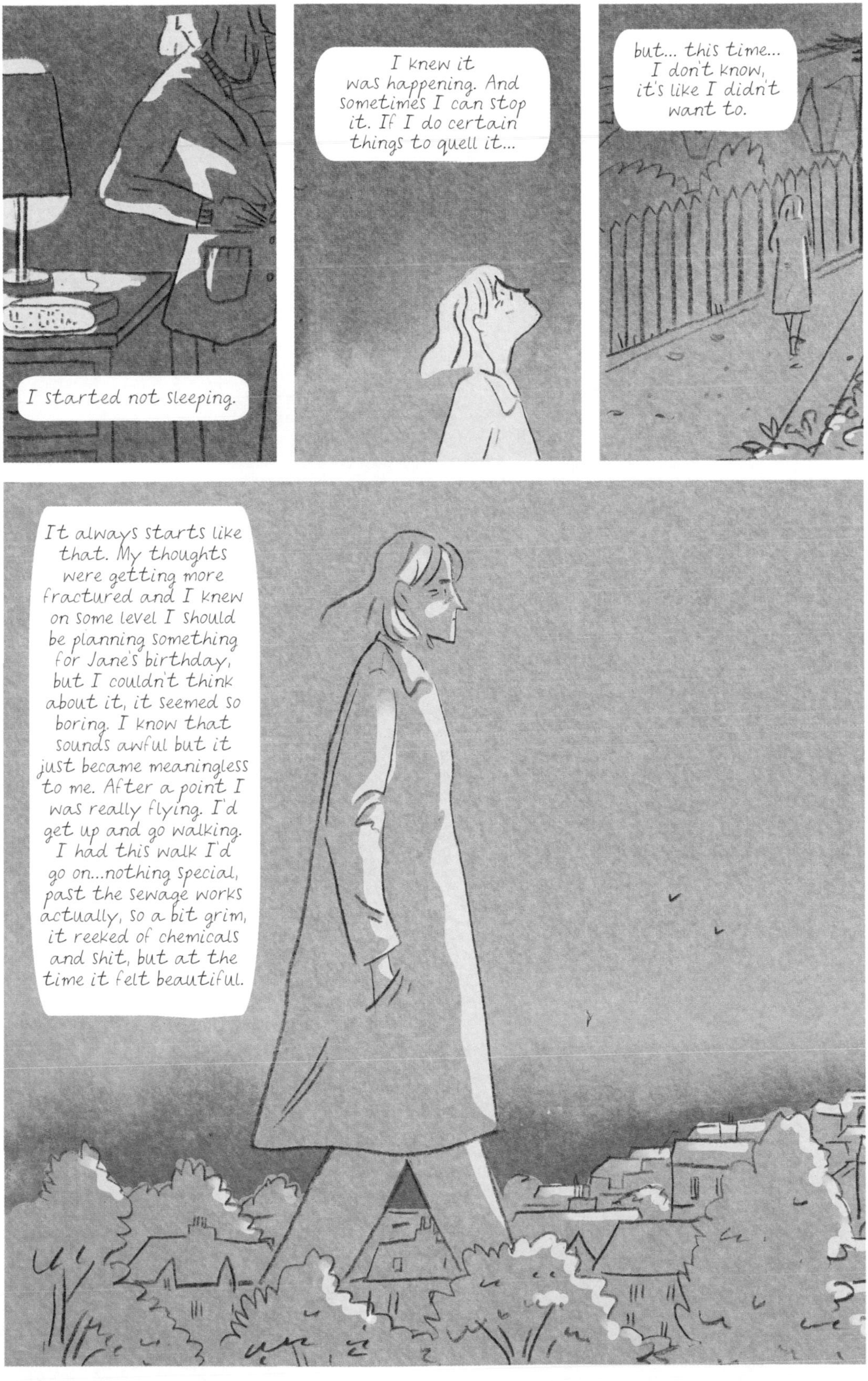
I started not sleeping.
I knew it was happening. And sometimes I can stop it. If I do certain things to quell it...
but... this time... I don't know, it's like I didn't want to.
It always starts like that. My thoughts were getting more fractured and I knew on some level I should be planning something for Jane's birthday, but I couldn't think about it, it seemed so boring. I know that sounds awful but it just became meaningless to me. After a point I was really flying. I'd get up and go walking. I had this walk I'd go on...nothing special, past the sewage works actually, so a bit grim, it reeked of chemicals and shit, but at the time it felt beautiful.

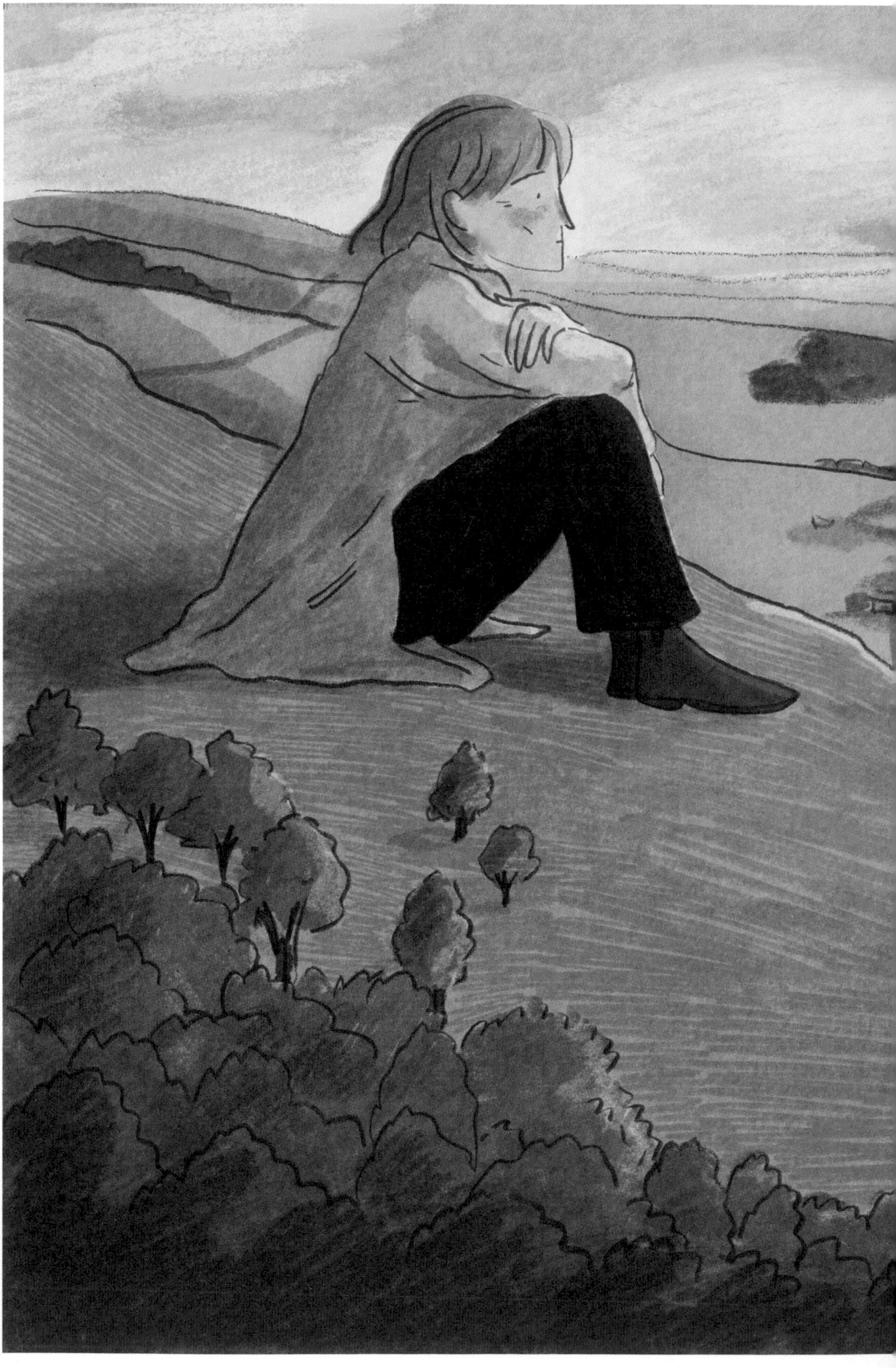

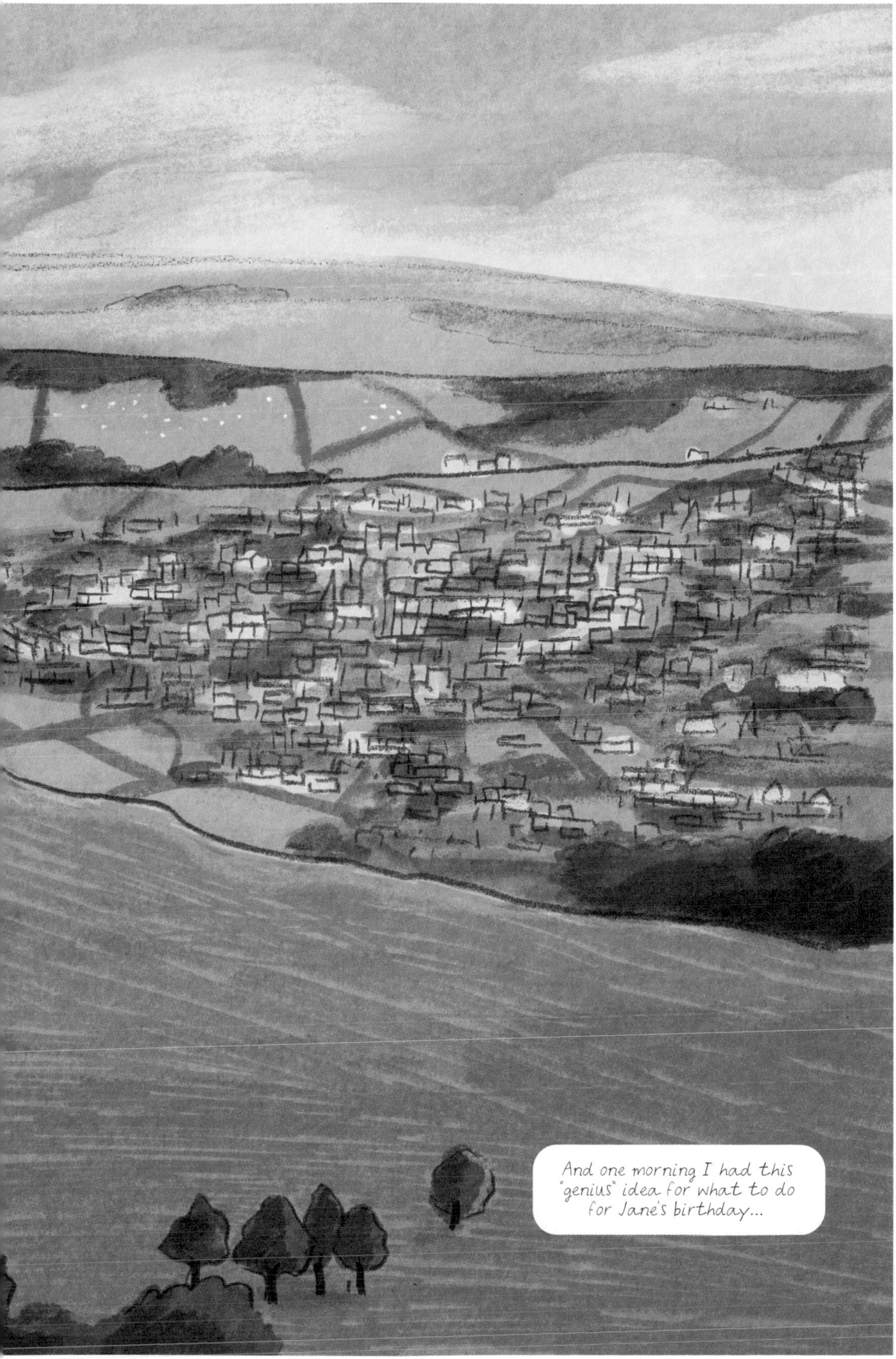
And one morning I had this "genius" idea for what to do for Jane's birthday...

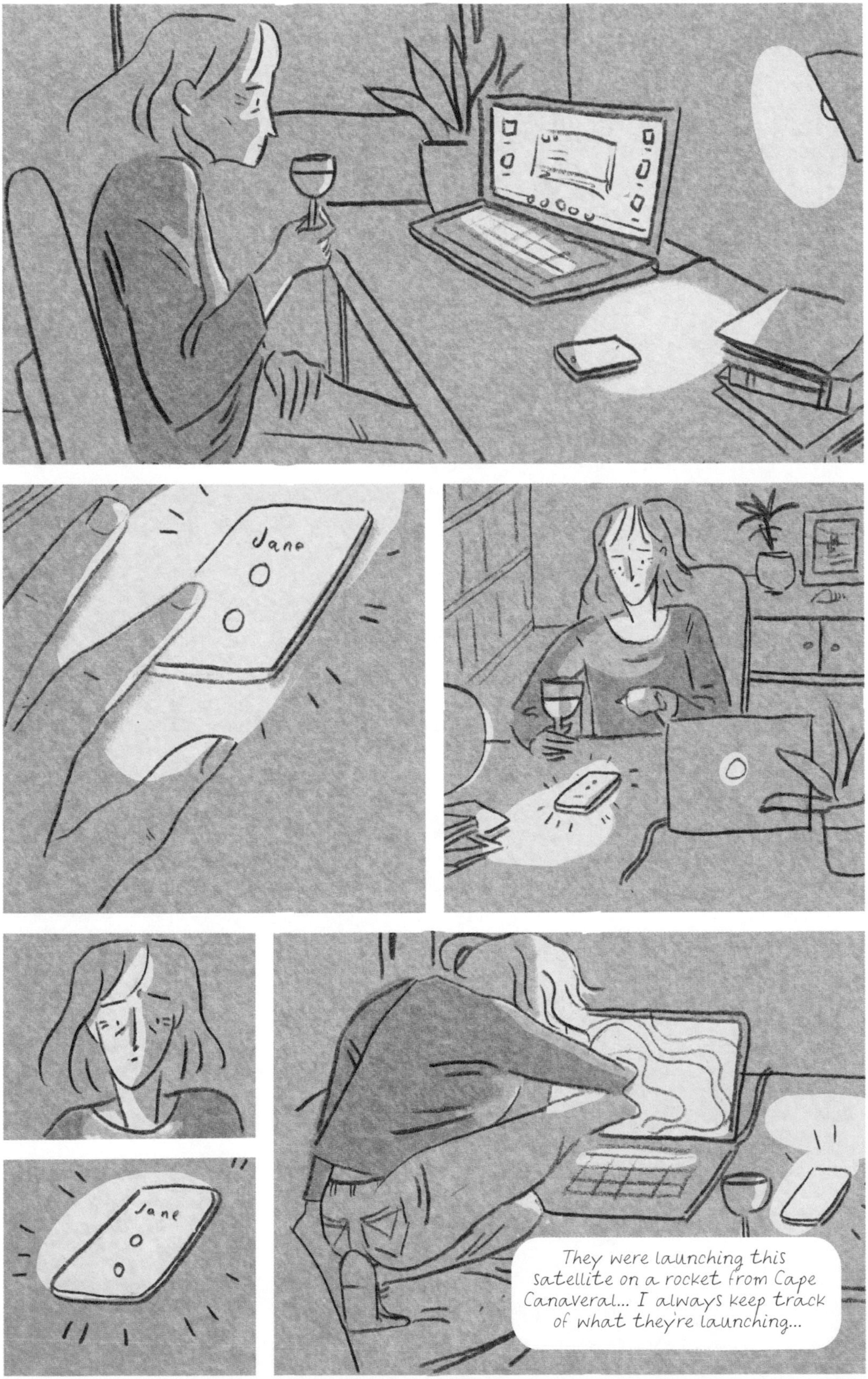
Jane
Jane
They were launching this satellite on a rocket from Cape Canaveral... I always keep track of what they're launching...

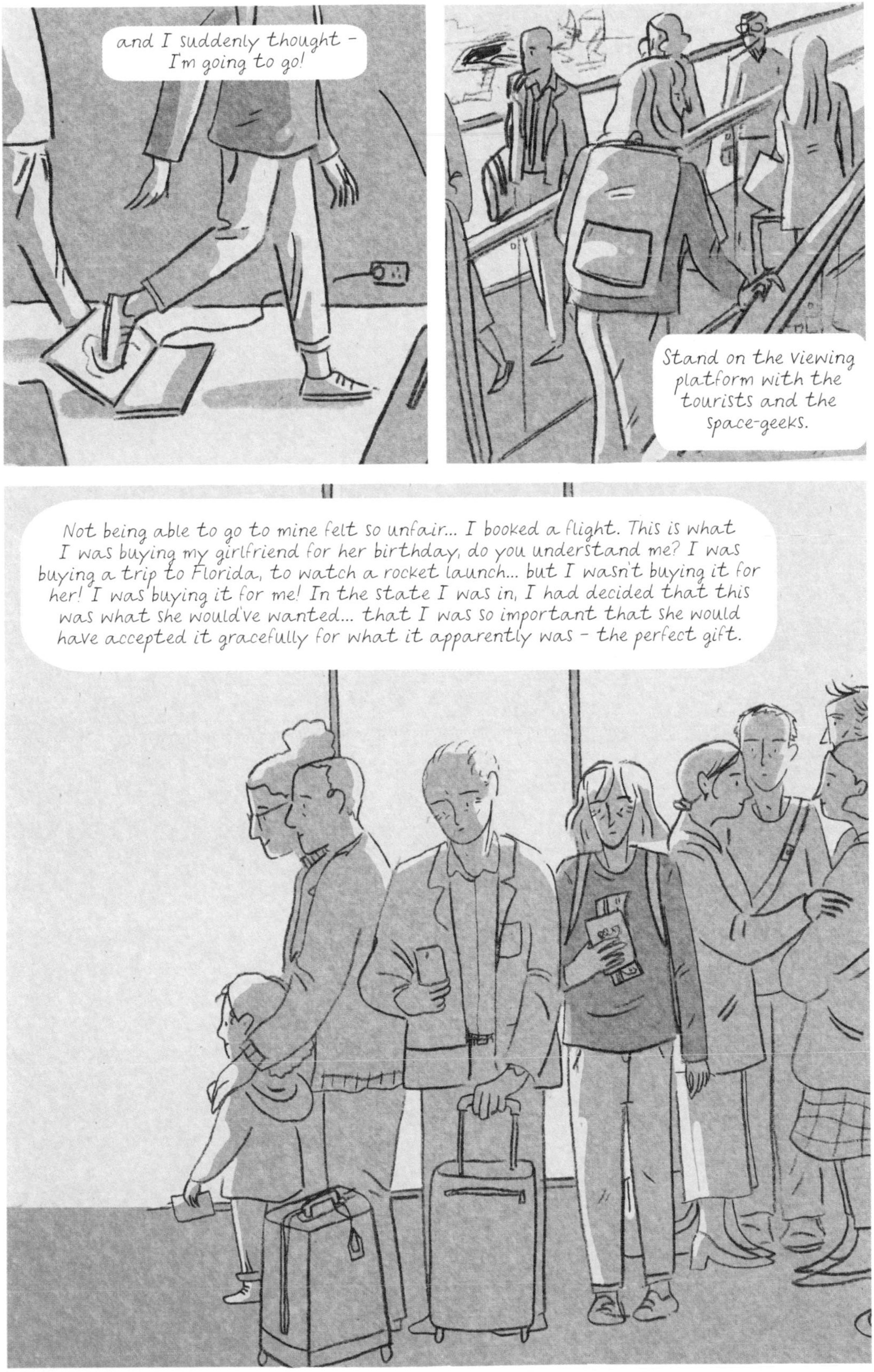
and I suddenly thought – I'm going to go!
Stand on the viewing platform with the tourists and the space-geeks.
Not being able to go to mine felt so unfair... I booked a flight. This is what I was buying my girlfriend for her birthday, do you understand me? I was buying a trip to Florida, to watch a rocket launch... but I wasn't buying it for her! I was buying it for me! In the state I was in, I had decided that this was what she would've wanted... that I was so important that she would have accepted it gracefully for what it apparently was – the perfect gift.

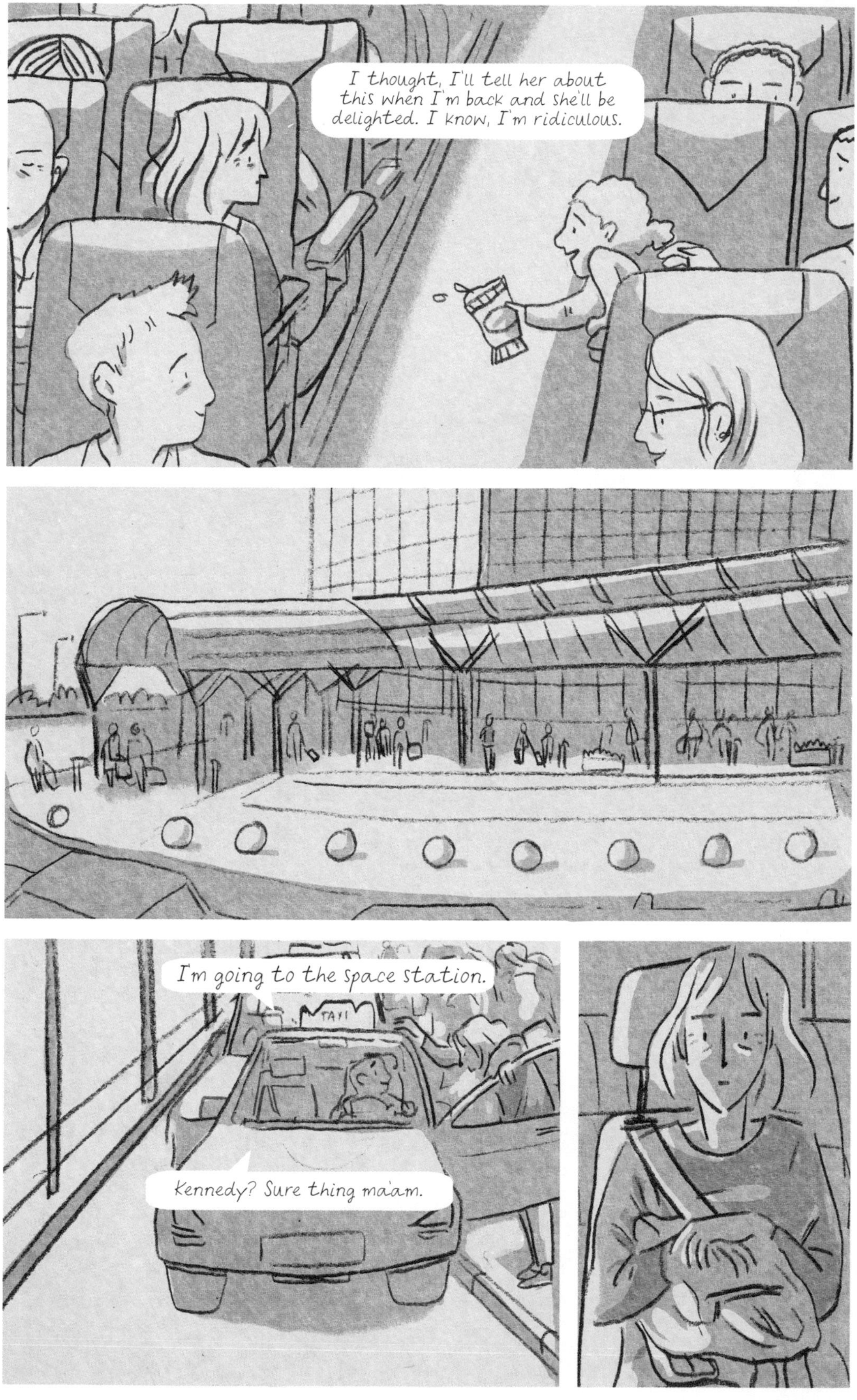
I thought, I'll tell her about this when I'm back and she'll be delighted. I know, I'm ridiculous.
I'm going to the space station.
TAXI
Kennedy? Sure thing ma'am.

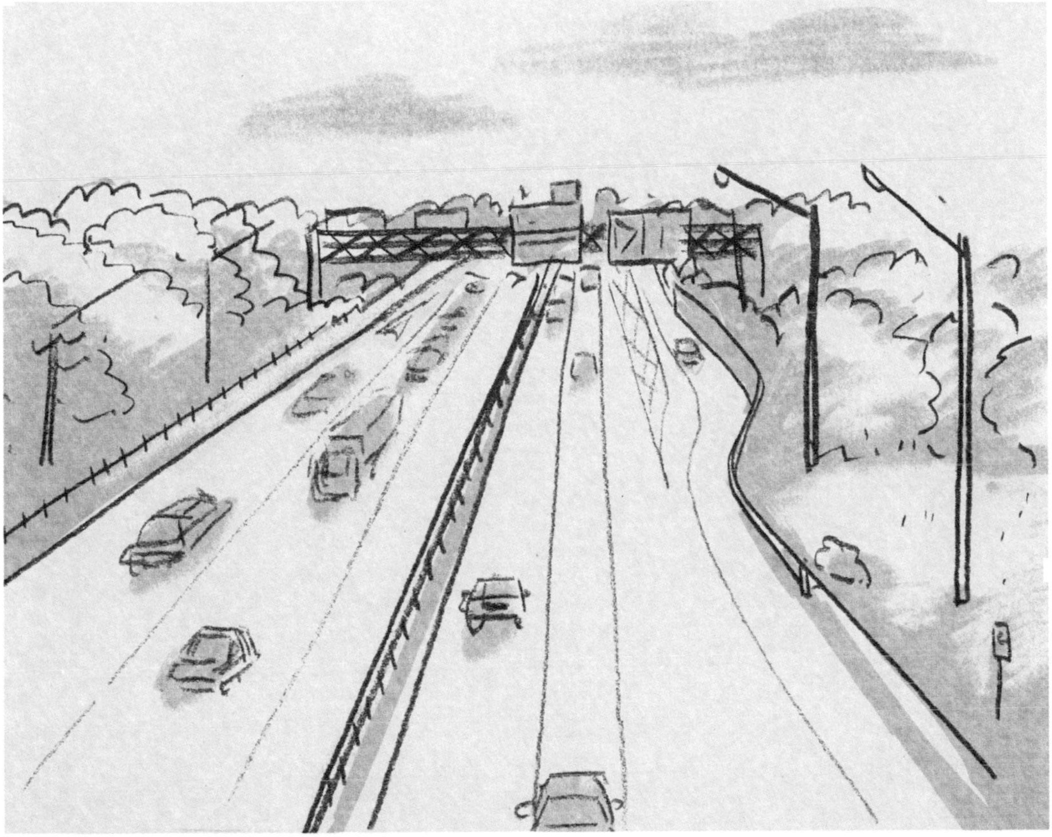

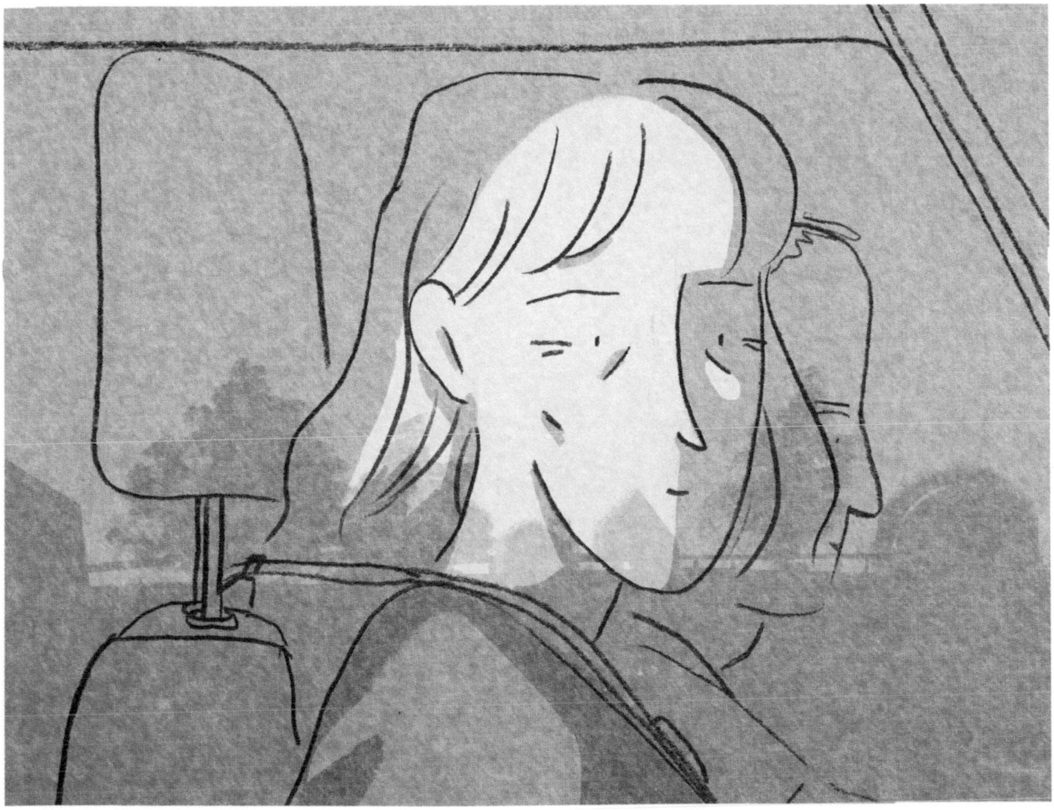

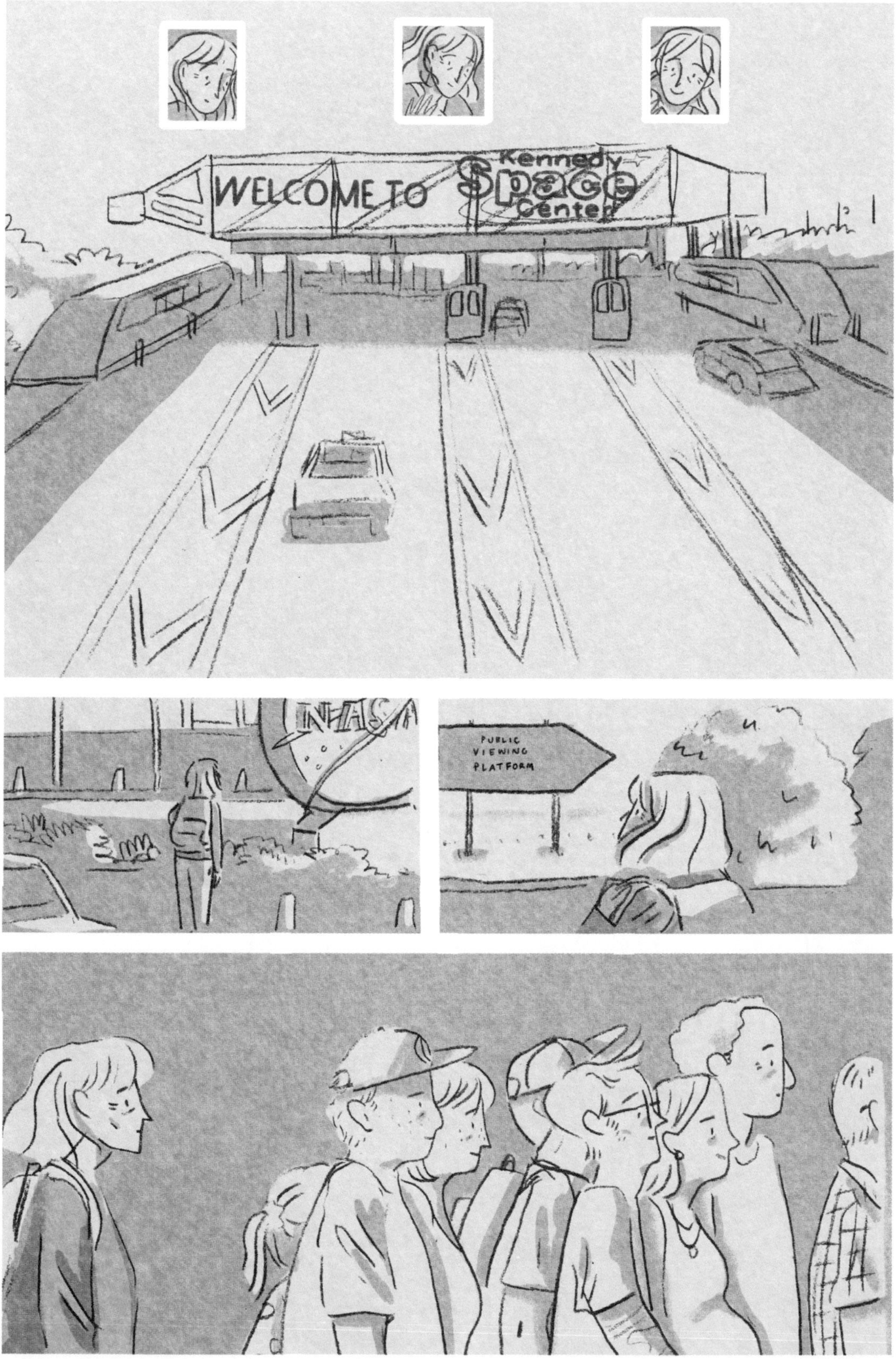
WELCOME TO Kennedy Space Center
PUBLIC VIEWING PLATFORM

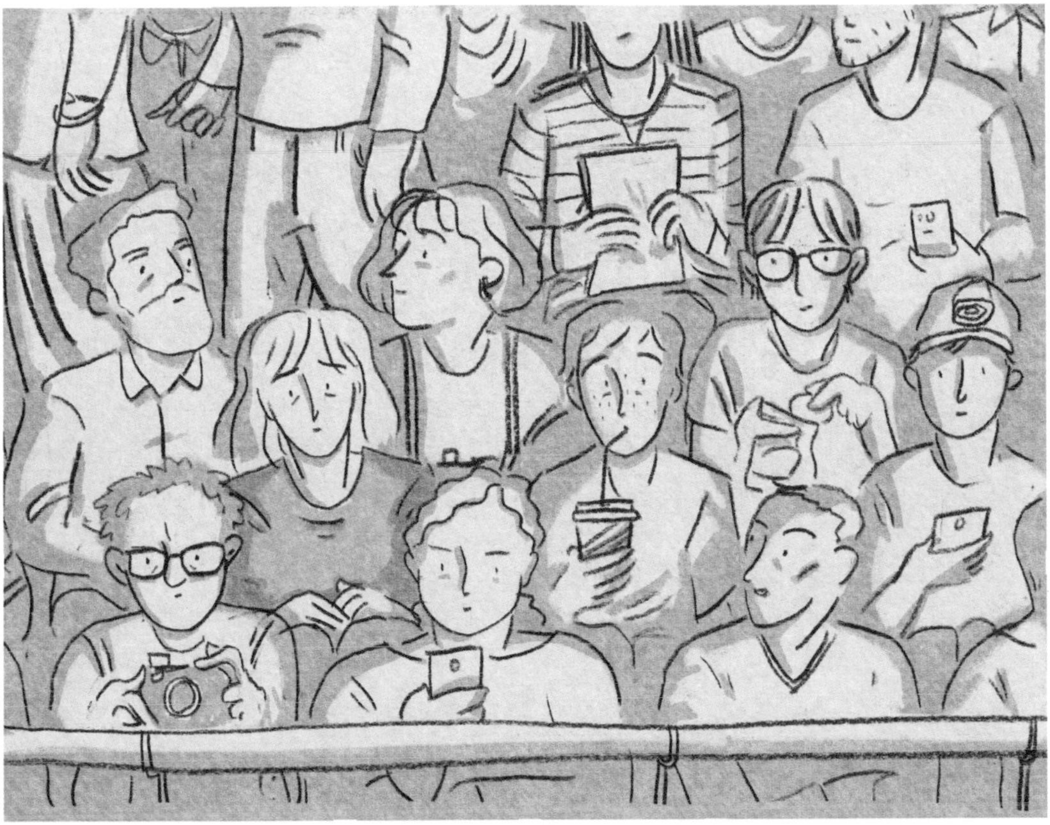

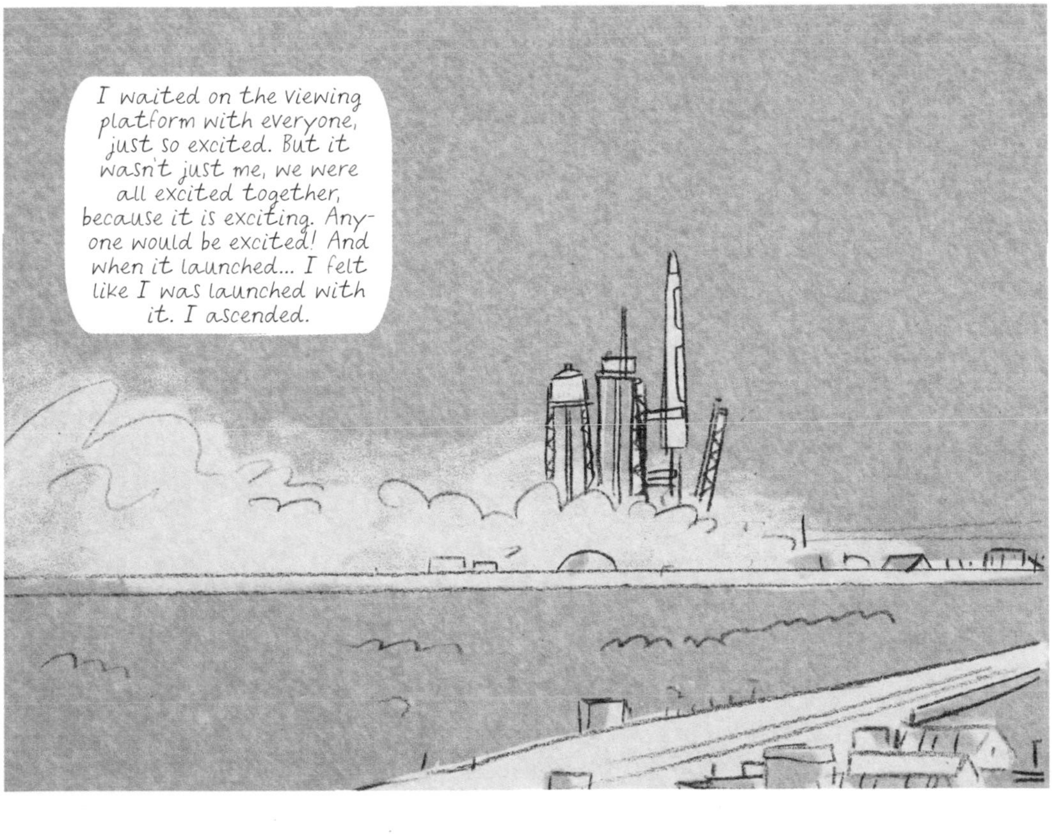
I waited on the viewing platform with everyone, just so excited. But it wasn't just me, we were all excited together, because it is exciting. Anyone would be excited! And when it launched... I felt like I was launched with it. I ascended.

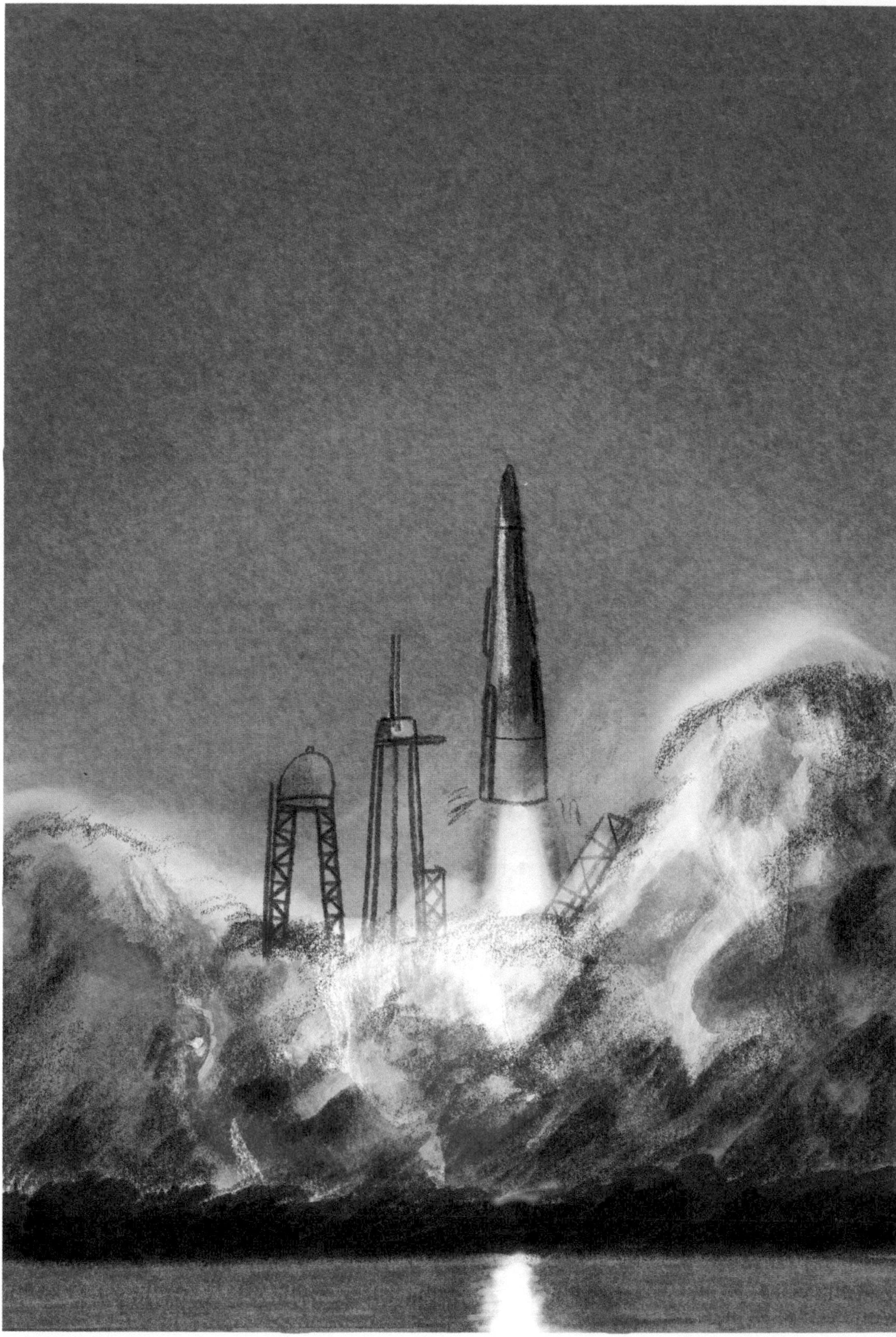

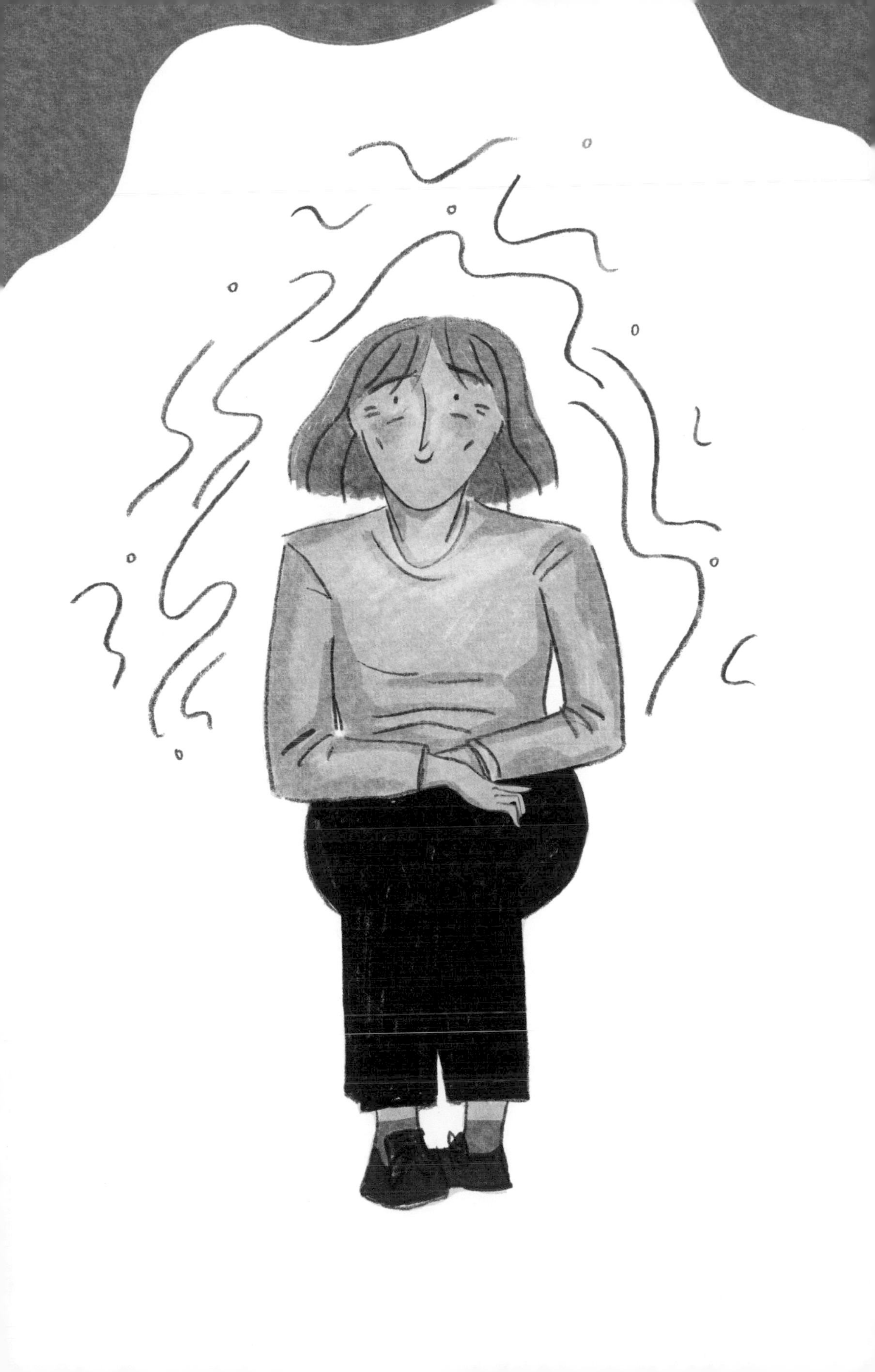

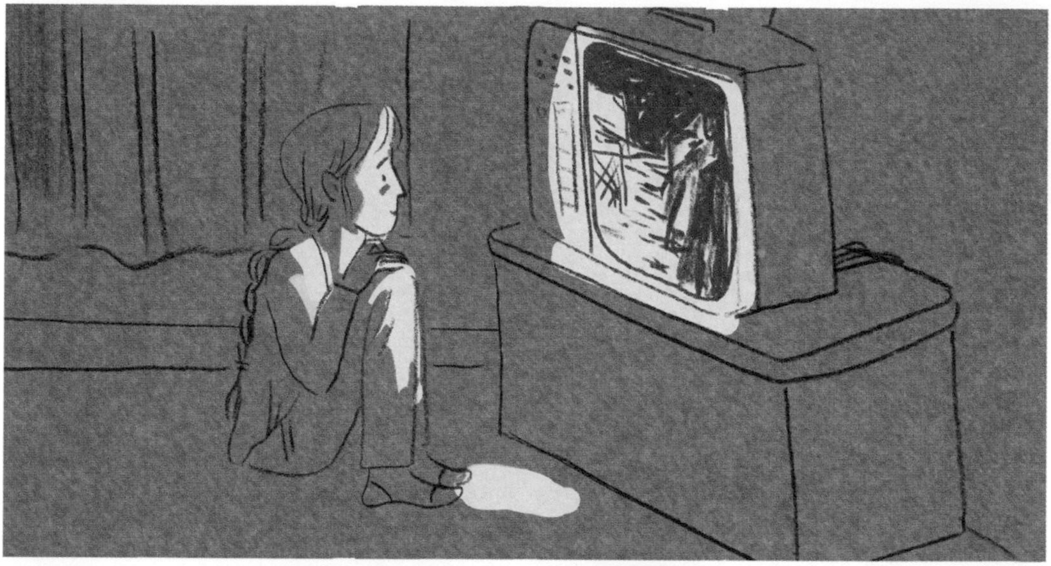
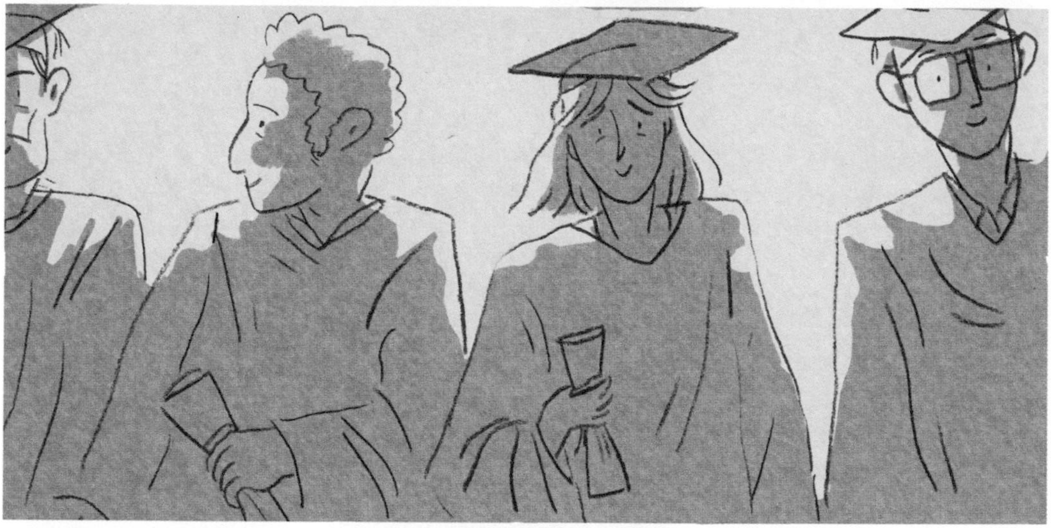
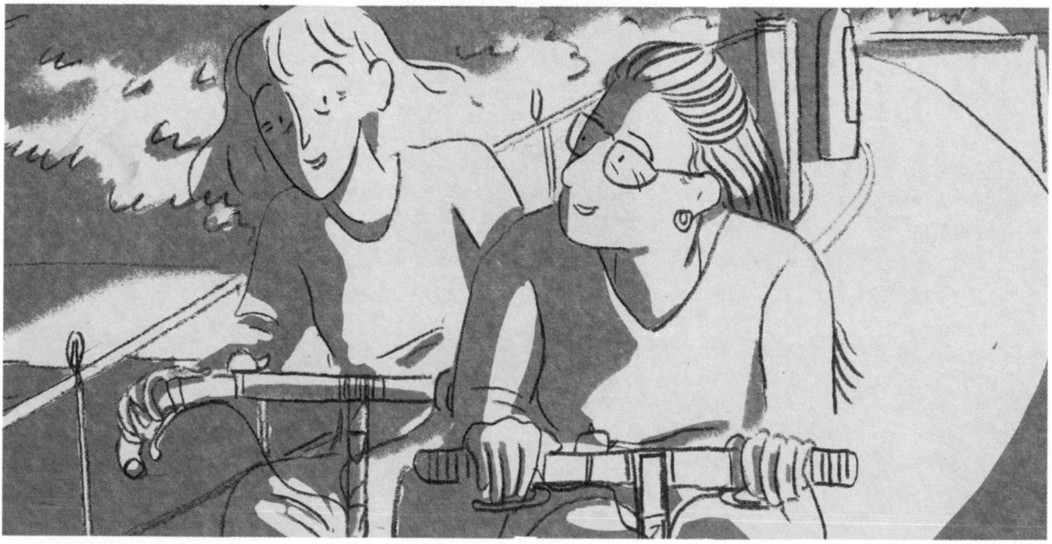

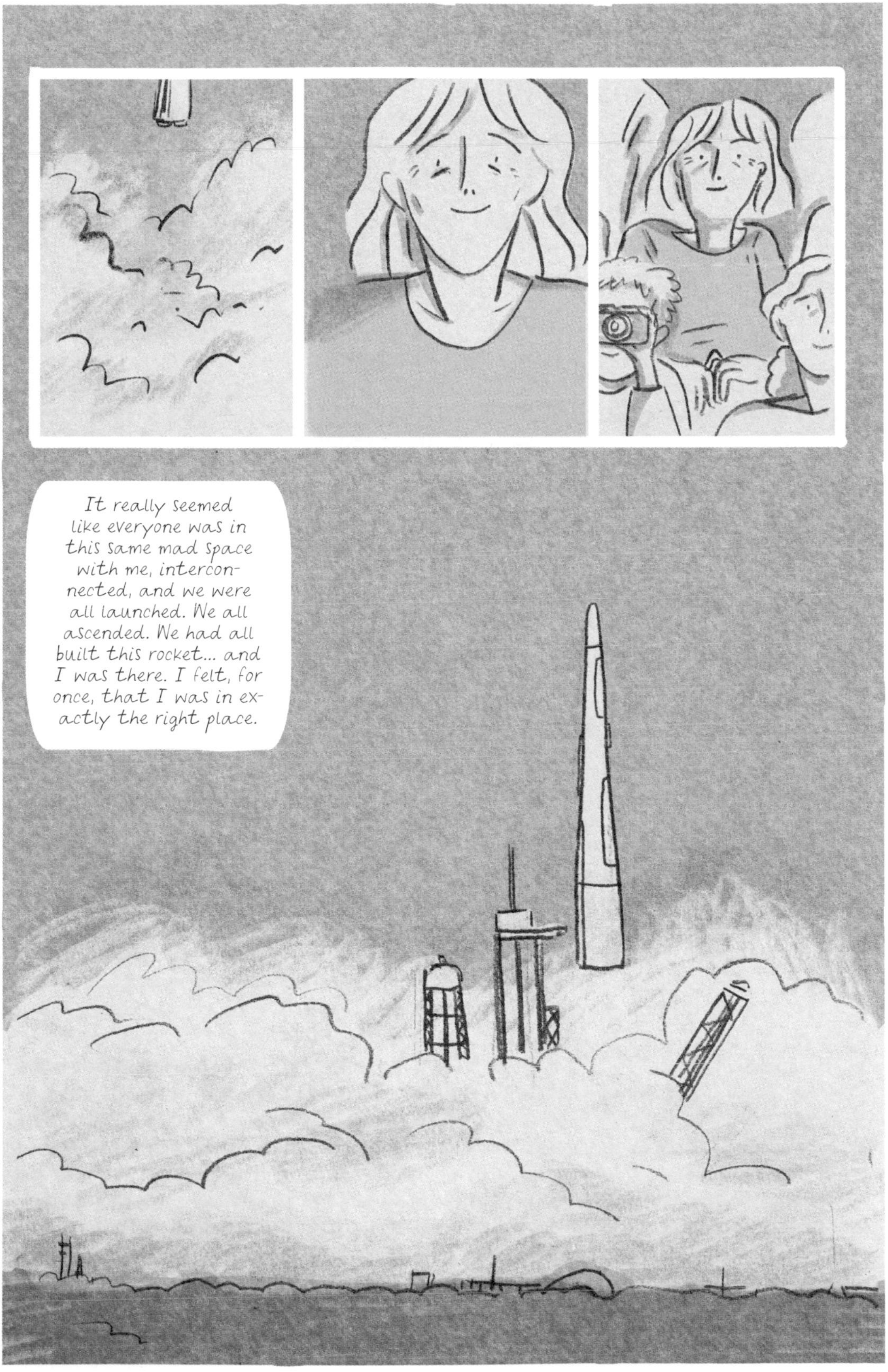
It really seemed like everyone was in this same mad space with me, interconnected, and we were all launched. We all ascended. We had all built this rocket... and I was there. I felt, for once, that I was in exactly the right place.

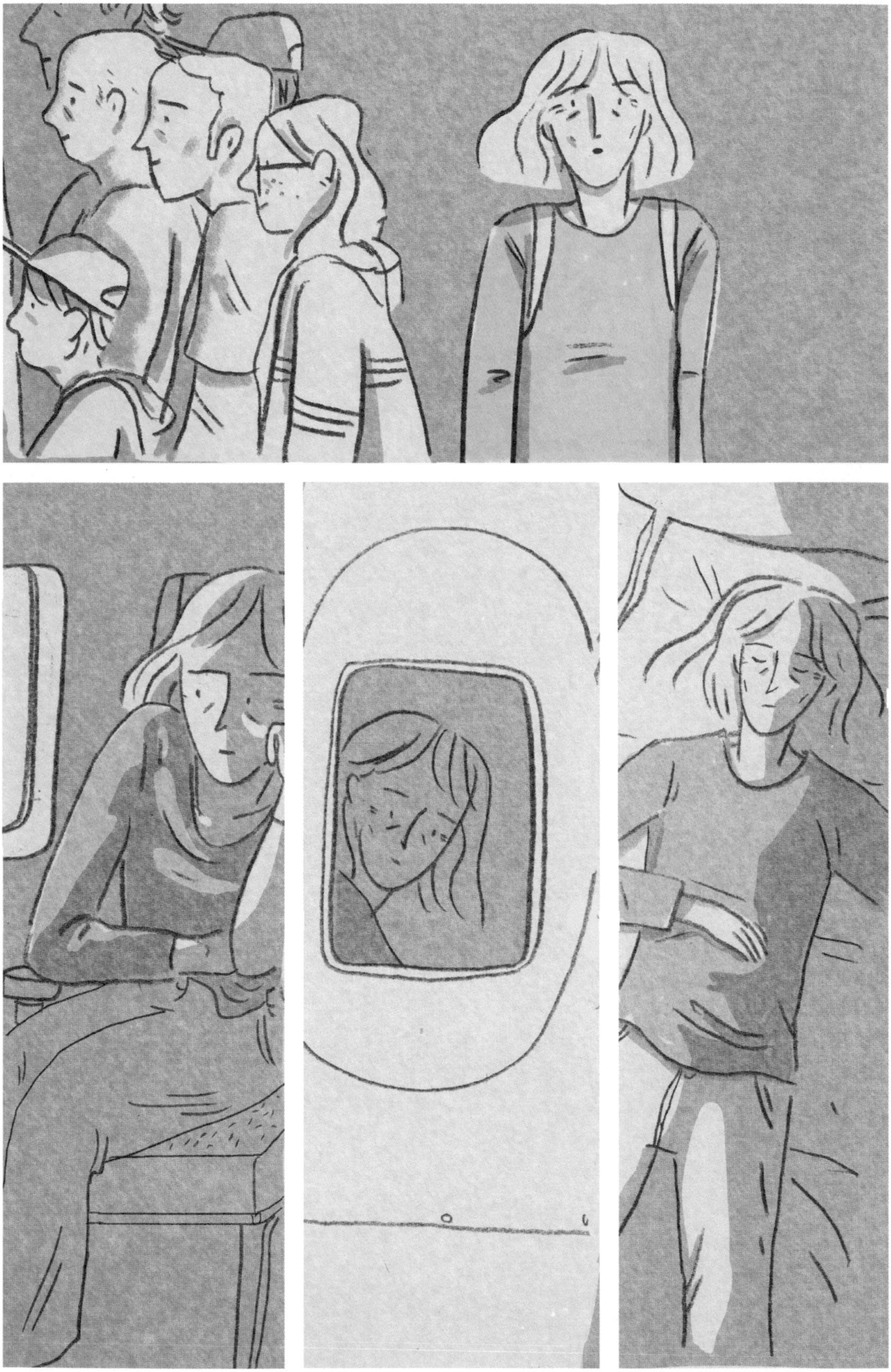

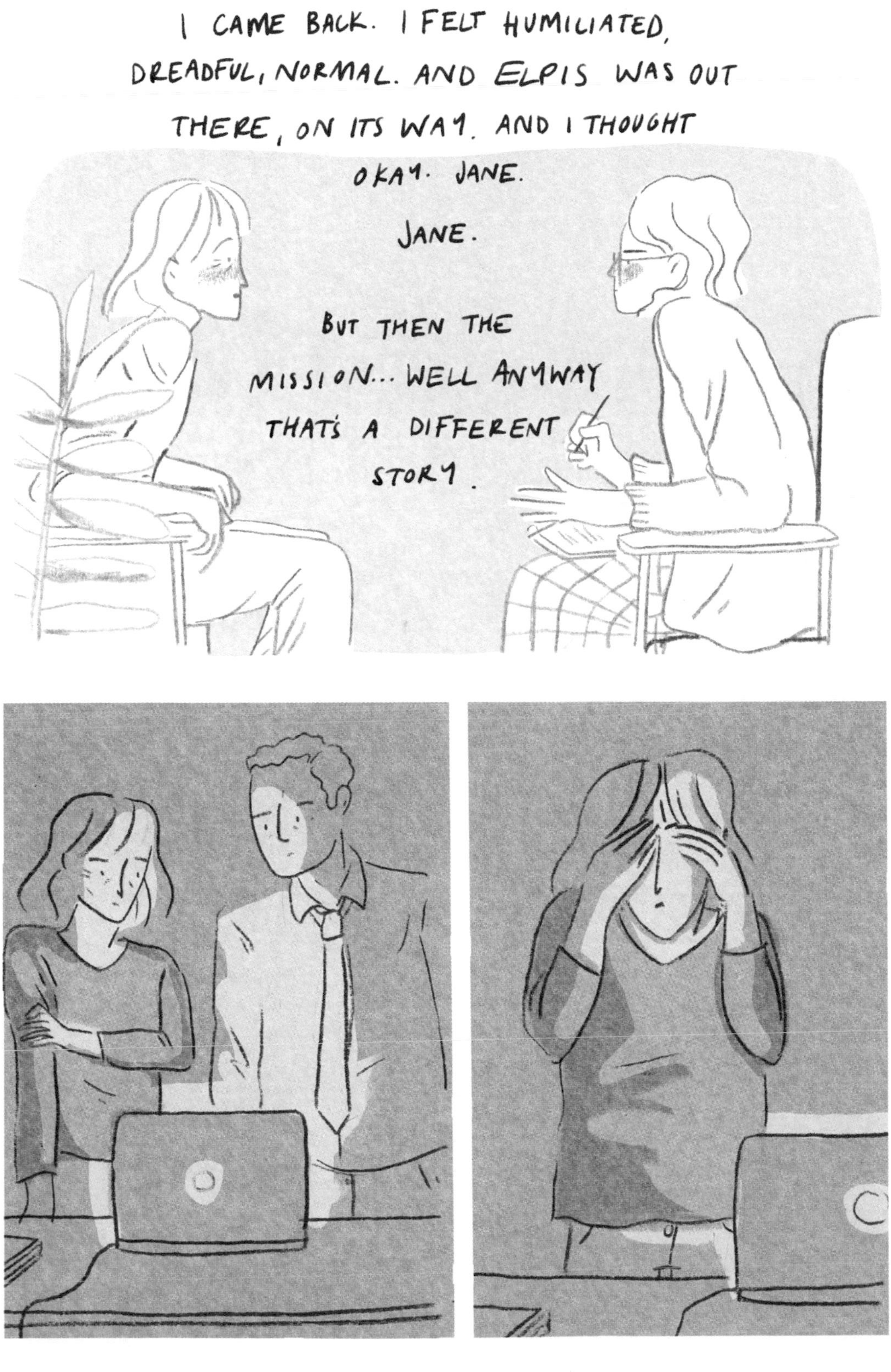
I CAME BACK. I FELT HUMILIATED, DREADFUL, NORMAL. AND ELPIS WAS OUT THERE, ON ITS WAY. AND I THOUGHT OKAY. JANE.
JANE.
BUT THEN THE MISSION... WELL ANYWAY THAT'S A DIFFERENT STORY.

Yep?

I just wondered...

Why can't we live on one of the planets that Kepler found?

Oh for... okay, do you know what, the thing about the planets that Kepler found, right...

Yes, pretty photographs and yes, all very exciting, but actually, it's not that exciting. The press get hold of something like that and they want a story.

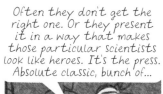

Often they don't get the right one. Or they present it in a way that makes those particular scientists look like heroes. It's the press. Absolute classic, bunch of...

Sorry, but... those Kepler planets, great, right? But they're not Earth 2.

Those planets are rotating in such a manner that one face of the plan- et remains locked toward the star. So there would be no night and day!

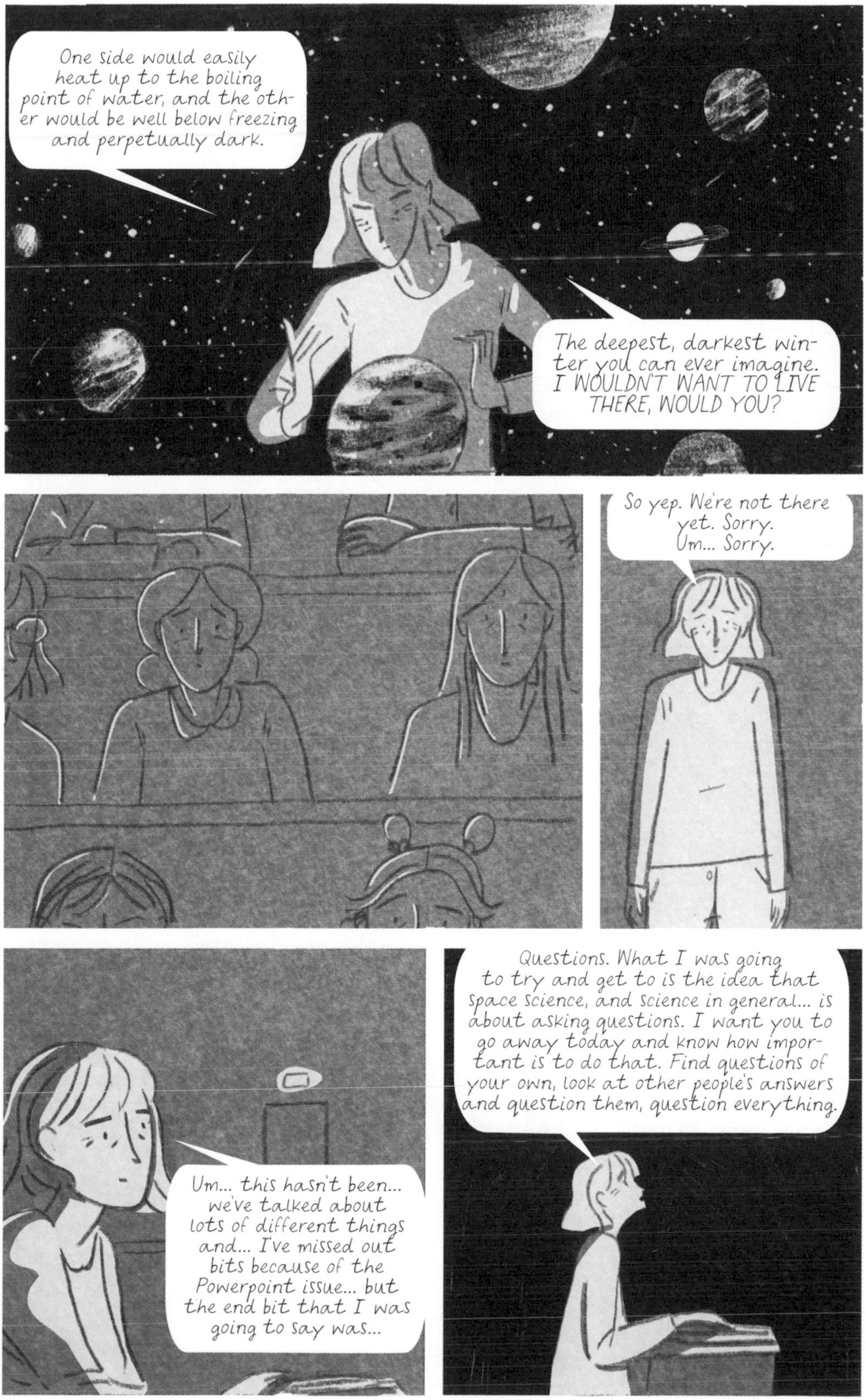
One side would easily heat up to the boiling point of water, and the other would be well below freezing and perpetually dark.
The deepest, darkest winter you can ever imagine. I WOULDN'T WANT TO LIVE THERE, WOULD YOU?
So yep. We're not there yet. Sorry. Um... Sorry.
Um... this hasn't been... we've talked about lots of different things and... I've missed out bits because of the Powerpoint issue... but the end bit that I was going to say was...
Questions. What I was going to try and get to is the idea that space science, and science in general... is about asking questions. I want you to go away today and know how important is to do that. Find questions of your own, look at other people's answers and question them, question everything.

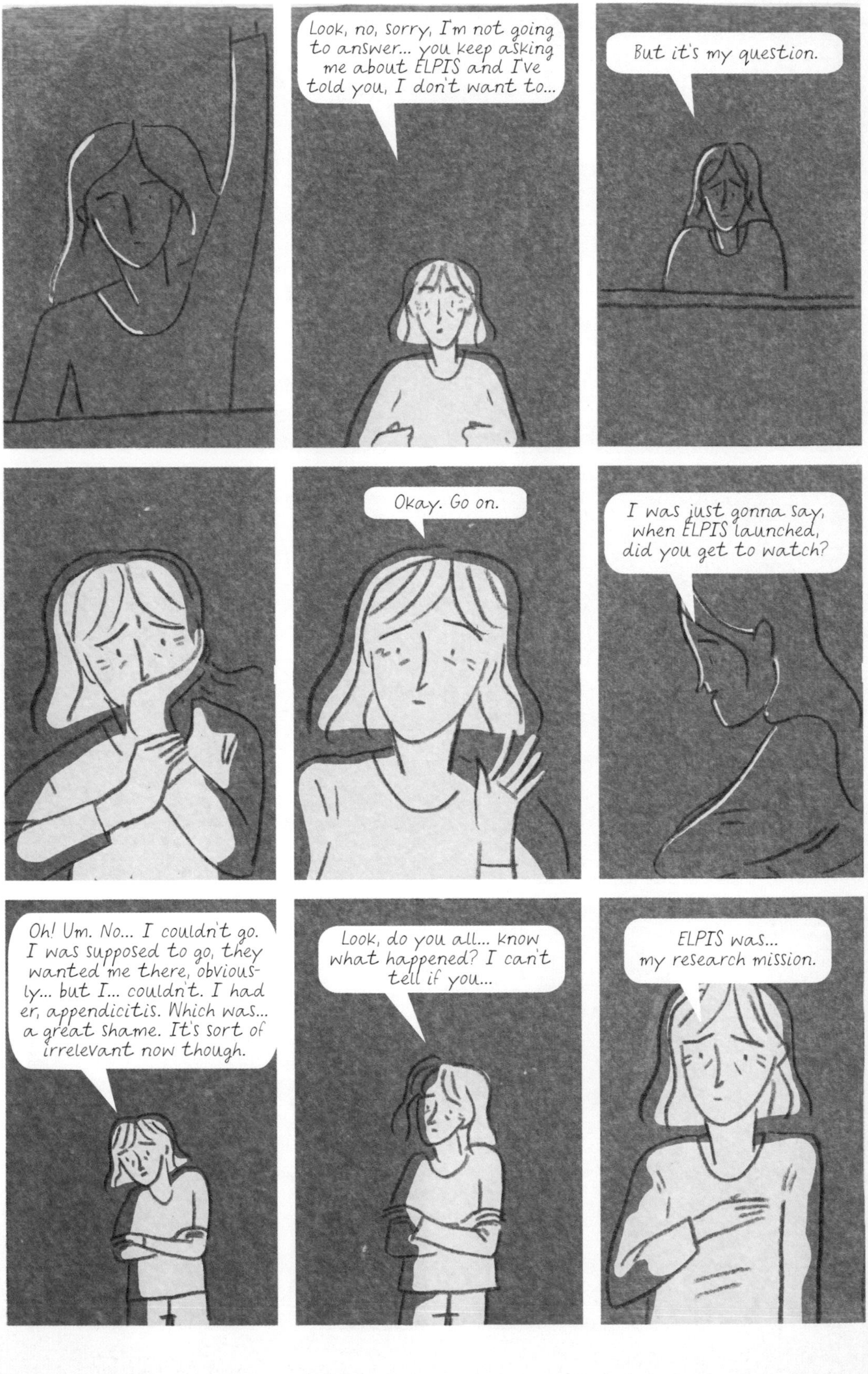
Look, no, sorry, I'm not going to answer... you keep asking me about ELPIS and I've told you, I don't want to...
But it's my question.
Okay. Go on.
I was just gonna say, when ELPIS launched, did you get to watch?
Oh! Um. No... I couldn't go. I was supposed to go, they wanted me there, obviously... but I... couldn't. I had er, appendicitis. Which was... a great shame. It's sort of irrelevant now though.
Look, do you all... know what happened? I can't tell if you...
ELPIS was... my research mission.

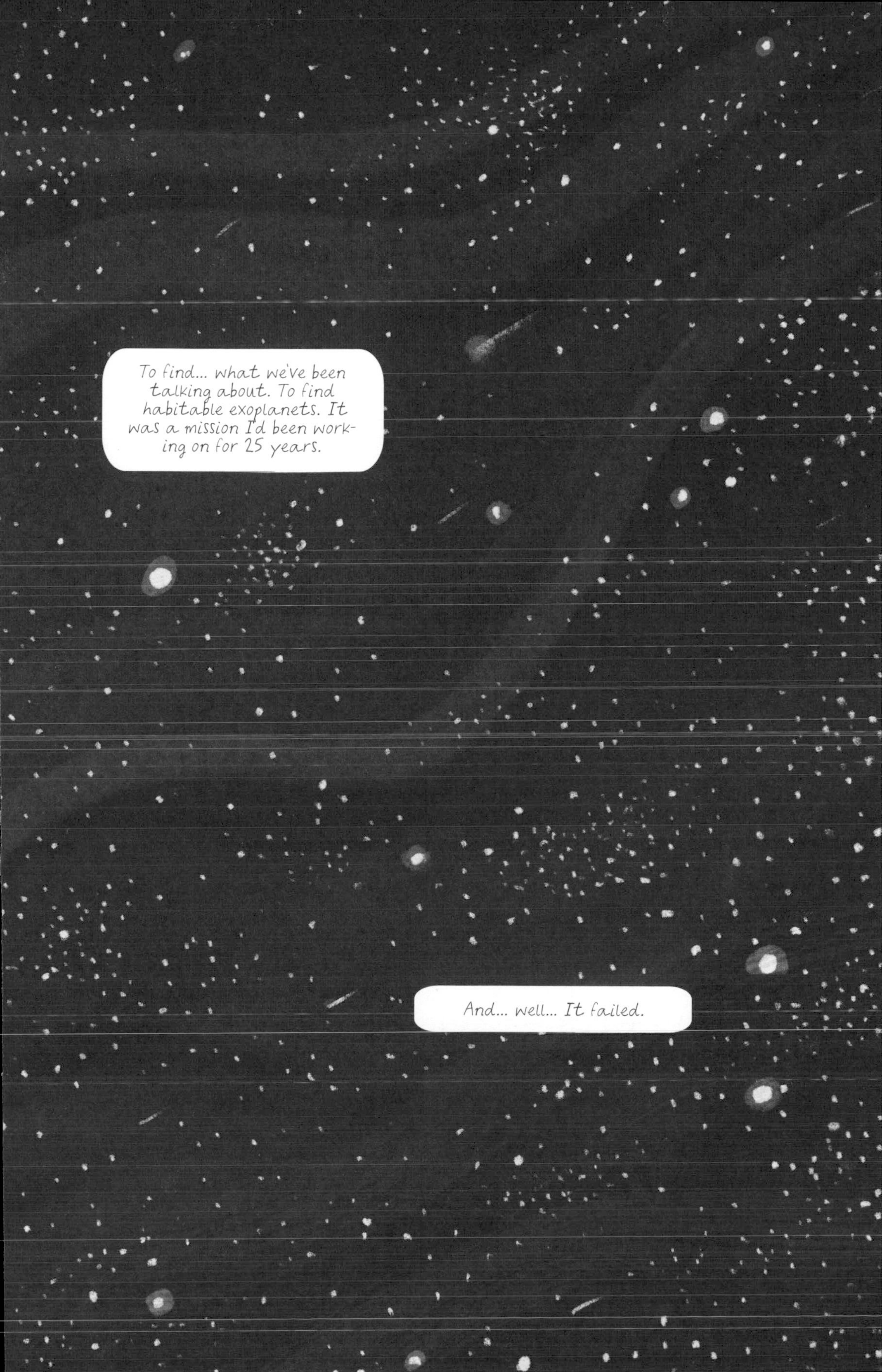
To find... what we've been talking about. To find habitable exoplanets. It was a mission I'd been working on for 25 years.
And... well... It failed.

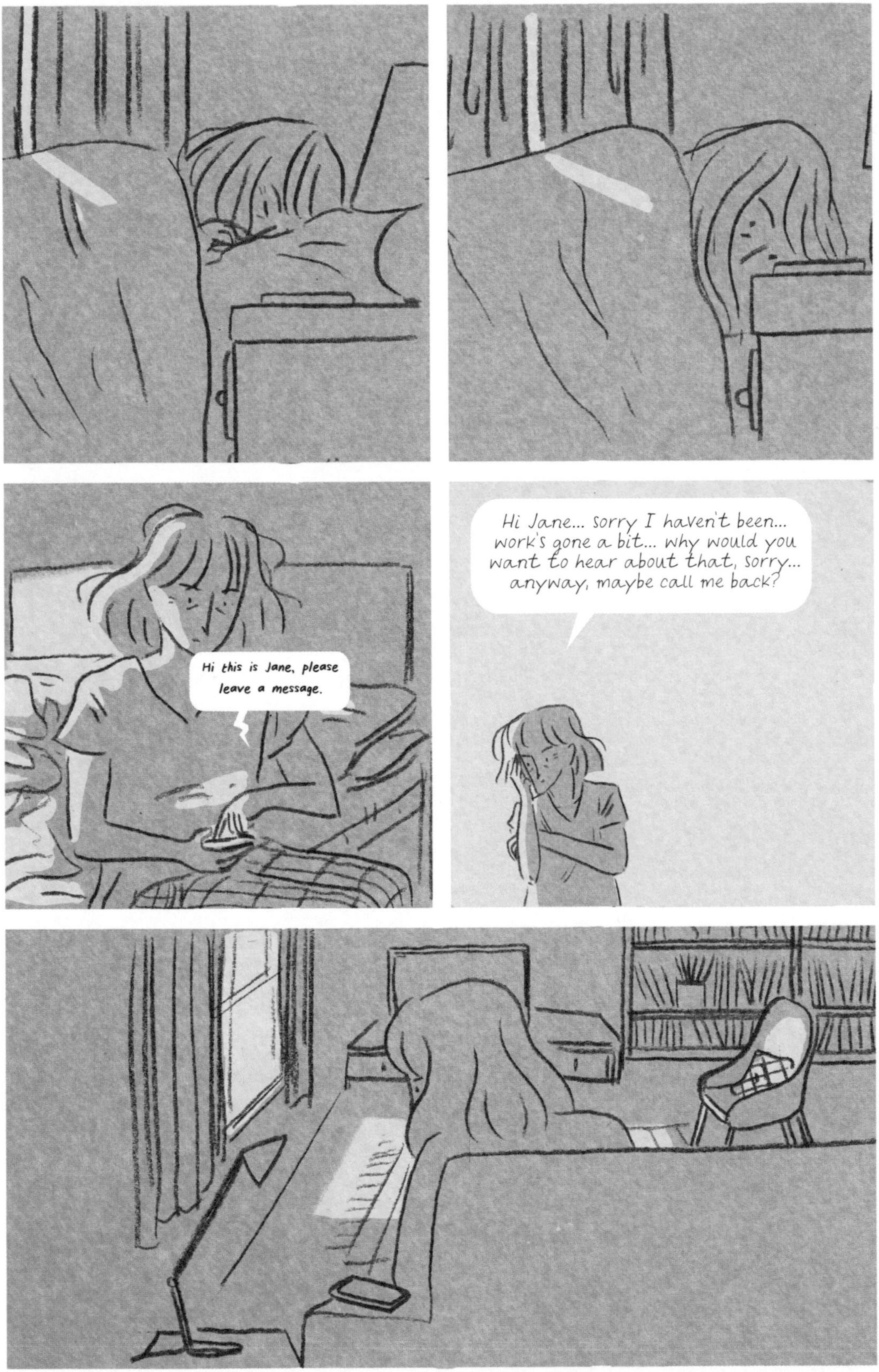
Hi this is Jane, please leave a message.
Hi Jane... sorry I haven't been... work's gone a bit... why would you want to hear about that, sorry... anyway, maybe call me back?

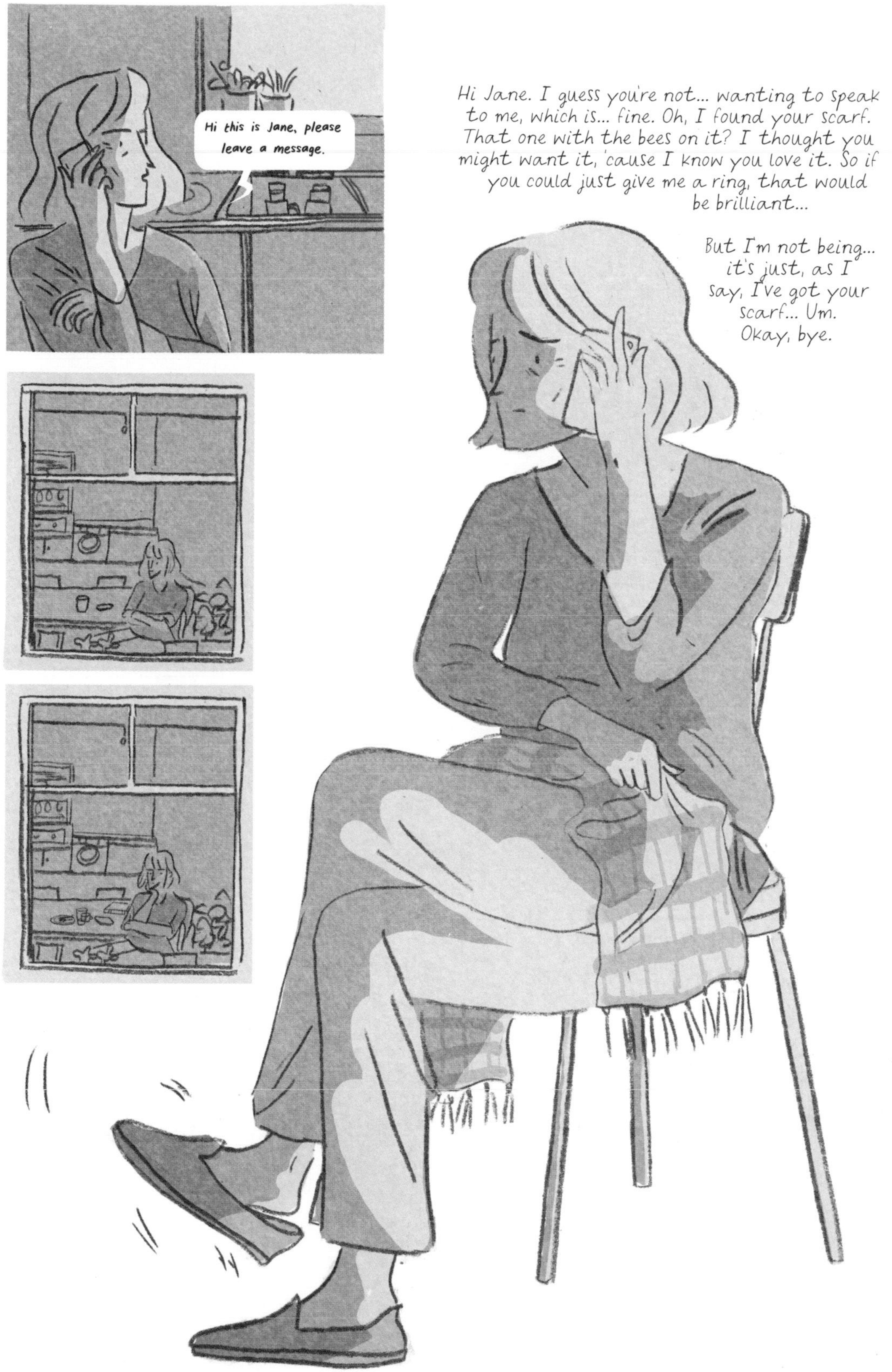
Hi this is Jane, please leave a message.
Hi Jane. I guess you're not... wanting to speak to me, which is... fine. Oh, I found your scarf. That one with the bees on it? I thought you might want it, 'cause I know you love it. So if you could just give me a ring, that would be brilliant...
But I'm not being... it's just, as I say, I've got your scarf... Um. Okay, bye.

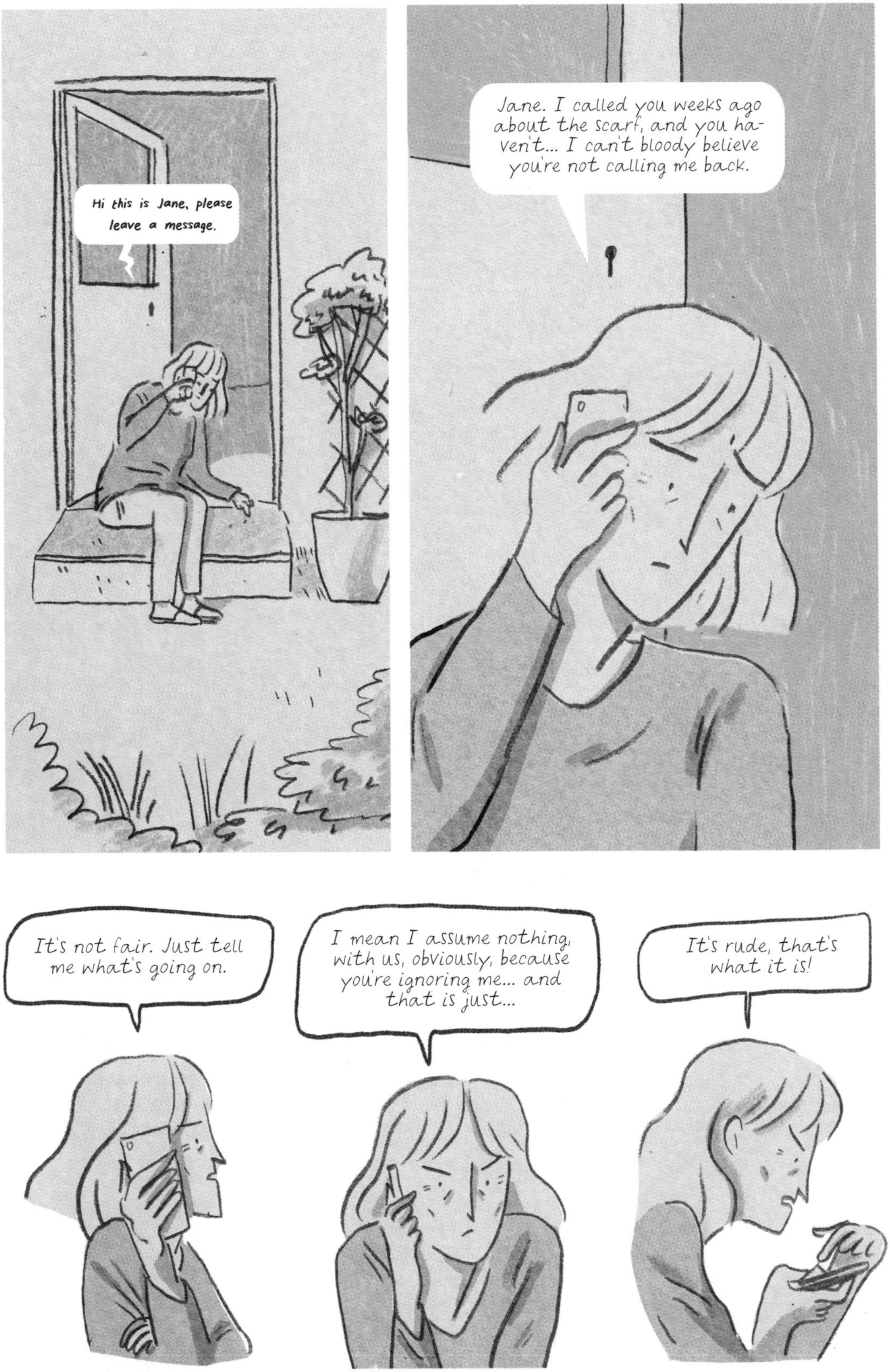
Hi this is Jane, please leave a message.
Jane. I called you weeks ago about the scarf, and you haven't... I can't bloody believe you're not calling me back.
It's not fair. Just tell me what's going on.
I mean I assume nothing, with us, obviously, because you're ignoring me... and that is just...
It's rude, that's what it is!

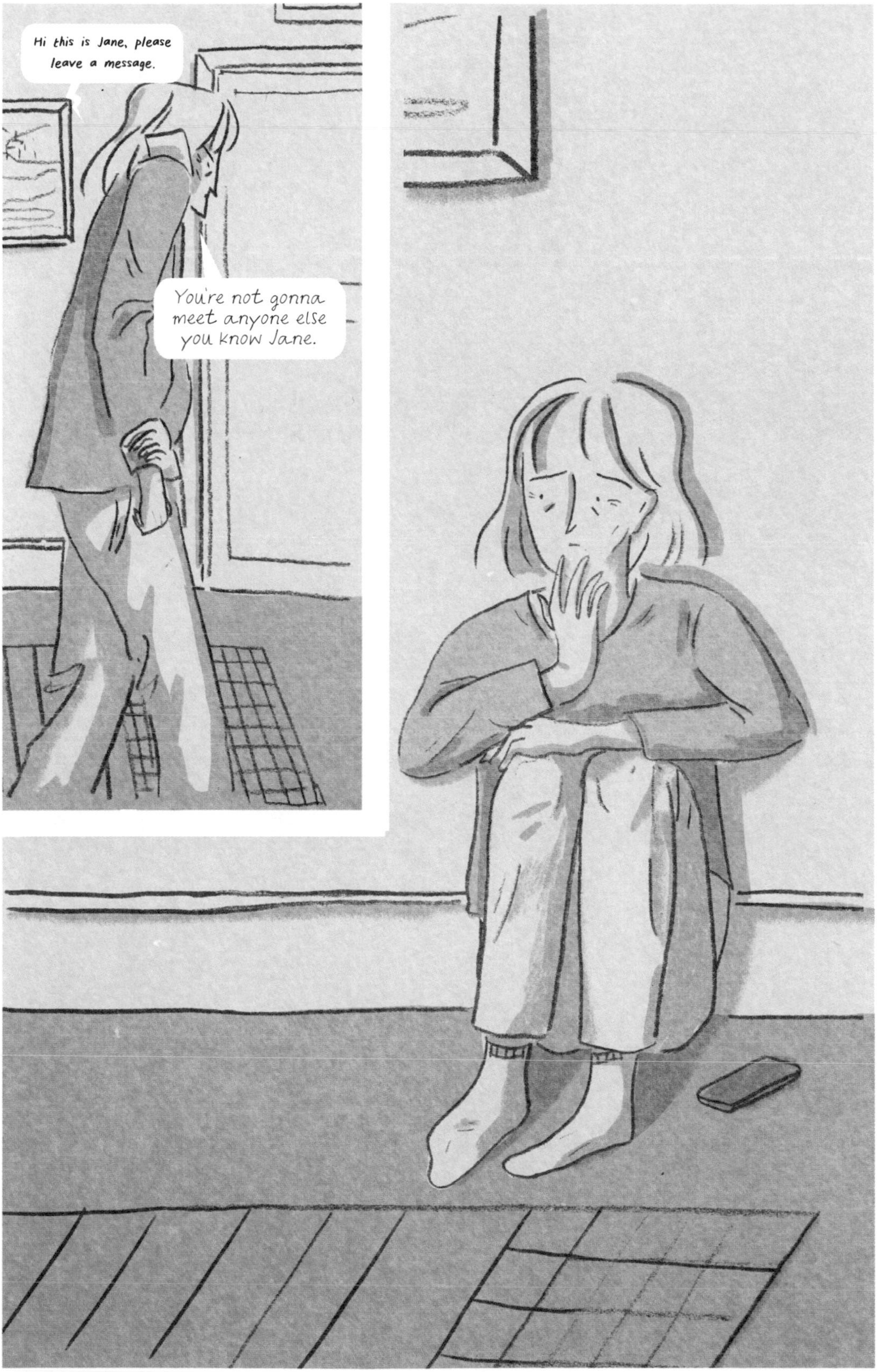

Hi this is Jane, please leave a message.
You're not gonna meet anyone else you know Jane.

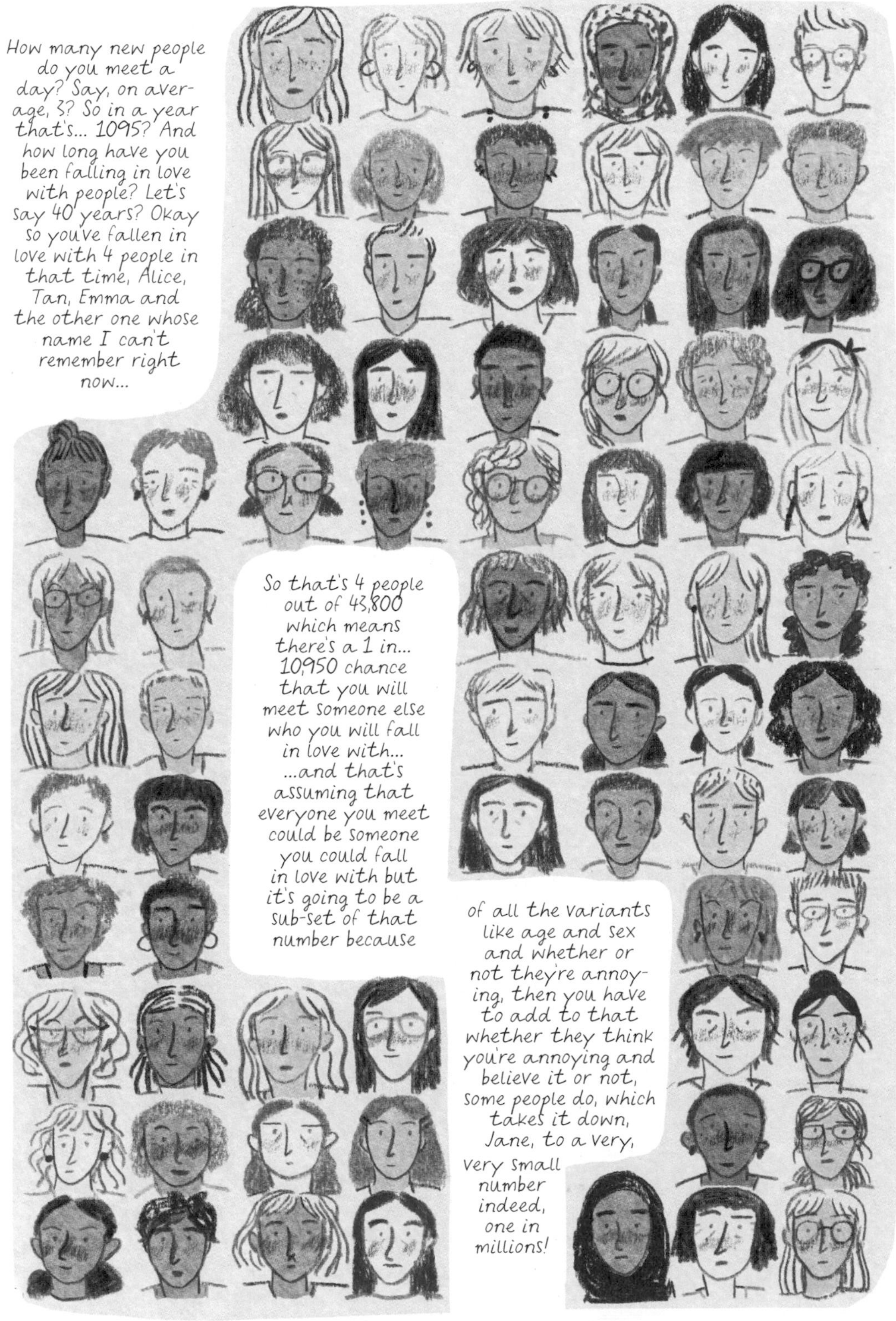
How many new people do you meet a day? Say, on average, 3? So in a year that's... 1095? And how long have you been falling in love with people? Let's say 40 years? Okay so you've fallen in love with 4 people in that time, Alice, Tan, Emma and the other one whose name I can't remember right now...
So that's 4 people out of 43,800 which means there's a 1 in... 10,950 chance that you will meet someone else who you will fall in love with... ...and that's assuming that everyone you meet could be someone you could fall in love with but it's going to be a sub-set of that number because
of all the variants like age and sex and whether or not they're annoying, then you have to add to that whether they think you're annoying and believe it or not, some people do, which takes it down, Jane, to a very,
very small number indeed, one in millions!

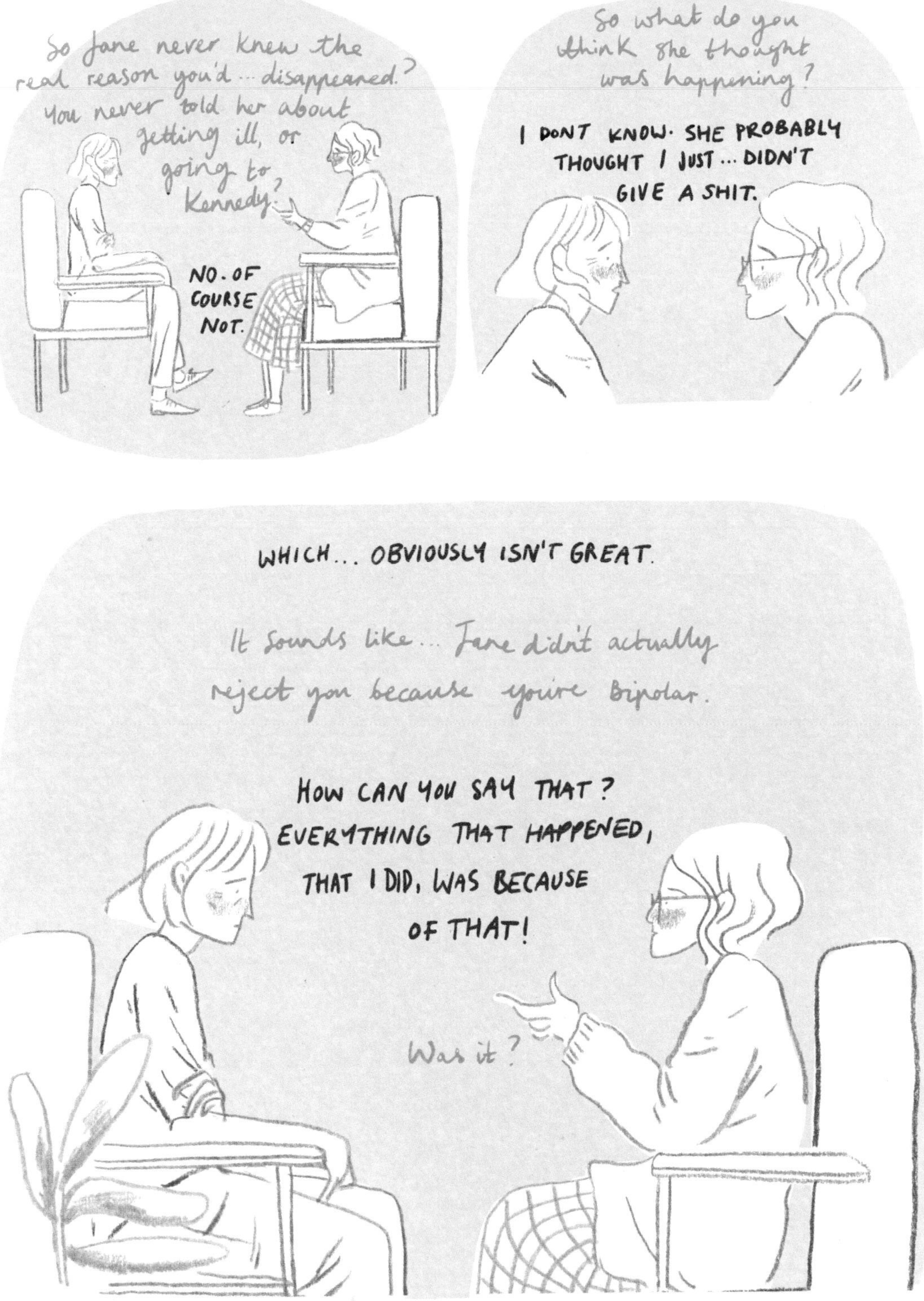

So Jane never knew the real reason you'd ... disappeared? You never told her about getting ill, or going to Kennedy?
NO. OF COURSE NOT.
So what do you think she thought was happening?
I DONT KNOW. SHE PROBABLY THOUGHT I JUST ... DIDN'T GIVE A SHIT.
WHICH ... OBVIOUSLY ISN'T GREAT.
It sounds like ... Jane didn't actually reject you because you're Bipolar.
HOW CAN YOU SAY THAT? EVERYTHING THAT HAPPENED, THAT I DID, WAS BECAUSE OF THAT!
Was it?

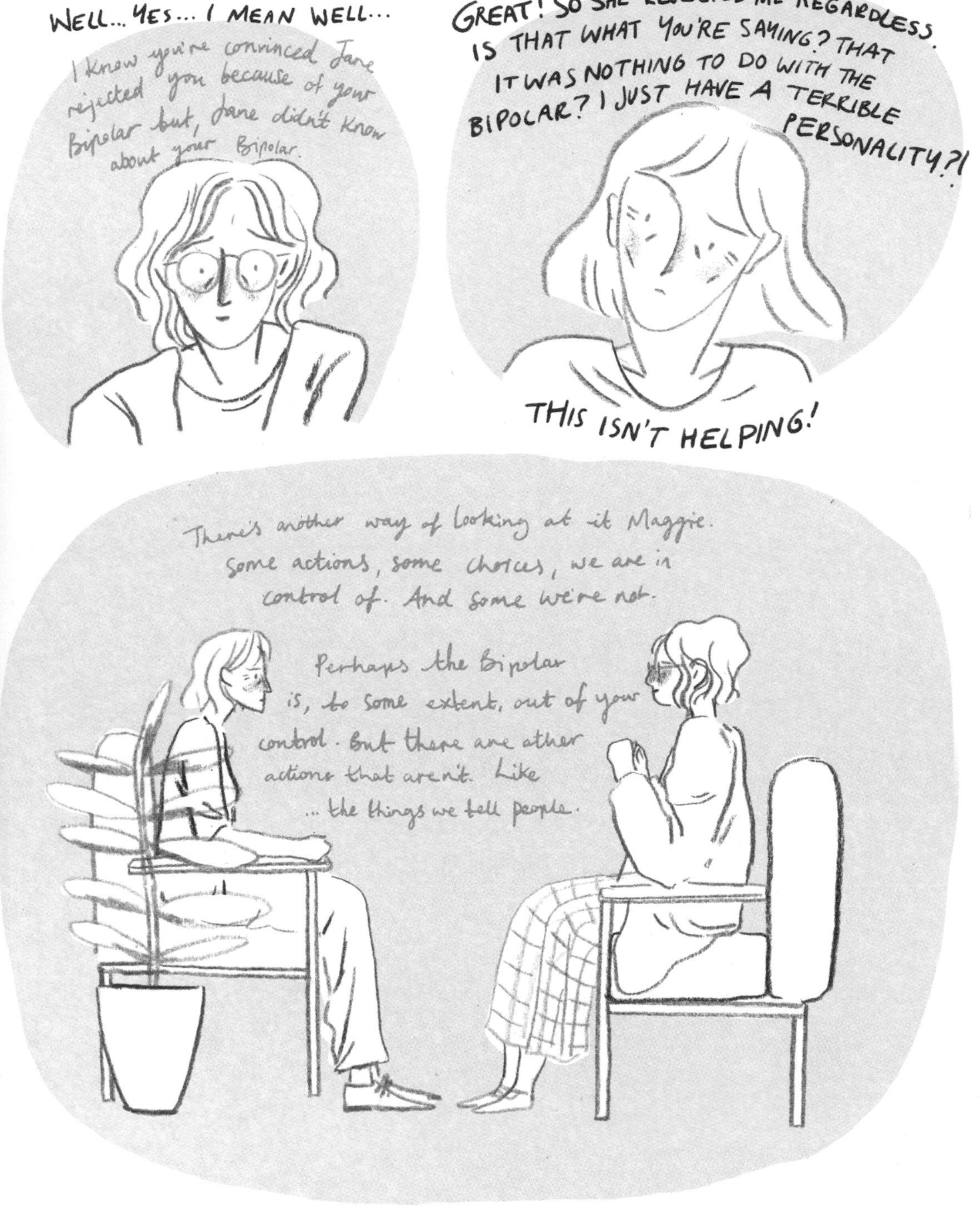
WELL... YES... I MEAN WELL...
I know you're convinced Jane rejected you because of your Bipolar but, Jane didn't know about your Bipolar.
GREAT! SO SHE REJECTED ME REGARDLESS. IS THAT WHAT YOU'RE SAYING? THAT IT WAS NOTHING TO DO WITH THE BIPOLAR? I JUST HAVE A TERRIBLE PERSONALITY?!
THIS ISN'T HELPING!
There's another way of looking at it Maggie. Some actions, some choices, we are in control of. And some we're not.
Perhaps the Bipolar is, to some extent, out of your control. But there are other actions that aren't. Like ... the things we tell people.

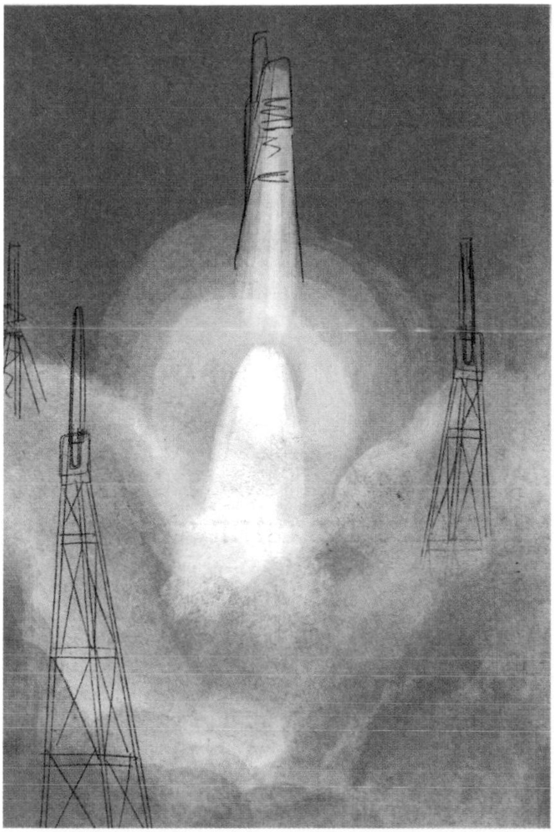
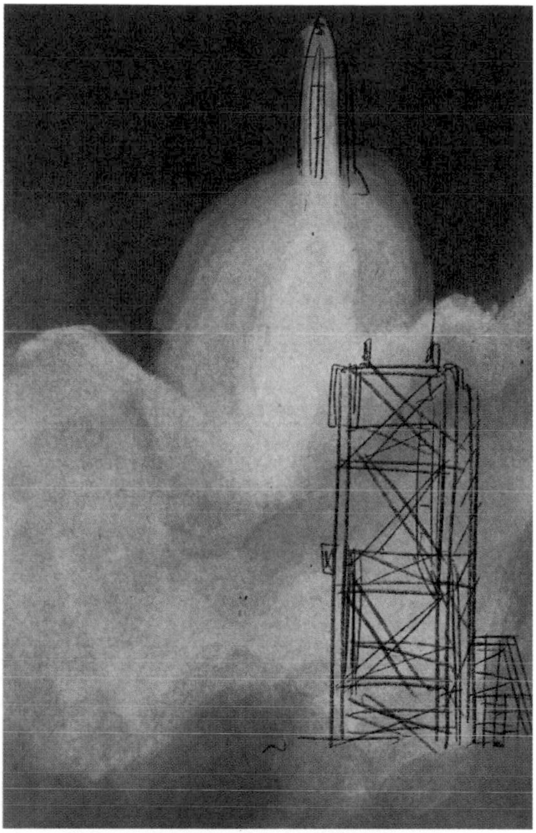
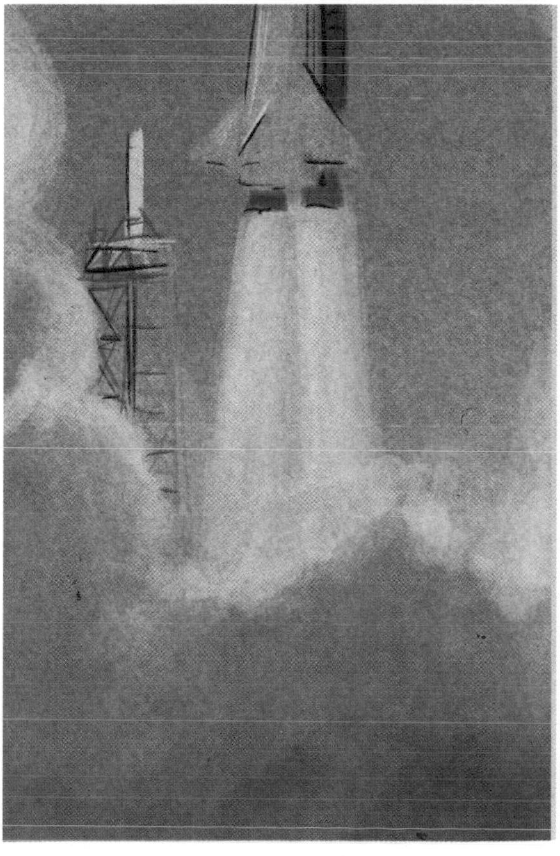
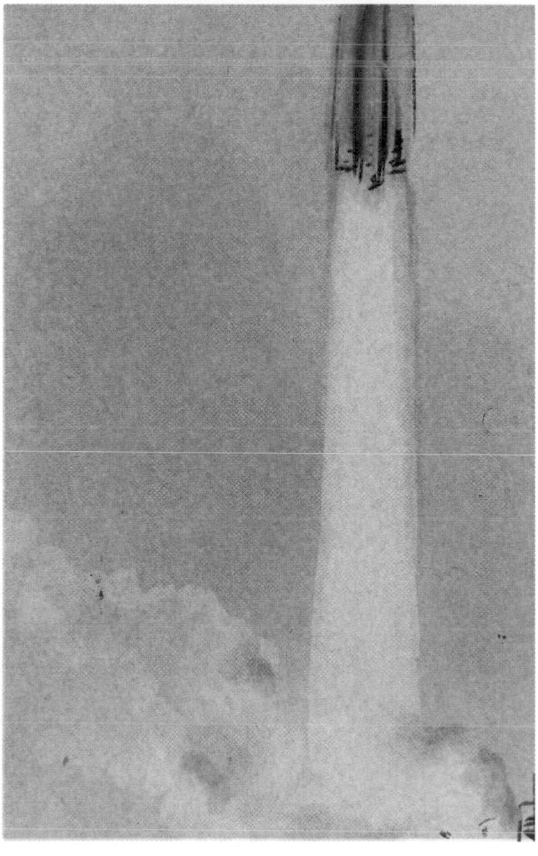

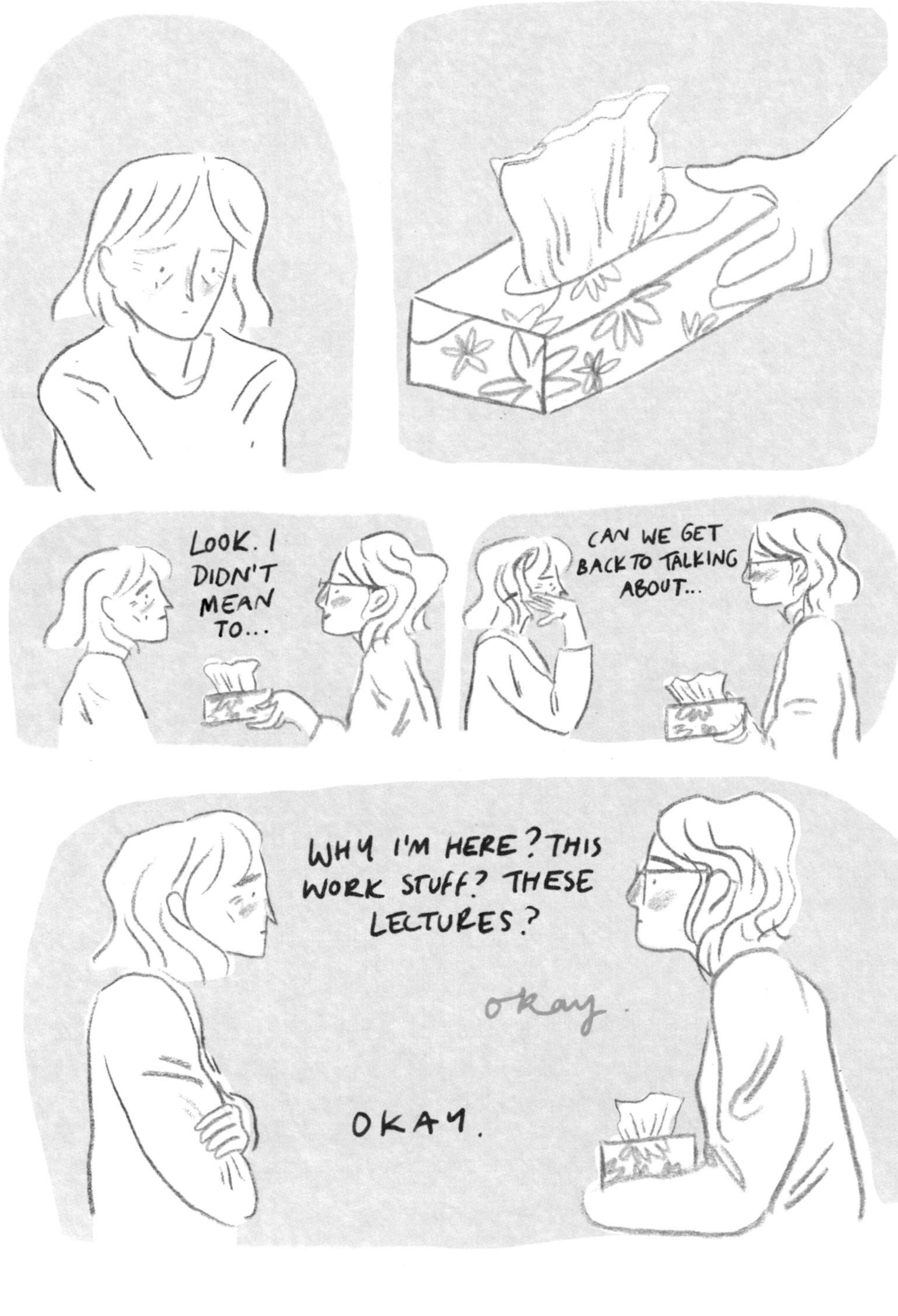
LOOK. I DIDN'T MEAN TO...
CAN WE GET BACK TO TALKING ABOUT...
WHY I'M HERE? THIS WORK STUFF? THESE LECTURES?
okay.
OKAY.

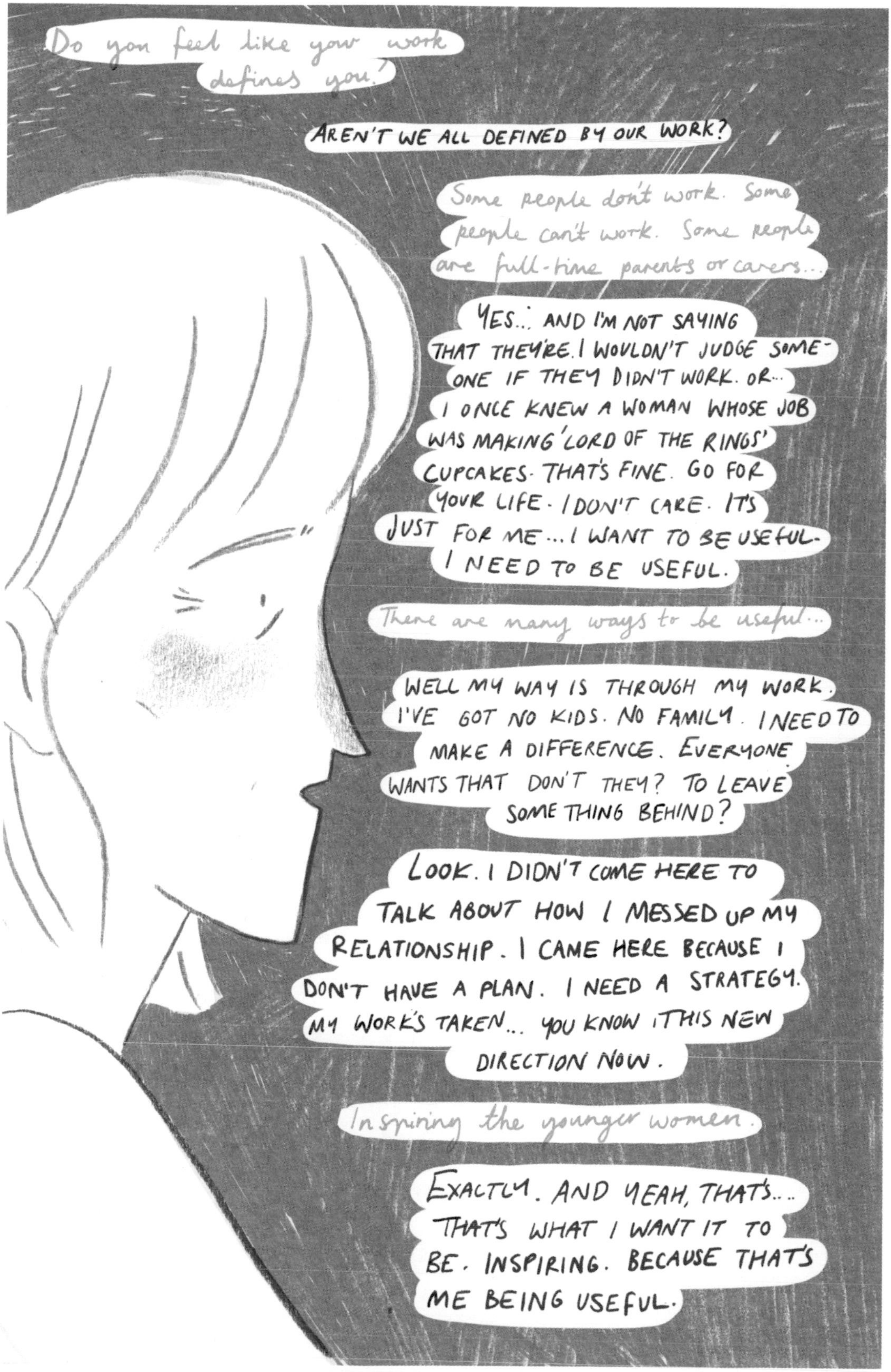
Do you feel like your work defines you?
AREN'T WE ALL DEFINED BY OUR WORK?
Some people don't work. Some people can't work. Some people are full-time parents or carers...
YES... AND I'M NOT SAYING THAT THEY'RE. I WOULDN'T JUDGE SOME-ONE IF THEY DIDN'T WORK. OR... I ONCE KNEW A WOMAN WHOSE JOB WAS MAKING 'LORD OF THE RINGS' CUPCAKES. THAT'S FINE. GO FOR YOUR LIFE. I DON'T CARE. IT'S JUST FOR ME... I WANT TO BE USEFUL. I NEED TO BE USEFUL.
There are many ways to be useful...
WELL MY WAY IS THROUGH MY WORK. I'VE GOT NO KIDS. NO FAMILY. I NEED TO MAKE A DIFFERENCE. EVERYONE WANTS THAT DON'T THEY? TO LEAVE SOMETHING BEHIND?
LOOK. I DIDN'T COME HERE TO TALK ABOUT HOW I MESSED UP MY RELATIONSHIP. I CAME HERE BECAUSE I DON'T HAVE A PLAN. I NEED A STRATEGY. MY WORK'S TAKEN... YOU KNOW. THIS NEW DIRECTION NOW.
Inspiring the younger women.
EXACTLY. AND YEAH, THAT'S... THAT'S WHAT I WANT IT TO BE. INSPIRING. BECAUSE THAT'S ME BEING USEFUL.

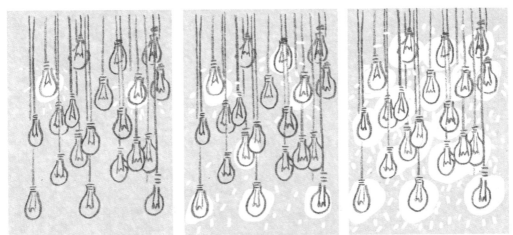

THAT'S A GOOD WAY OF PUTTING IT ACTUALLY! I'M GOING TO BE INSPIRING THEM. EXACTLY. AND THAT'S WHY THIS IS IMPORTANT! BECAUSE... YES... IF ONE OF THEM GOES ON TO BECOME A SPACE SCIENTIST, AND DOES THEIR OWN MISSION LIKE THE ONE I WAS DOING, AND... YOU KNOW... I LOVE THAT IDEA... THAT THEY'D BE SAT IN THE THAT AUDIENCE HAVING A LITTLE TWINKLE OF AN IDEA. THAT SPARKLY FEELING IN THEIR CHEST

BECAUSE I MADE THEM FEEL LIKE THAT WAS POSSIBLE. I MEAN THAT'S BIG RIGHT? THAT'S.... THAT'S WHAT I FELT WATCHING THE MOON LANDINGS... THAT'S WHY IT'S IMPORTANT, THATS WHY I'M PANICKING... BECAUSE IN ORDER FOR THEM TO HAVE THAT, I NEED TO BE AMAZING!

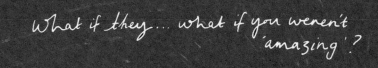

What if they... what if you weren't 'amazing'?

WHAT DO YOU MEAN?

Well, sometimes... when we... strive for perfection, we relinquish our humanity.

WHO SAID THAT?

oh, err... Sorry if I made it sound like I was quoting someone, it was just me.

I KNOW WHAT I NEED TO DO.
I'LL JUST DO A POWERPOINT. FILL IT WITH PICTURES. THEN IF I START TO PANIC, I'LL SHOW THEM A VIDEO WHILST I TAKE TIME TO GET MY SHIT TOGETHER.
Maggie-
YES. THAT'S IT.
YES! I'LL JUST PLAN IT REALLY WELL. THEY DON'T NEED TO KNOW ABOUT ME. MY STUFF. THAT'S WHAT WAS FREAKING ME OUT.
THEY JUST NEED TO KNOW ABOUT THE SCIENCE. THANKS FOR TODAY.
LOOK. BUT I'M GOING TO BE HONEST I DON'T THINK THIS IS REALLY FOR ME. SORRY TO WASTE YOUR TIME.
But-
HOW MUCH DO I OWE YOU?

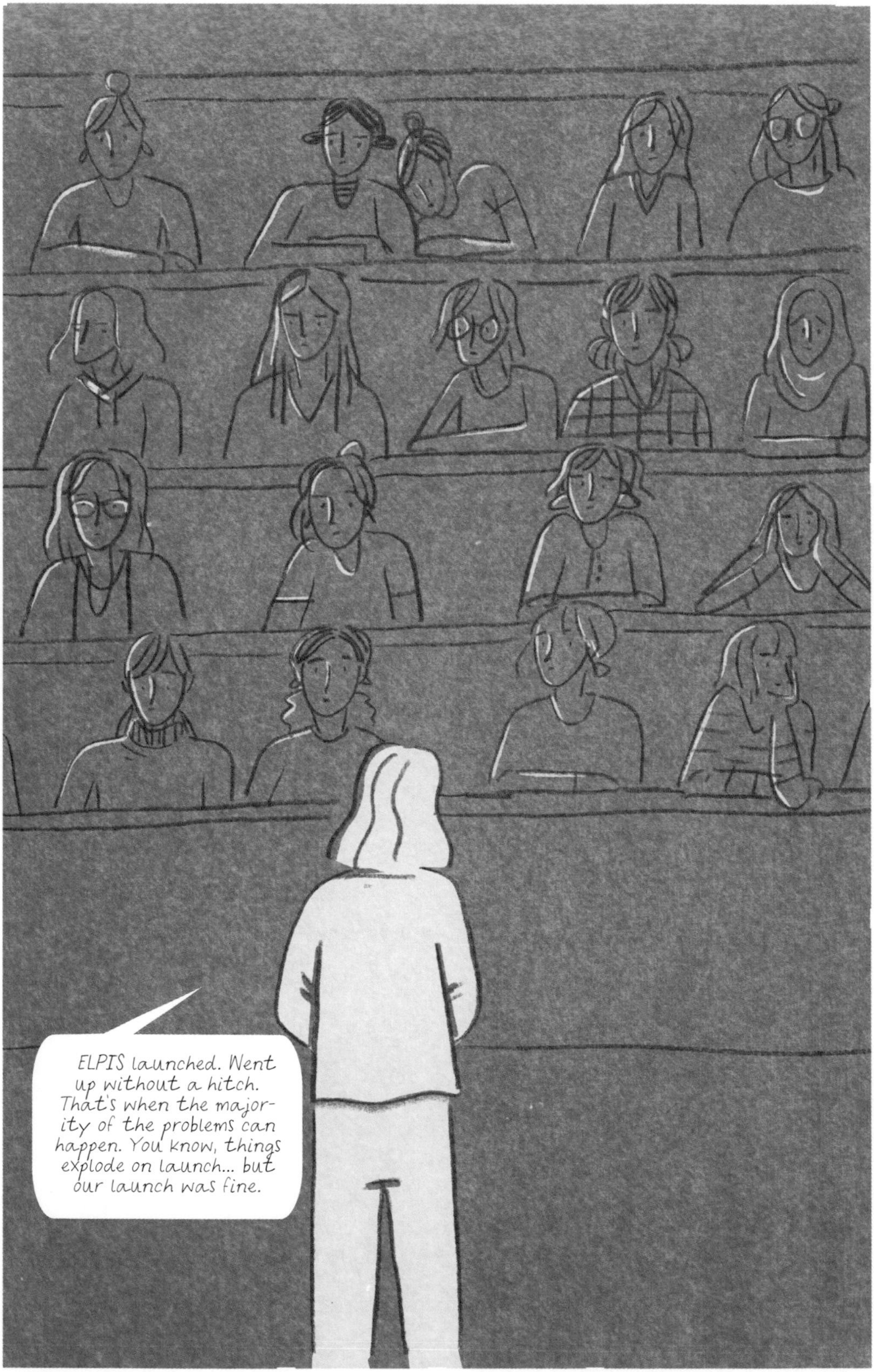
ELPIS launched. Went up without a hitch. That's when the majority of the problems can happen. You know, things explode on launch... but our launch was fine.

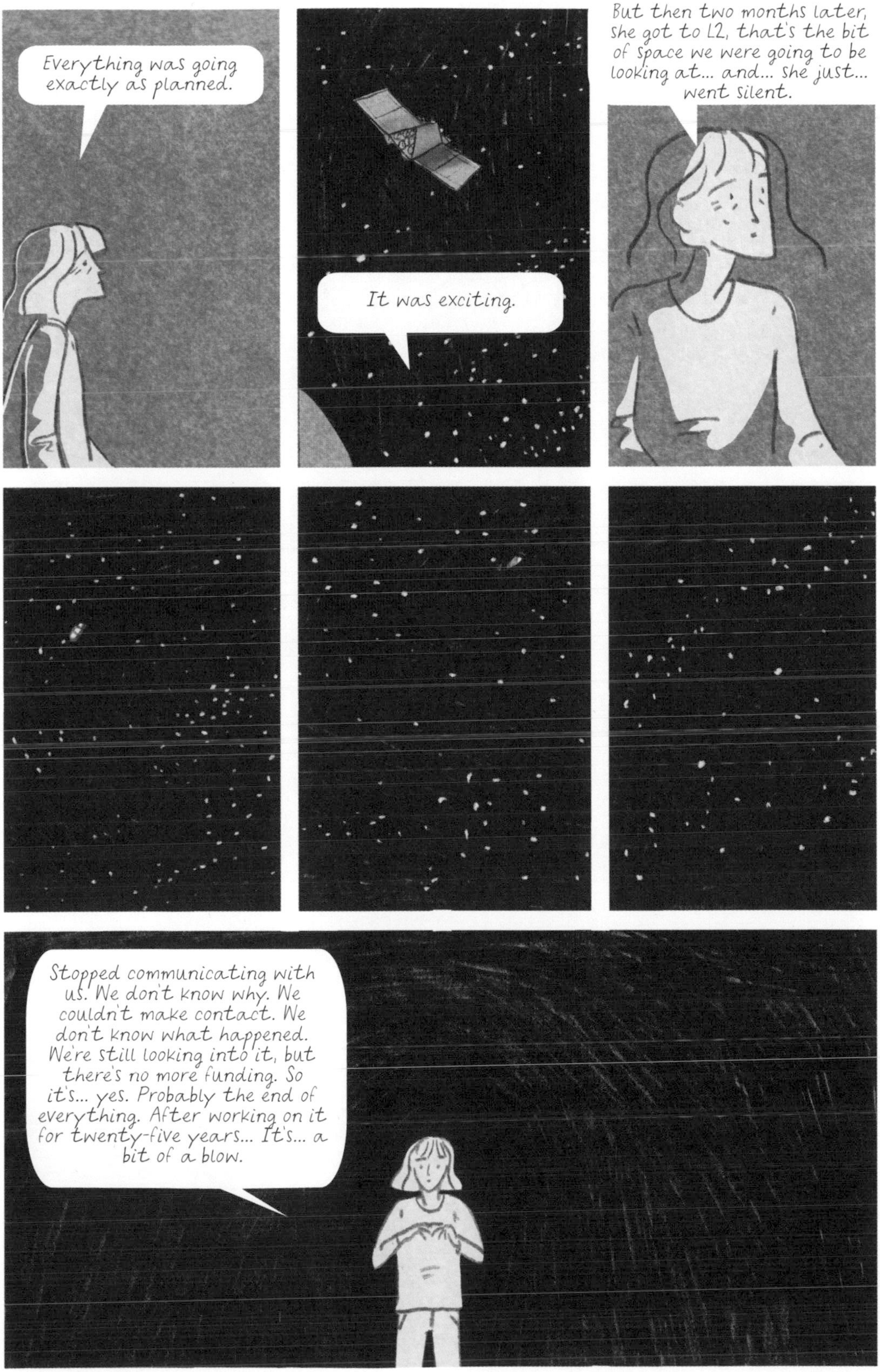
Everything was going exactly as planned.
It was exciting.
But then two months later, she got to L2, that's the bit of space we were going to be looking at... and... she just... went silent.
Stopped communicating with us. We don't know why. We couldn't make contact. We don't know what happened. We're still looking into it, but there's no more funding. So it's... yes. Probably the end of everything. After working on it for twenty-five years... It's... a bit of a blow.

Sorry, I realise now you were just being... curious.

How do you justify the cost of a space mission, when it fails?

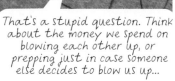
That's a stupid question. Think about the money we spend on blowing each other up, or prepping just in case someone else decides to blow us up...

It's not like the money for that mission was gonna be like... a hospital.

And like, we're damaging the planet and we need a new one. And this could have helped. Probably still has.

It's true, everything she said... But also, I didn't start off doing this for that reason... I got into this because... just because... it's exciting! I was just curious, that's all.

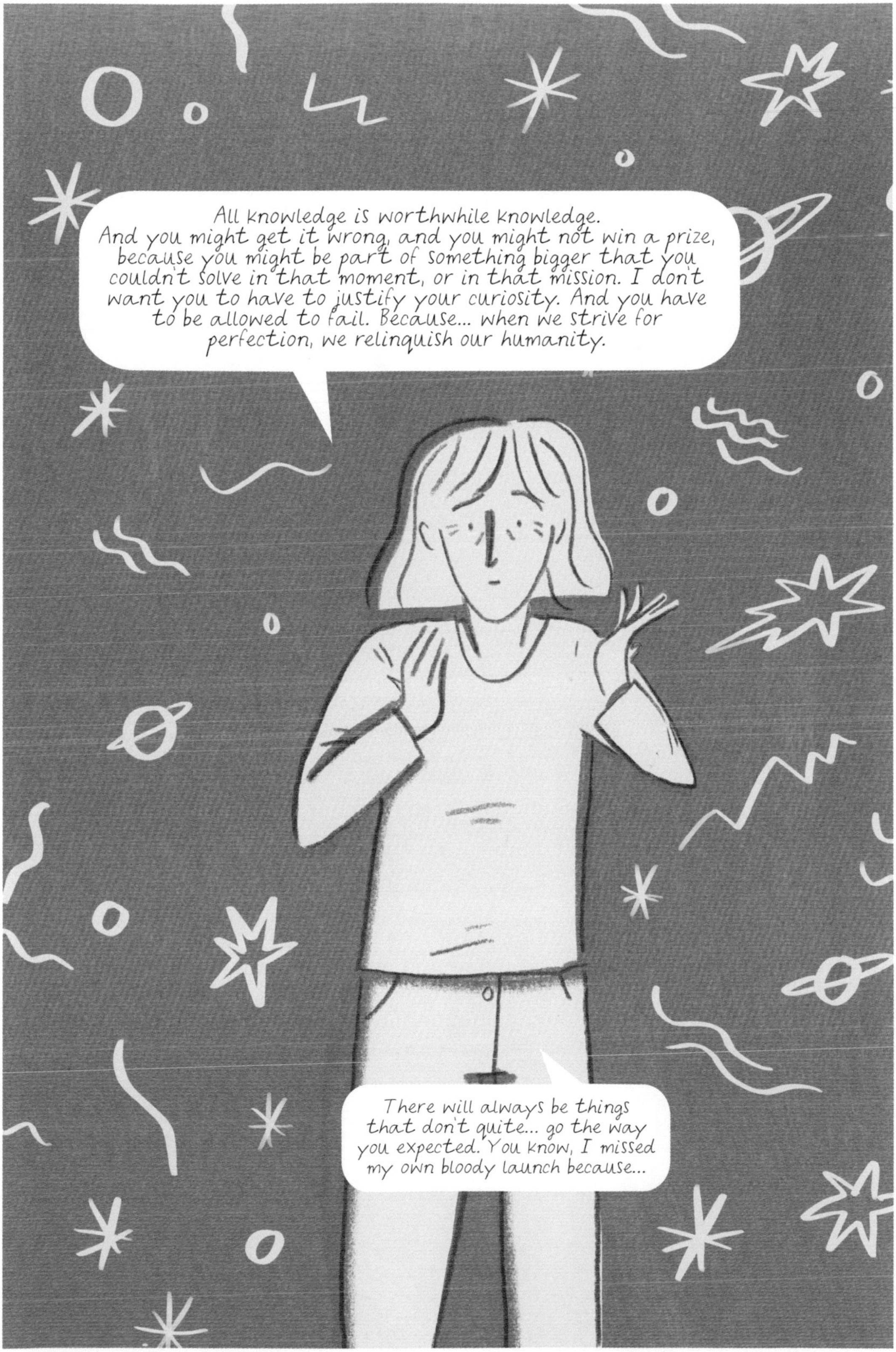
All knowledge is worthwhile knowledge. And you might get it wrong, and you might not win a prize, because you might be part of something bigger that you couldn't solve in that moment, or in that mission. I don't want you to have to justify your curiosity. And you have to be allowed to fail. Because... when we strive for perfection, we relinquish our humanity.
There will always be things that don't quite... go the way you expected. You know, I missed my own bloody launch because...

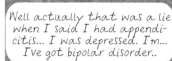
Well actually that was a lie when I said I had appendicitis... I was depressed. I'm... I've got bipolar disorder..

That's why I wasn't at the launch. I don't know how much you know about depression... it's not like when you're sad. You feel nothing. You would LOVE to feel sad. Sorry if I'm telling you something you already know. There's more awareness about it now isn't there? Leaflets and things. We never had any of that.

This isn't relevant. Does anyone want to know anything else about ELPIS? Last chance.

So... is that it? Are we not going to find Earth 2?

No! My mission failed. That's all I meant. But there are loads of other missions being planned all the time. So someone else probably will. I'm sure they will. It might be you, you never know! But it won't be me. That's all I meant love.

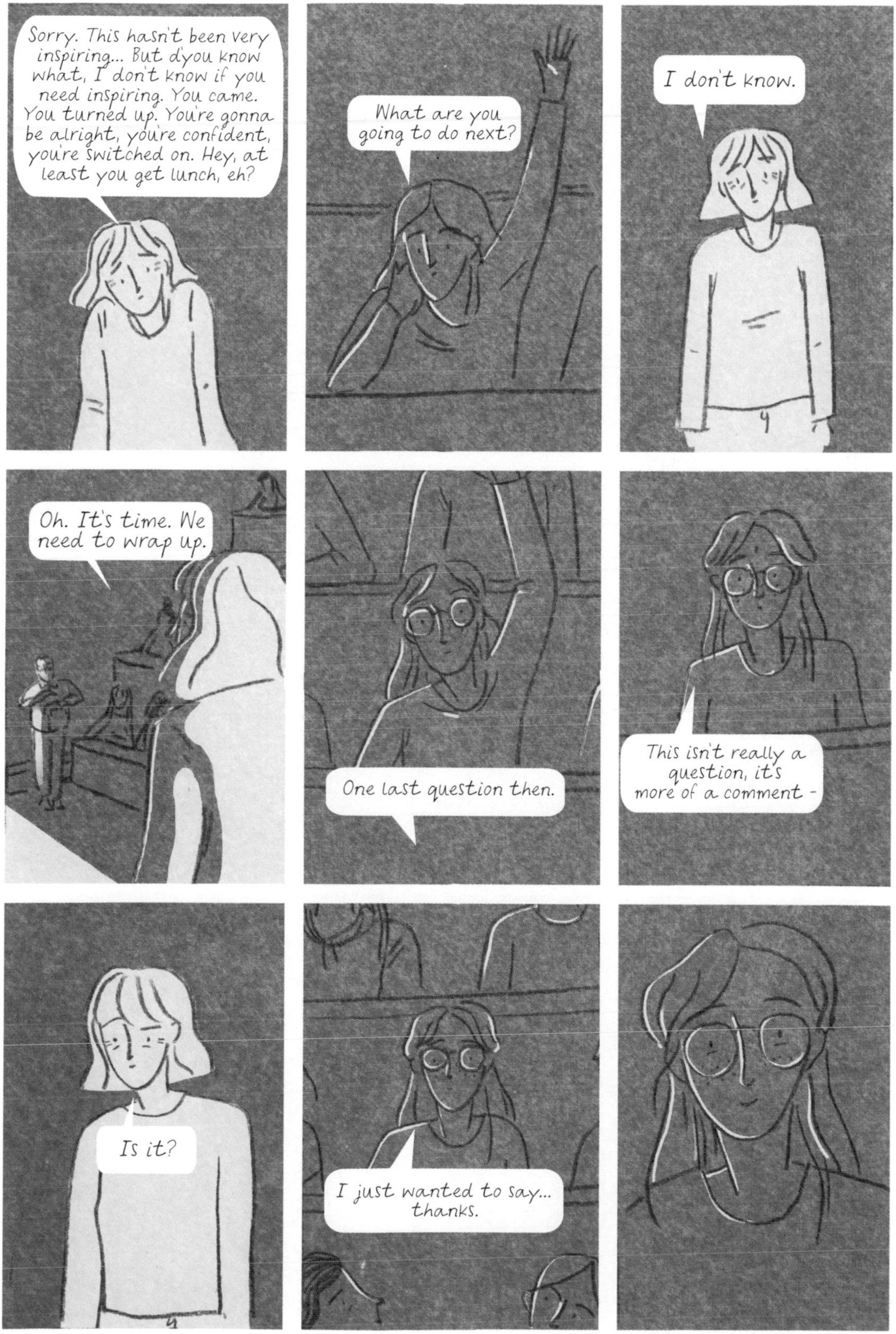
Sorry. This hasn't been very inspiring... But d'you know what, I don't know if you need inspiring. You came. You turned up. You're gonna be alright, you're confident, you're switched on. Hey, at least you get lunch, eh?
What are you going to do next?
I don't know.
Oh. It's time. We need to wrap up.
One last question then.
This isn't really a question, it's more of a comment -
Is it?
I just wanted to say... thanks.

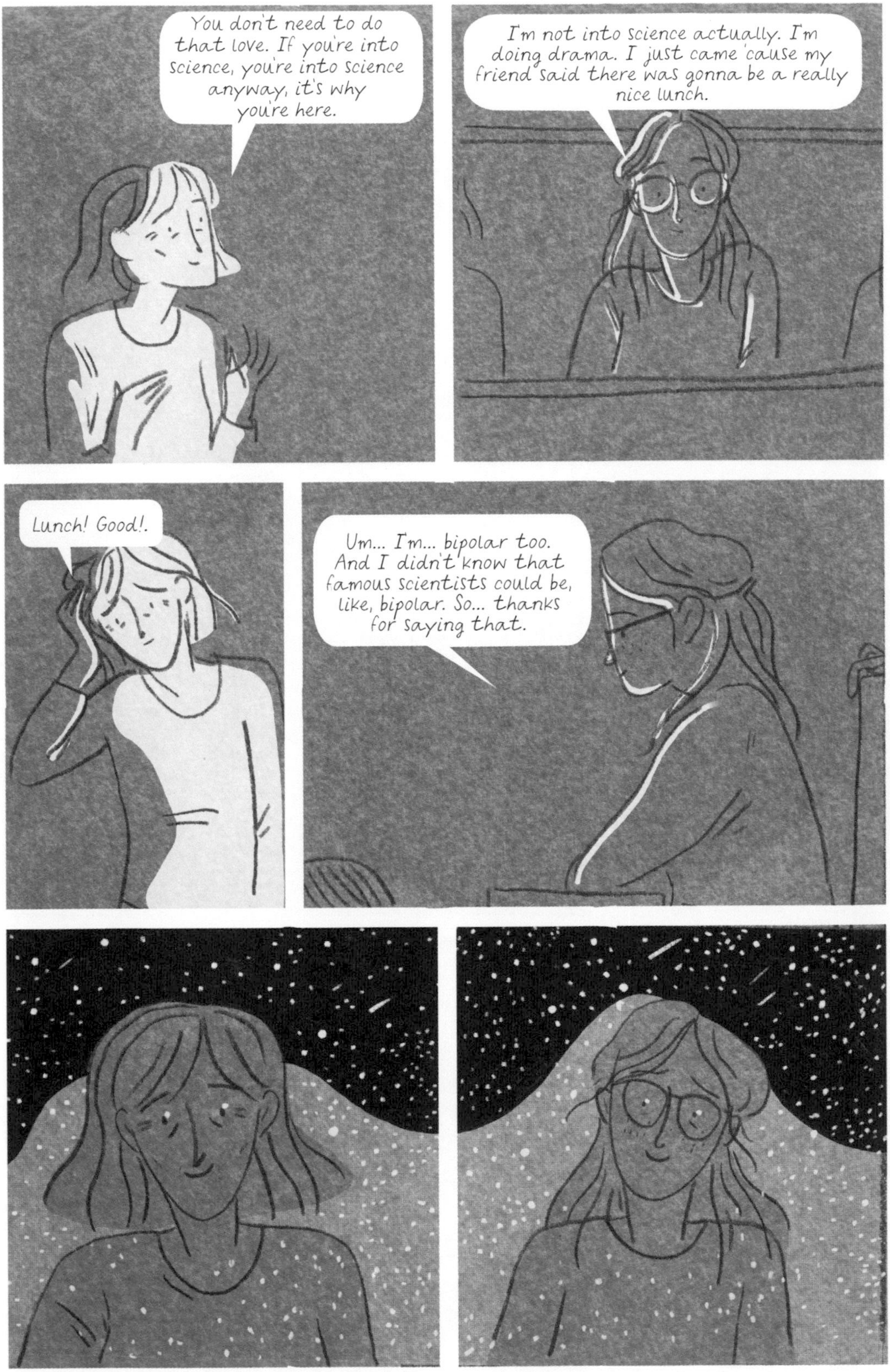
You don't need to do that love. If you're into science, you're into science anyway, it's why you're here.
I'm not into science actually. I'm doing drama. I just came 'cause my friend said there was gonna be a really nice lunch.
Lunch! Good!.
Um... I'm... bipolar too. And I didn't know that famous scientists could be, like, bipolar. So... thanks for saying that.

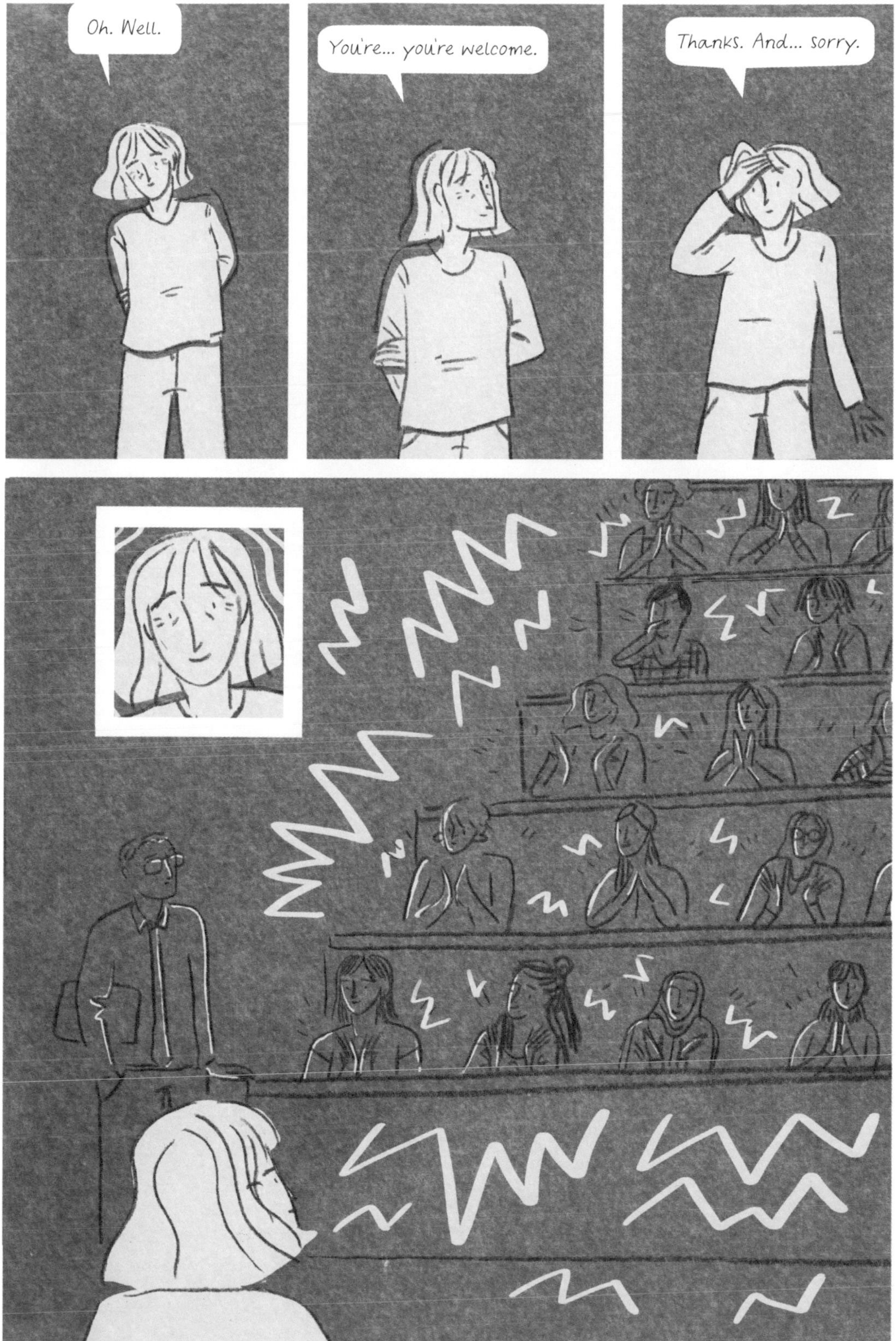
Oh. Well.
You're... you're welcome.
Thanks. And... sorry.

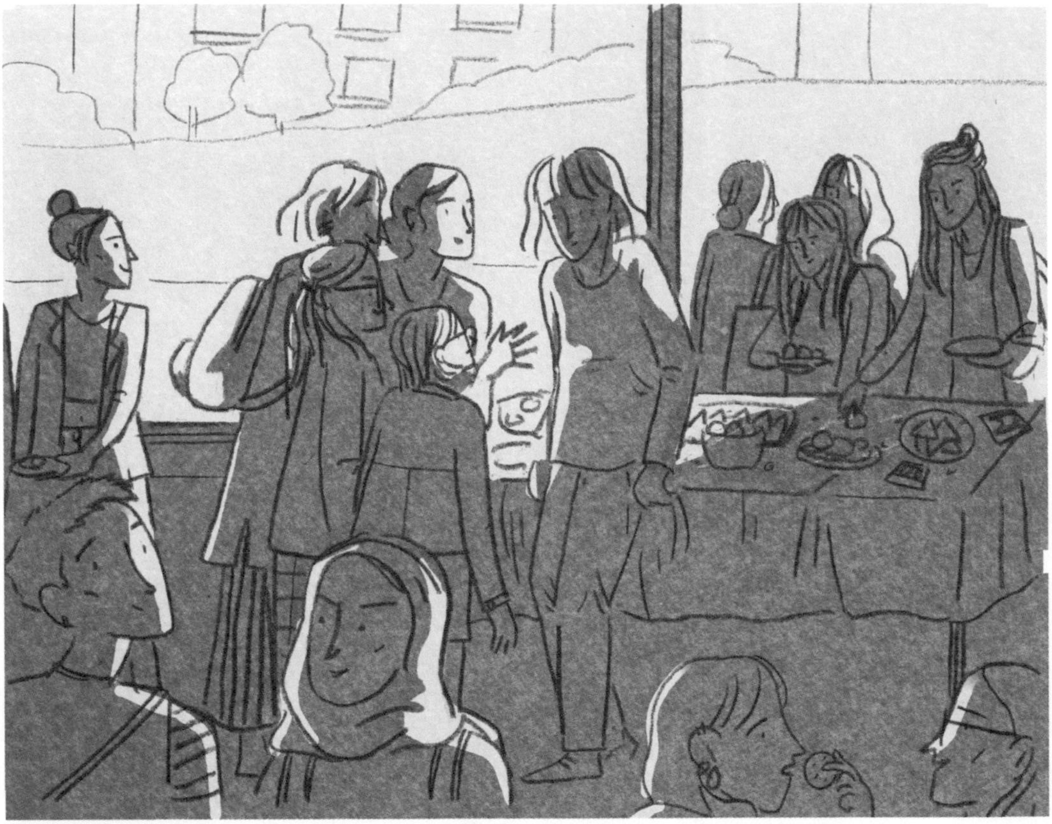

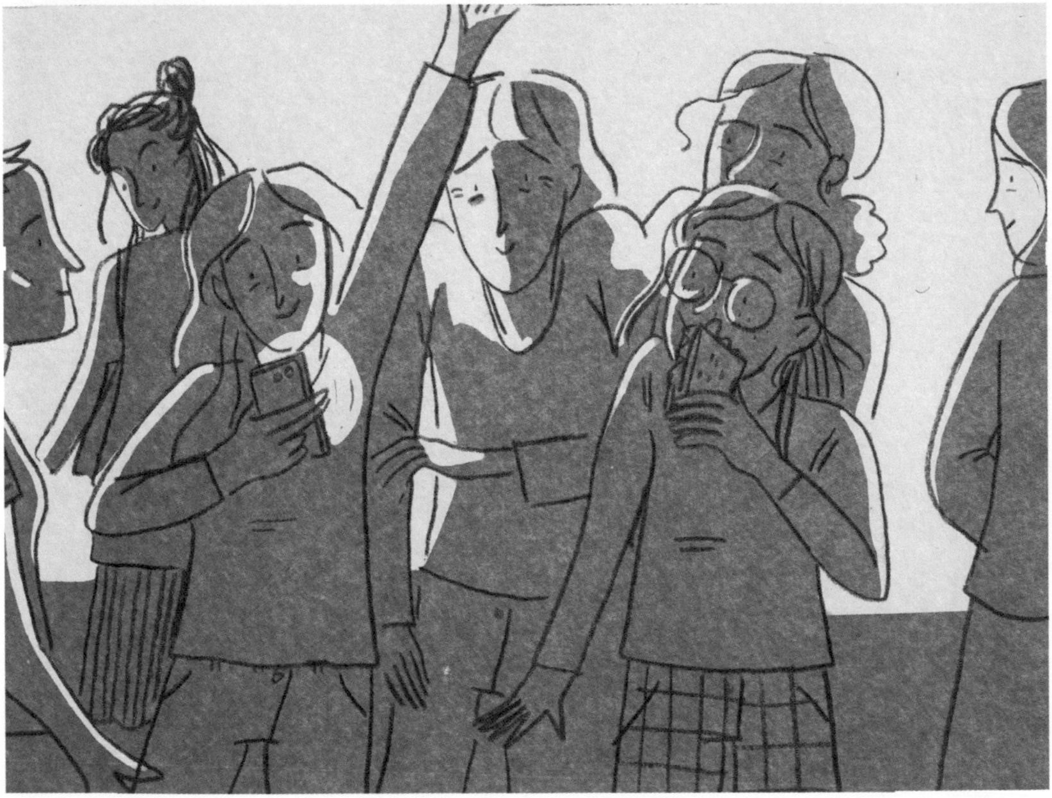

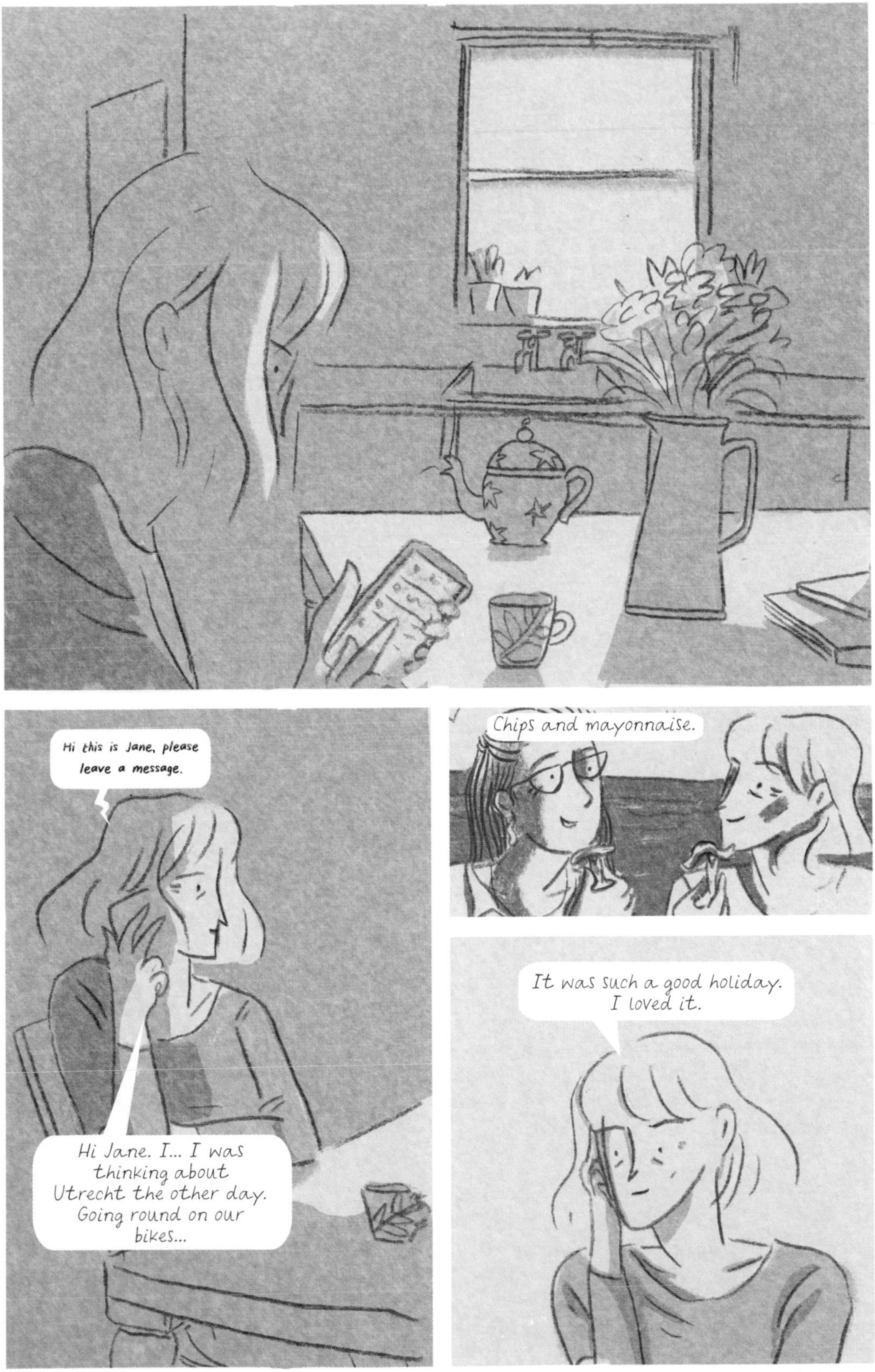
Hi this is Jane, please leave a message.
Hi Jane. I... I was thinking about Utrecht the other day. Going round on our bikes...
Chips and mayonnaise.
It was such a good holiday. I loved it.

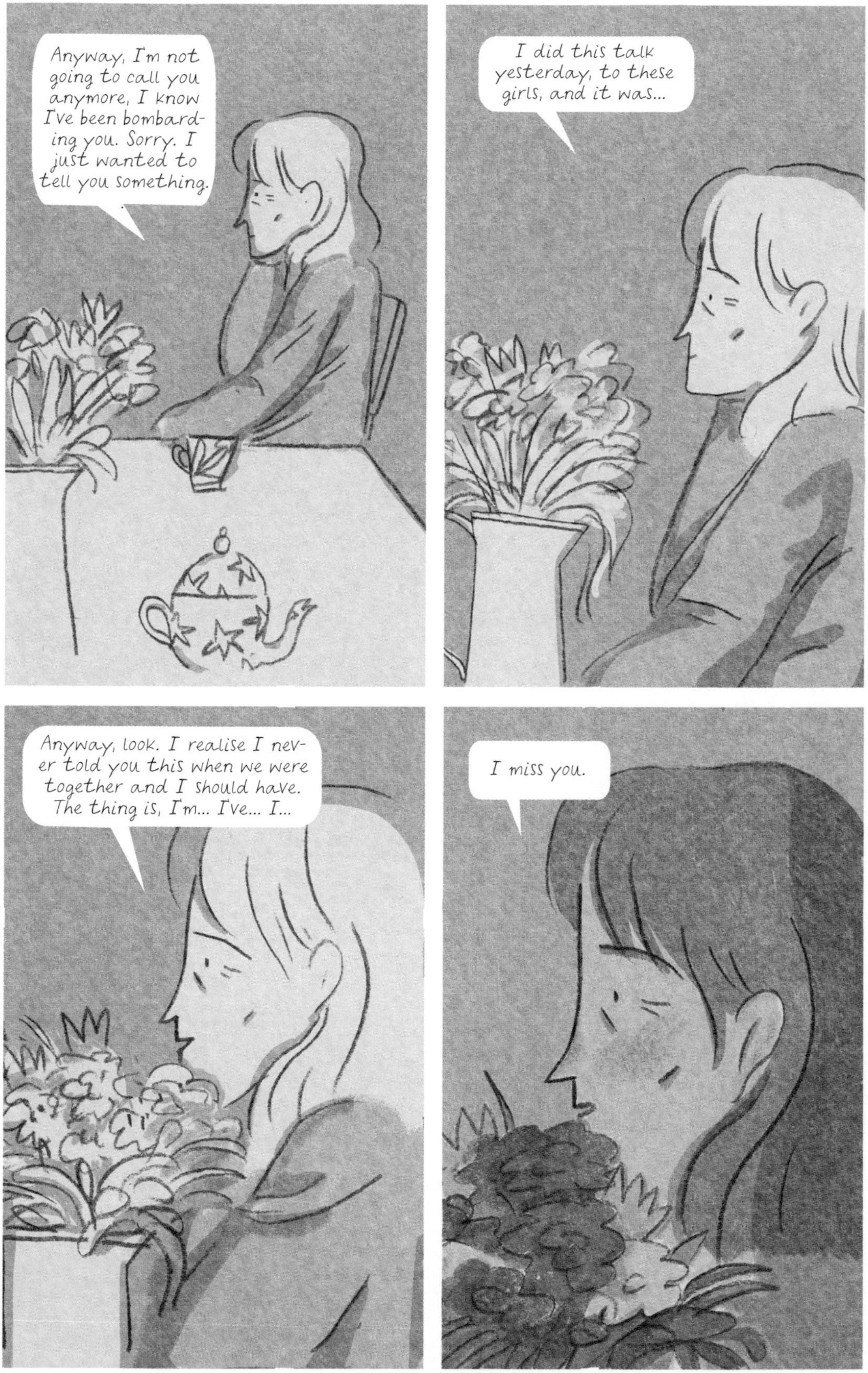
Anyway, I'm not going to call you anymore, I know I've been bombarding you. Sorry. I just wanted to tell you something.
I did this talk yesterday, to these girls, and it was...
Anyway, look. I realise I never told you this when we were together and I should have. The thing is, I'm... I've... I...
I miss you.

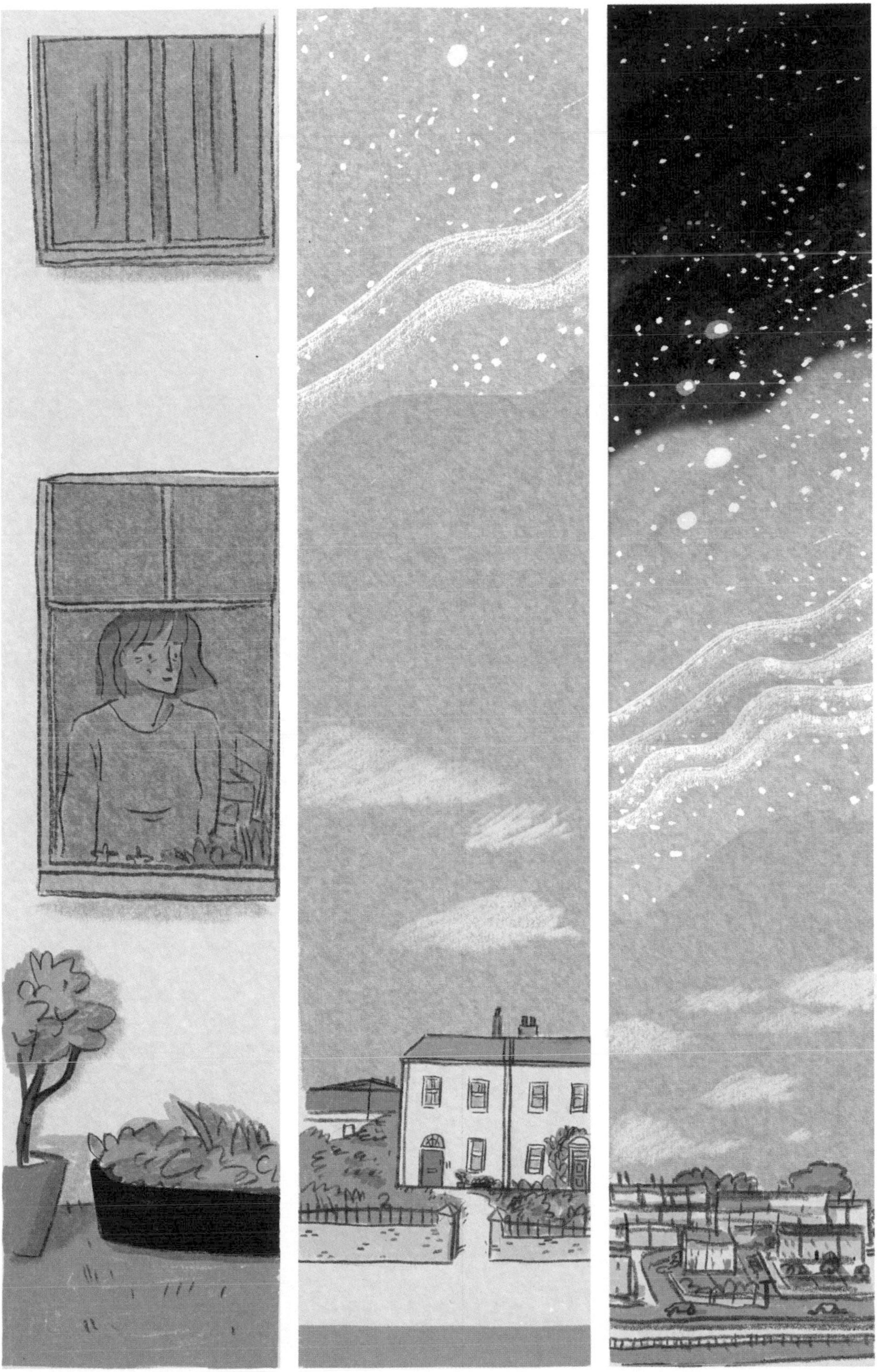

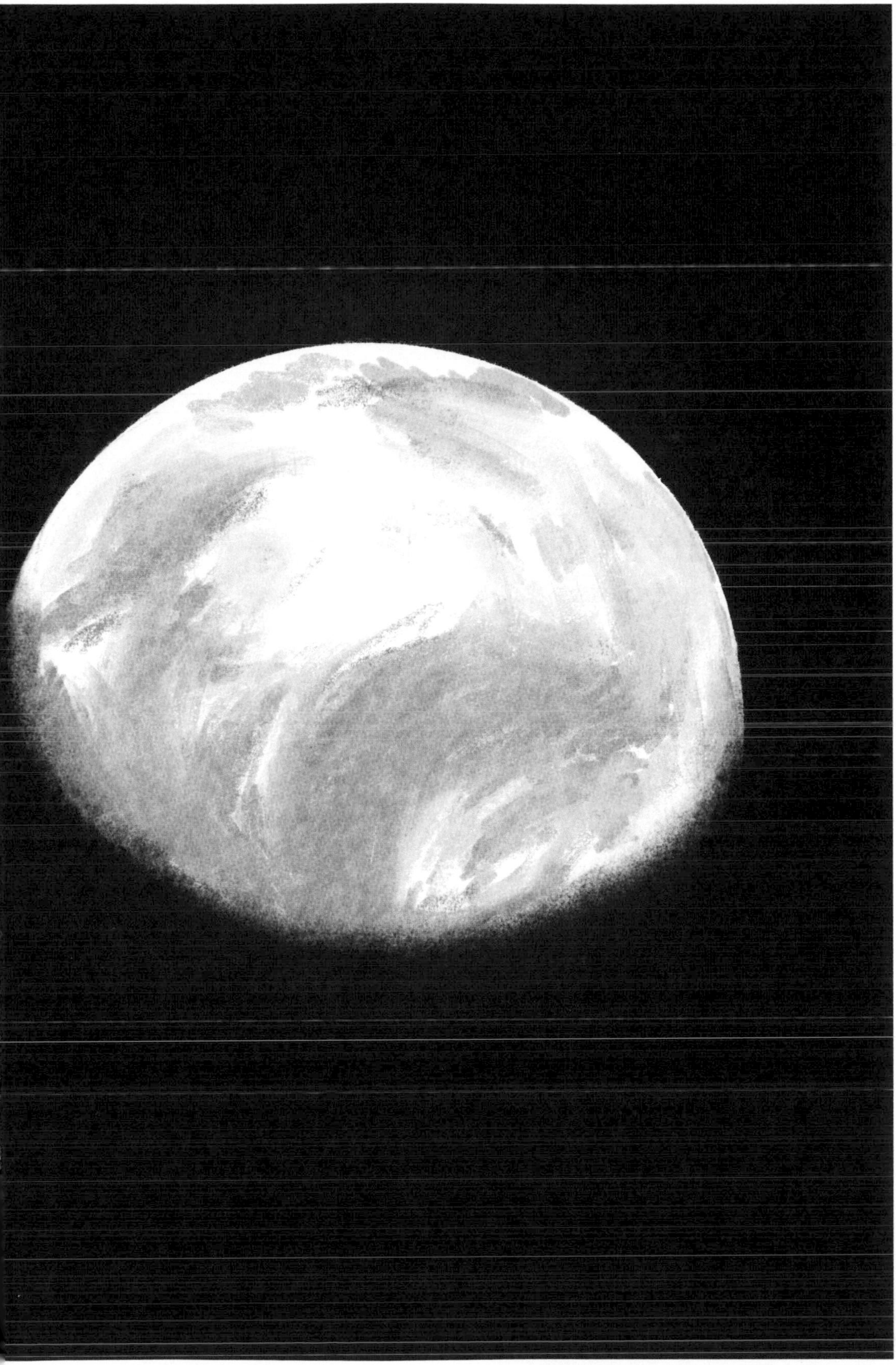

Acknowledgements

Molly: 'Lights, Planets, People!' started life as a stage play. It was conceived at China Plate's This Is Tomorrow, then co-commissioned by Norwich Arts Centre, Warwick Arts Centre and Nuffield Southampton Theatres. It was produced by Emily Williams. It won the Norfolk Arts Award for Theatre. Special thanks to the original LPP crew – Betty Atkins, Dave Guttridge, Mark Hannant and Karen Hill.

Thanks to Sandra Chapman and Don Pollacco at the University of Warwick Physics Department. Thanks also to Steve Waters, Ben Musgrave and the University of East Anglia Research Group.

Thanks to Etta for your friendship and support.

And to Grace, for everything; and to Frank, for absolutely nothing.

Lizzy: Many thanks to Arts Council England for supporting us in the making of this book. Thanks to Avery Hill for always being the good guys and to Molly for asking me to collaborate on her wonderful text. Thanks to Dan and Lisa for being the people who connected us.

Thanks, as always, to Owen. The best one, as it turns out.

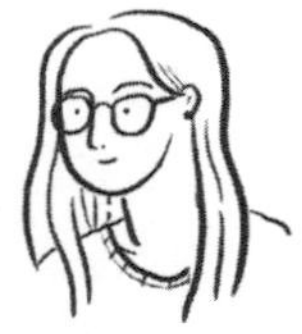

About the authors

Molly Naylor is a poet, scriptwriter, performer and director. Her stories and plays have been broadcast on BBC Radio 4 and she has performed at festivals and events all over the world. Her first poetry collection 'Badminton' was published in 2018. Her most recent collection 'Stop Trying to be Fantastic' was published by Burning Eye Books in 2020. She is the co-creator and writer of Sky One comedy 'After Hours'. She wrote and performed the acclaimed spoken-word shows 'Whenever I Get Blown Up I Think Of You' and 'My Robot Heart'. Her first feature film 'I'll See Myself Out' is in development.

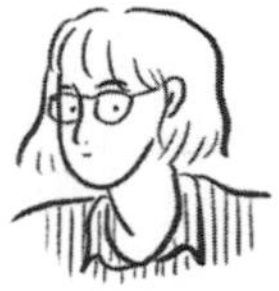

Lizzy Stewart is an illustrator and author. She has published three picture books for children. Her debut 'There's a Tiger in the Garden' won the Waterstone's Children's Book Prize in 2017. Her first book for adults 'Walking Distance' was published by Avery Hill in 2019 and a collection of her short story comics were published as 'It's Not What You Thought It Would Be' by Fantagraphics (US) in 2021. Her next book 'Alison' will be published by Serpent's Tail in 2022.

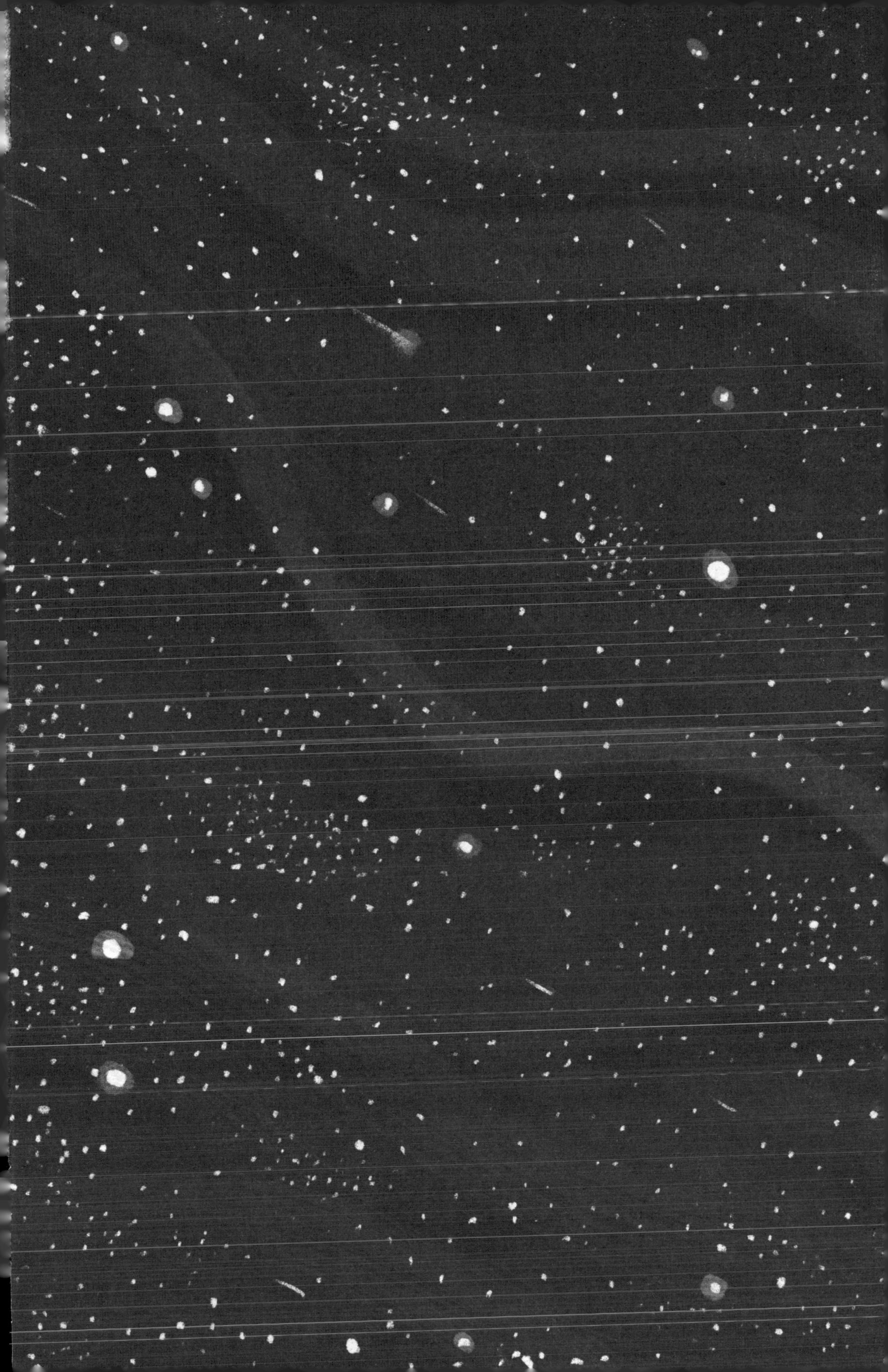

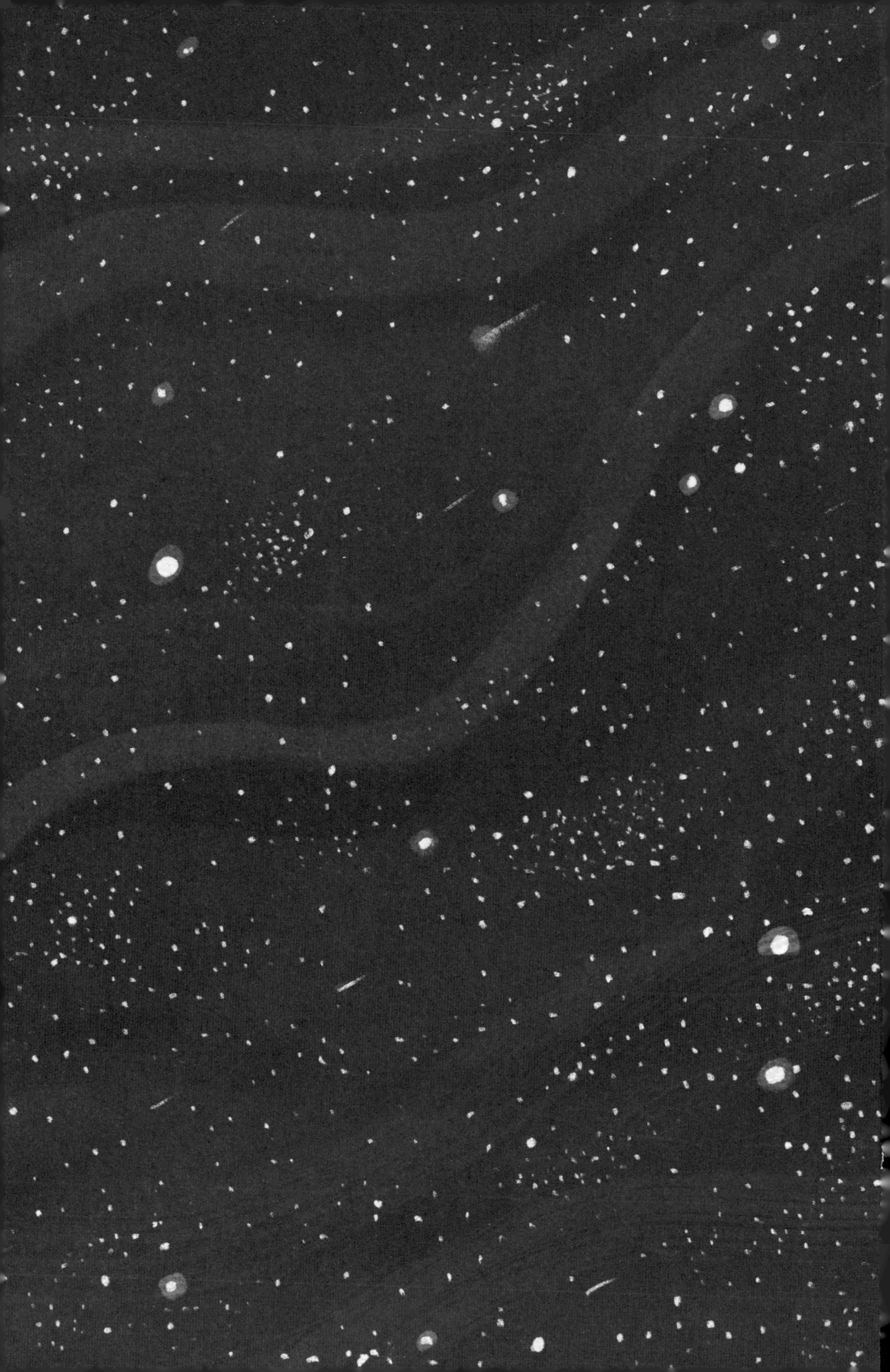